MANAGEMENT GUIDE TO OVERSEAS OPERATIONS

MANAGEMENT GUIDE TO
OVERSEAS OPERATIONS

Business Looks Abroad—
at Its Opportunities and Responsibilities

Edited by Huntington
DAN H. FENN, JR.
Assistant Editor of the Harvard Business Review

McGRAW-HILL BOOK COMPANY, INC.
New York Toronto London 1957

PREFACE

THIS BOOK, the eighth in an annual series, is based on the proceedings of the 26th National Business Conference, sponsored by the Harvard Business School Association on June 16, 1956. In many ways it is similar to it predecessors, for a conscientious effort has been made to catch the ideas of the conference in words designed for reading instead of listening. But in one basic way it is different: turning away from the internal needs of modern administrative practice, it focuses on an area of increasing concern to American business and to the world.

The topic of this book developed from a sense of responsibility, at the Harvard Business School and within the leadership of its Alumni Association, to the growing interest and activity in overseas business operations. This concern was partly for the improvement of skills and techniques in foreign operations; it was also for the enlargement of our understanding of the implications carried by United States business programs abroad. As Dean Stanley F. Teele pointed out in his welcome, the School now reflects that concern in a number of ways.

The authors of this book eloquently declare that we are living in a new kind of world today. The balance sheets of our businesses, the daily life in our country is affected in a myriad of ways by the vigorous competition we face from an opposing philosophy. The democratic and the communist ideals are vying for the support of vast millions of uncommitted peoples, and that competition is felt throughout our society. Its outcome may well determine the pattern of lives to be lead by our children.

This competition is brought sharply into focus by Ambassador Mehta's remarks in this book. One cannot help but feel, in his words, the sturdy determination of his people—and others like them —to walk their own path through the world. They will choose the best from the competing systems which are seeking to attract their support; it is up to us to see that they choose more from us than from the communists.

We hope, of course, that the people of these new nations will find our business practices—our management skills and tools—useful in their own situations. We hope, further, that they will agree with us that our economic system, with its emphasis on the maximum degree of freedom, can be helpful to them in solving their pressing problems. But most of all, we hope that they will join with us in our continuing effort to build a society founded on the dignity and worth of the individual. We hope they will share with us the challenge and the adventure of striving to find ways, each in his own land, whereby men can work ever more productively and harmoniously on common tasks.

The fulfillment of these hopes depends, in substantial part, on our technical efficiency in overseas operations, the calibre of our international business managers, and the spirit which we reflect in our day-to-day relationships. All of us who have had a part in the preparation of this book trust that it will be useful to businessmen in a hard-headed, practical way; we hope, further, that it will point to some specific ways in which the executive's efforts can relax and improve the general climate of international politics. Finally, we are even optimistic enough to hope that it may contribute some slight amount to the strengthening of the democratic cause in its conflict with authoritarianism, wherever the latter may be.

I say "we" advisedly, for many hands and minds have contributed to the chapters that follow. First of all, of course, come the authors of the comments; then the businessmen whose "questions from the floor" are reported here; and then those 1200 Harvard Business School alumni and guests who provided the sounding board for the speakers and panel members. But more specifically, I would like to extend my thanks to Professor Edward C. Bursk, Editor of the Harvard Business Review, who served throughout as editorial consultant; to three able, hard-working, and imaginative assistants whose help was invaluable, Mrs. Warren M. Little, Mrs. John Montgomery, and Miss Abigail J. S. Lewis; and finally, to Mrs. John S. Gibson, Miss Louise B. Morse, Miss C. Moyra Laing, and Miss Joan E. Foster, who played indispensable parts in the organization and preparation of the book.

Dan H. Fenn, Jr.

CONTENTS

Part One

OVERSEAS BUSINESS AND THE
NATIONAL INTEREST

A PROSPECTIVE FOR BUSINESS ABROAD

John J. McCloy

THE SUBJECT OF THIS BOOK seems to me peculiarly appropriate and timely. We are passing through another exacting period which calls for a re-examination of the policies and practices that govern our relations with the rest of the world. The continuing revolution in the technique of warfare, the new leadership and changing tactics of the Soviets, the great shifts of power, and the rise of many new and uncommitted nations have made this re-examination necessary. Our government has emphasized, and events proclaim, that we are at another turning point in international affairs; and public policies are being weighed and measured anew. It is no less fitting and important that the business community should take similar action with regard to its activities in the international sphere.

As I consider the role of United States business in the world, I

Note: Mr. McCloy is Chairman of the Board, The Chase Manhattan Bank, a former President of the World Bank, and former High Commissioner to Germany.

3

cannot help but be impressed again with the vast physical changes that have occurred in our operating environment in recent years. It still startles me, for example, to contemplate the tremendous advance in the art of communication and the extent to which the world has thereby been shrunk. A short while ago I visited the research laboratory of one of our greatest communication systems and I was really amazed at the devices of the future which were being forecast and planned there. Thought, in an infinite variety of forms, can already be transmitted in a flash. In about two years we shall be able to travel to Europe in something like four hours—about the same time it now takes to journey by train from New York to Boston.

With the globe grown so small, it is little wonder that political power and influence have tended to become polarized around relatively few units. Whether we like it or not, our own country has become one of these—indeed, perhaps the first among them. Today the United States holds responsibilities for leadership of a political, economic, and moral character that are unmatched in all history.

I do not need to go into great detail on why we find ourselves in this position. The weight of our resources, the state of our technical arts, the institutions we have fashioned—all these have something to do with it. But no matter what the reasons, the fact is that today the United States accounts for no less than 40% of the world's industrial output. This in itself makes our nation a decisive factor in any balance sheet of world affairs.

Hardly less important in shaping our position has been the rise of another great power. The Soviet Union, with its allies, controls one-fourth of the earth's land surface and one-third of its people; it has gained command of all the techniques of modern industry and warfare. Only recently a prominent European told me about a visit he made to the Academy of Science in Russia. This school of advanced learning has an enrollment of considerably over 100,000, with branches scattered throughout the land. It boasts up-to-date equipment which is the equivalent of anything we possess.

It may be that there is not much else in Russia but politicians and scientists—since that is where the Soviet leaders apparently believe their future lies—yet the facts of Soviet strength are sobering and impressive and cannot be laughed off. We are uncomfortably aware that the Soviet Union is an aggressive power guided by principles that are the antithesis of all that we ourselves cherish.

UNITED STATES ENTANGLED

In the face of all this, it is impossible indeed to visualize America as an isolated economy, standing alone in its own corner, with its interests and contacts growing continually smaller, while the Soviet Union reaches out to dominate the work and life of other lands. Such a picture becomes all the more unnatural when we contemplate its implications in terms of our national safety and security. In this day of the hydrogen bomb, soon to be carried by missiles that span continents, no nation—not even the United States—can stand alone. We need the help of allies and friends—of the 310 millions in Western Europe, the 190 millions in Latin America and Canada, and as many of the 850 millions in Free Asia as will work with us. Quite as clearly, they desperately need our good will and strength.

Today these political and military necessities are facts of life for every businessman. Standing beside them, moreover, is a corollary development that is more strictly economic in character. I refer to the growing shortage of certain key raw materials in the United States and our need to look abroad for an increasing supply. Our statistical position on such items as iron ore, petroleum, copper, and other metal ores, and the prodigious rate at which we are consuming them are well known. Suffice it to say that in the next two decades we must at least double our imports of these and other materials if we are to maintain our strength and our standard of living.

While these needs of the United States—political, military, and economic—have been growing, profound developments have been occurring elsewhere among nations who are our friends. Strong nationalism has taken hold in many of the underdeveloped areas of the world. Great new countries have emerged, full-scale, to play their independent roles in world affairs—India, Pakistan, Burma,

Vietnam, Indonesia, and soon the Gold Coast, Nigeria, and perhaps others. These are lands which traditionally have not looked toward the United States as a major source of trade and investment. Today they urgently require help in their development. Living standards are low; capital and technical skills are woefully scarce. Yet in spite of great needs, the atmosphere of extreme nationalism in these countries breeds obstacles to outside assistance, particularly in the form of private investment.

There is one final trend in the background that I would mention —and it applies both to the underdeveloped countries and to ourselves: the increasing role of government in matters that bear on world economic affairs. This tendency has been carried to its extreme in the newer countries, where government often acts as the arbiter and manager of enterprise in a manner with which we in the West do not always sympathize. We must, of course, recognize that these governments are trying to crowd a century of economic development into a generation, and they are under great pressure from their peoples. Even so, it seems probable that in their zeal they have allocated too large a role to government—and I believe experience is bound to prove this to them.

Looking to the positive side, perhaps the most helpful role taken up by governments in the postwar years is in the field of cooperative effort among two or more nations. The work of the international agencies is a case in point. The World Bank, for example, can and does make a contribution which increases the opportunities for private business throughout the area of its operation. The same can be said for the various technical assistance programs; for the activities of the Organization for European Economic Cooperation, for the Colombo Plan in Southeast Asia; and for work carried out under the Geneva Conference—the General Agreement on Tariffs and Trade.

Certainly, there is no denying that one of the profound changes for world business since the war has been this vast growth in the role of government, both domestically and in the international field.

It is a trend which people in all lands, including the United States, must watch with a continuing vigilance, reassuring themselves constantly that government is indeed acting to serve the best interests of its citizens.

THE NATIONAL INTEREST

These, then, are some of the broad developments of recent years that have a bearing on both the responsibilities and opportunities that face American business in its operations abroad. What do these developments add up to—and what is their meaning for our international business?

I believe it can be said that the international activities of our business today are tinged with the national interest as never before. When a United States company ships specialized machinery to Western Germany, it helps strengthen an area which is vital to us. When one of our metal producers develops a new copper supply in Africa, he contributes both to our future defense and to our standard of living. And when an investment firm provides dollar funds for capital imports into India, it affords much-needed help to a nation whose friendship we value highly.

This does not mean that the national interest is the sole or even the primary consideration in determining the shape and extent of our foreign trade and investment. The interests of shareholders and employees continue to be paramount factors, and private business cannot be expected to carry out ventures that are inconsistent with them. Yet a third consideration must often be added today to the interests of shareholders and employees—and in a degree never before recognized. That factor is the public interest. Management's problem is to be cognizant of all three and move ahead in harmony with each of them.

Let us look for a moment at the record of United States business, and determine how it is discharging this international responsibility. The degree to which business today is contributing to the world economy is not generally appreciated. All told, our companies now provide products to other countries which have an estimated value of $35 billion yearly. Of this total some $15 billion represent direct exports, while the remaining $20 billion constitute the output of branches and subsidiaries located abroad. This is a huge total indeed. It is almost as great as the entire national product of West Germany, which today is a major exporting power, and it is larger than that of all Italy. Moreover, this contribution is being made throughout the whole Free World—to the industrial countries of Western Europe, as well as to Latin America, Southeast Asia, and other areas.

The impact of our exports is readily evident in most sections of the globe. Our heavy construction equipment can be seen building roads, dams, and railroads the world over; electrical equipment is going into new power facilities; specialized machinery is being installed in new factories; and much of Western Europe and Asia still uses our agricultural materials. Indeed, analysis of our export list shows that almost three-fourths of the shipments are either necessary food and raw materials or machinery essential to manufacturers. This high proportion is itself an index of the significant role which our exports play in the countries receiving them.

But when one turns to the activities of branches and subsidiaries abroad, he enters an area where our contribution tends to be underestimated. United States companies have, of course, made a huge capital investment in other lands—a total of almost $18 billion at the last counting. But much more than money has been poured into these endeavors. They represent the main channels through which other countries reap the benefits of our research and techniques of management and manufacturing.

Again, it is not only the underdeveloped countries that benefit from this process. Take Great Britain, for example: there are 800 United States firms operating there, leaving their mark on such diverse fields as chemicals, autos, heavy machinery, and food processing. As a matter of fact, a recent study of these companies suggests that competition in Britain is stronger, prices are lower, and many management standards are higher because of their influence. Moreover, and this is of great importance to Britain, exports are undoubtedly larger than they would otherwise have been.

The benefits from both trade and foreign investment do not flow only one-way, as I have already suggested. Companies would not engage in foreign business if it failed to be profitable. Somehow or other, I am never much impressed by statements that our exports are less than 4% of our gross national product or that foreign earnings which are remitted to the United States represent a very small return on capital investment. I know that many firms remit only a part of their earnings—a good share is used for further expansion. I am more impressed by the fact that a certain large machinery producer with which I am familiar exports a third of its product. I am interested in the program of another domestic producer of national repute, with whom I do business, that has almost half of its investment overseas.

Furthermore, averages can be misleading. The fact is that business abroad provides a very essential margin for a great many important companies in the United States today. Nor must we forget the significance of the raw materials which the United States obtains from other lands. Life would be rather complicated for us without the oil of Venezuela and the Middle East, copper from Chile and Africa, and, in growing measure, iron ore and newsprint from Canada. There is not a shadow of a doubt that United States business, with its great needs and vigorous activity, is making an indispensable contribution to the growth and welfare of the Free World, while it maintains the health of enterprise in our own country.

But the past decade has been an unusual one in many respects. It has been a period of extraordinary expansion and adjustment and we have been left with a legacy of unsolved problems, both political and economic. In the face of these problems, what is the outlook for United States business abroad and where can we best concentrate our efforts, both for the public and for our own interest? These are not easy questions. For my own part, I have only a few rather broad observations which I hope may help point the way for some of our thinking.

TOUGHER COMPETITION AHEAD

First, I think it is clear that we all must expect heavier competition in the period ahead. I recently took a rather extended trip through the Middle East and was impressed with the variety and number of visiting engineers and salesmen who are traveling that road. I saw them everywhere—in Beirut, in Cairo, in Damascus, and even in the remote vastnesses of Arabia. In addition to Americans, there were Germans, Dutch, French, and even some Japanese. Perhaps these gentlemen had remained in the shadows on my previous trips, but for some reason I suddenly was highly conscious of them, particularly of any who were bankers! It is no secret that the Germans in particular have been making a strong bid for trade in the Middle East—helped in the initial stages, at least, by some rather generous credit arrangements facilitated by the government at Bonn.

The same trend is evident in Latin America, a market which is closer to us and one which we may have taken too much for granted in recent years. In 1947 the United States supplied two-thirds of Latin American imports. Admittedly this was artificially inflated by wartime developments, but even so our share had come down to 52% by 1950. Since then it has gradually slipped to 48%.

Our experience in Latin America and the Middle East raises many questions for which I do not pretend to have the final answers. How are our prices? Are we staying competitive on this score? I am told, for example, that in the field of heavy electrical equipment, sales of United States companies to Latin America have dropped a third since 1951, whereas those of Britain and West Germany have risen 50%. Is price a factor here? What about credit?

Then again, I notice that the number of farm tractors we ship to Latin America is off 30%, while those provided by West Germany and Britain are up 24.5%, a total now actually greater in number than ours. Other producers seem to ship diesel tractors, while many of ours use gasoline. Are we adjusting to the changing needs of the market? Does this make a difference?

And above all, what about dollar availability? The big increase in our exports last year was to Western Europe, while shipments to friendly neighbors like Brazil and Colombia slipped lower, apparently because of lack of dollar exchange.

I personally doubt that the world as a whole suffers from any general dollar shortage or that it will in the near future. Not only are our military and aid expenditures in other countries likely to stay fairly heavy for some time, but our imports should also continue to grow. Indeed, if our economy operates at the high level of which it is capable, imports a decade hence may exceed $16 billion, a rise of more than a third. But dollars from these imports will, of course, not be spread evenly throughout the world, so the dollar problem may continue to plague individual nations and cause some distortion in the normal pattern of trade.

It is clear, then, that we must be prepared for greater competition in the period ahead—in terms of price, quality, and monetary exchange considerations. It might even be that some of our friends in countries like Britain, Germany, and Japan, which must export or die, will have to sharpen their pencils more than we. In these circumstances it may turn out that the recent trend toward establishing branches or subsidiaries in such countries is a middle ground that works increasingly to the advantage of all.

But there is another source of competition that is rising to confront us—one that I mentioned earlier as being less friendly and more apt to play the game by its own rules. I refer to the growing activity of the Soviet bloc in world markets and particularly to its efforts to expand trade relations with the underdeveloped countries. This is certainly not a matter to be taken lightly. The Soviet Union now has an industrial capacity second only to ours, and it is expanding rapidly. The day will come when the Soviet Union too will have its surpluses, and it will have fewer compunctions about costs and relations with allies in disposing of them.

Indeed, one of Russia's most dangerous weapons is its ability to use foreign trade as a deliberate instrument of foreign policy, regardless of cost. We see it at work in the Middle East and Southeast Asia. Last year the Soviet bloc provided a market for one-fourth of Egypt's exports, as against only 14% in 1954. It has taken over a major part of external trade with Afghanistan and is a growing source of supply to Burma, India, and Indonesia. *The New York Times,* for example, recently reported that about 25% of Burma's imports are now flowing from the Soviet bloc.

Given all its political strength, we could make a mistake and exaggerate the Soviet Union's competitive position. There is a rigidity in the Soviet approach to trade that must result in some very serious limiting factors. Trade arrangements are made with other nations on a bilateral basis; and thus far the items that the Soviet has had to offer have been limited in number, and delivery has not always been good. Both Argentina and Britain, for example, have found Soviet deliveries taking longer than expected. Furthermore, there are a number of indications that the flow of Soviet supplies has not been satisfactory.

But I do not think we can take any very great satisfaction from these particular incidents. Past experience should demonstrate that the Soviets are capable of remarkable achievements in industrial production in spite of certain crudities of approach. We have to look the facts squarely in the face and determine just what the extent of the Russian competition is likely to be, both in its effect on the trade of the Free World nations and on us. I do not expect us to be the loser in this new phase of the continuing struggle with the Soviets. But it is another factor that will act to keep us on our toes.

Nor is the challenge limited only to the export field. Assistance that might be offered to underdeveloped countries in the form of investment to aid their growth may be of even greater importance. Already the Soviet Union has extended credits to these countries amounting to more than $500 million. For the Western world, economic assistance is a complicated process in which governments, international organizations, and private business all must cooperate. Yet it is not a task of unmanageable proportions. While it is true that there are at least one billion people in these areas, as compared with our population, which is barely one-sixth as great, the vital fact is that our $400 billion economy carries about three times the productive power of all the underdeveloped areas combined.

The United States is long on capital and relatively short on manpower, while the underdeveloped countries are just the reverse. Of course, their capacity to absorb increased capital is limited. Today, total annual investment in the underdeveloped areas is in the area of $13 billion. Foreign sources, public and private, finance something more than one billion of this amount. It is estimated that an additional one to two billion dollars yearly is about all that could be handled in the near future—less than is being spent in 1956 by one of our largest corporations. This sum obviously will not produce any revolutionary results overnight, but revolutionary results are not attainable in most countries. What this money can do is to assure a steady progress that at least gives hope of a stable and more productive future. The only alternative to such help appears to be for us to stand by in the race of production and population growth, a solution which will never be acceptable.

Certainly the United States can afford the investment necessary for the underdeveloped countries. The big issues are how to organize it, how to manage it, and particularly how to enlist the support of private capital. The record of our companies in the lesser developed countries can only be labeled a mixed one. We have been most successful in areas where opportunities to develop resources or markets appear abundant, and where outside capital has been welcome. Certain countries in Latin America and the Middle East stand out in this regard. On the other hand, we have been least successful in Southeast Asia, an area that urgently needs assistance.

There are many explanations for this mixed record of investment in the underdeveloped areas. Very often one of the most important reasons is the extreme nationalism to which I have already referred. Frequently this finds an outlet in the form of restrictions and discriminatory practices that sharply limit the activities of foreign businessmen. Sometimes the threat of expropriation hangs over the investor, and there is always the possibility of political change and even war. We cannot overlook the fact that at times in the past investors have suffered some brutal losses in the foreign field.

In the face of all this I feel somewhat puzzled and uncertain as to the best way to build up needed investment in the underdeveloped countries. Thus far in the postwar period we appear to have favored a mixed approach, with both government and private business contributing. It needs to be recognized, however, that a mixed system of this character creates problems of its own, particularly in areas that may run into exchange difficulties. How do private investors and government creditors queue up in such an event? Is there danger of a kind of Gresham's Law operating here, with government investment driving out the private, no matter how good the latter?

WHAT OF THE FUTURE?

Perhaps there are no final answers to the questions about business assistance and no immediate solutions to the problems confronting the private investor in the underdeveloped lands. We may be faced with the alternative of either doing nothing and letting governments carry on alone by default or of moving ahead in the face of all the uncertainties, exercising reasonable caution and considerable courage. Of these two alternatives, I very much prefer the latter. Moreover, I am optimistic enough to believe that the underdeveloped countries themselves will gradually come to recognize the great advantages to be gained from private foreign investment.

Such countries should never be allowed to forget that it is the private investor who often works in the most dynamic sectors of the economy—those which are capable of maximum growth and can earn essential foreign exchange. Moreover, it is private investment which usually carries with it the technical and management skills that are as scarce and necessary as capital itself. It is no accident that over one-third of United States imports from Latin America are produced by companies that represent United States investment—imports that are highly valuable to us and enable the Latin Americans to buy machinery and other items that are even more important to them.

For our part, if we are to move ahead with foreign investment, particularly in the underdeveloped lands, our businessmen must gain an intimate knowledge of the countries involved—knowledge not only of the economic forces at work, but of the political forces as well. It is not enough to have a vague impression that the communists in a particular country are gaining ground, or that the balance of payments in a particular year looks shaky. We need men who possess the same detailed knowledge and understanding of other lands that the Bostonian has of Massachusetts. In no other way can we even begin the task of evaluating risks.

Men of the type needed for our foreign business are not created overnight. For this reason, among others, progress on the problem of foreign investment in the underdeveloped lands may not be rapid. Yet such progress seems inevitable to me. Just as I cannot imagine this nation living in isolation, I cannot see United States business, with its immense stock of capital and technical know-how, standing apart from the billion people or so who will benefit from the assistance we can bring to them.

For the West, such assistance is not merely a matter of helping other lands build up their own strength as a counter to possible Soviet encroachment, although that can be an important by-product. Rather, investment in the lesser developed countries seems to me to be a natural expression of our times, an inevitable challenge and outlet for the talents and energies of the more advanced sectors of the Free World economy. I have no doubt whatsoever that the necessary institutions and arrangements will emerge to give body to this expression.

QUESTIONS AND ANSWERS *

From the floor: You have mentioned two areas in which the United States Government could act to stimulate investments overseas: tax

---

* In a subsequent meeting, Mr. McCloy answered questions pertaining to his formal presentation; this section of the chapter is drawn, more or less verbatim, from the discussion that took place at this meeting. George P. Baker, James J. Hill Professor of Transportation, Harvard Business School, acted as moderator.

relief and government guarantees against expropriation. Would you comment further on these?

Mr. McCloy: This matter of expropriation—of political risks, in other words—is always a major consideration in determining whether or not to move into a foreign country. However, as an observer of capital investment flow abroad, I have found that concern over political disturbances and expropriation diminishes as stability develops in overseas areas and the exchange situation is improved. The circumstances in Venezuela and Mexico are good examples. Although government intervention by way of a guarantee is important, the real impetus for investment comes from the businessman's feeling that stability has, in fact, been established. In other words, the flow of capital is induced by a fundamental belief that the conditions are stable, rather than by any government crutch. If an executive feels that a situation is shaky, he is unlikely to invest even though the government has provided him with guarantees.

Tax relief, on the other hand, is more of a major factor. We are all so tremendously conscious of tax relief these days that I think concessions of this kind would be effective.

From the floor: You have mentioned the importance of learning the ways of a country. Have you a specific suggestion along these lines?

Mr. McCloy: Personally, I put an enormous stress on this matter of language. We need an entirely new teaching technique in this country! It is ridiculous to think you have mastered a language once you have taken French I and French II or German I and German II. Both better teaching and more sustained effort on the part of the student are required if we are going to be able to speak to these people in their own tongues. And if we cannot communicate with them, the crucial decisions are going to be made on the basis of hearsay and hunch.

From the floor: Are these underdeveloped countries, which are trying to do so much in such a short time, wrong in placing the emphasis upon domination, regulation, and guidance from their governments?

Mr. McCloy: By and large, my answer would be, "Yes, they are wrong." The most effective way to develop techniques and know-how—which is what they most need—is through private enterprise, because it is more flexible. Certainly, our best business talent is not found in the departments of government but in our business concerns. It is difficult for the government to enlist these people—to take them away from their companies and send them overseas on aid programs. Everybody from the president of the concern on down is in a tizzy over losing them, and they themselves don't want to go because their pension rights and their positions in the firm are jeopardized. This reluctance of people to enter government work may not be so widespread in underdeveloped countries, but in general I think it is unwise for them to overstress government domination and neglect private activity.

In spite of the socialistic trends described by Ambassador Mehta,* I have a feeling that the Indians themselves are going to learn before very long that they will have a more flexible, more active, more dynamic economy if they stress private investment instead of government action. At least they will benefit as much from it as they will from government programs, or from business that is directed and controlled by the government.

From the floor: Do you see any evidence of a movement in this country to develop programs which might counteract the communist penetration of underdeveloped areas?

Mr. McCloy: I see many evidences of such programs in our government policy, but I do not know how much of an urge there is on the part of private enterprise to throw its money in as a barrier against communist encroachment. This is such a political matter that most businessmen feel it is a governmental responsibility. However, I will say, speaking from my own bank's point of view, that we would never have started the American Overseas Finance Corporation unless the government had talked about the possibility of private cooperation with the government in order to meet the growing communist competition. I cannot foresee very large profits in this effort

* See page 241.

for a substantial period of time—though we are not doing this for philanthropic reasons, since we have our stockholders' interests to protect. But I do believe that private enterprise should experiment in this kind of effort, with the cooperation of the government in certain fields. Business must do all that it can, within its obligations to its stockholders and its customers, to assist the government. This is essentially a national obligation which I feel large public or quasi-public institutions, such as a large bank, must recognize.

From the floor: What is the AOFC?

Mr. McCloy: We formed the American Overseas Finance Corporation because of our sense of responsibility to the national interest, and because certain government officials specifically said to us that the banks ought to play a larger part in financing the export trade of the nation. We were asked why we were not involved in it to a greater extent. The government offered the facilities of the Export-Import Bank, and we brought a group of banks together into a private corporation to stimulate interest in financing exports.

The original concept called for the Export-Import Bank to guarantee a portion of the risk for a fee. But in practice the Export-Import Bank has had some difficulty guaranteeing a part of this risk because our rates, subject to income taxes, have been somewhat higher than the rate that they are able to set. Consequently, the work of the AOFC recently has been slowed up, though we have had a very heavy amount of business and many inquiries from corporations asking to do business with us simply because we are non-governmental. Some of the banks that are involved in this AOFC experiment are reluctant to go forward with their original vigor, despite the volume of business, because we have not been able to secure the guarantees as rapidly and as fully as we first thought.

Fundamentally, the AOFC is an experimental enterprise. We are trying to build up business and experience, with the thought that eventually we will dispose of some securities in the corporation to other exporters and perhaps to the public when it is ready to invest. Then there will be genuine equity capital in the venture, rather than just depositors' money. So far, there is justification for confidence in the experiment. After ten months of operation, we are in the black and are growing—which is very comforting—though we need more volume and smoother cooperation between government agencies and the company before the AOFC becomes a really profitable enterprise when judged by the, returns of the banking business in general. We are hopeful that both of these needed factors will develop.

AMERICAN BUSINESS ABROAD AND THE NATIONAL INTEREST

Herbert Hoover, Jr.

THE PAST QUARTER-CENTURY has seen extraordinary changes in the world situation. A great war has been fought, and the entire structure of relationships abroad has been radically altered. In the midst of this changing scene, it is most fitting that we devote our earnest attention to the future of American business abroad.

One of the major factors affecting that future is the unpredictable character of Soviet economic policy, controlling the lives of hundreds of millions of people. In this connection, we have heard a great deal in the past year about the new Soviet economic offensive. What is it, and where is it going? Is it a genuine movement toward peaceful economic expansion, or is it an attempt to spread communist political domination over new areas of the free world? Is the American system capable of coping with this development? What are the opportunities and responsibilities of United States business as we look ahead into the future? These and many other questions

Note: Mr. Hoover is former Under Secretary of State.

20

arise as we watch the pattern of a new type of Soviet aggression unfold in the far corners of the world.

I would like to explore the answers to some of these questions, because our conclusions may have much to do with the shaping of our governmental and our commercial policies for many years to come.

COMMUNIST CHALLENGE—
DEMOCRATIC RESPONSE

As we look back in history, we find that the communists expanded their domination over many parts of the world in the twenty-five years prior to Stalin's death in 1953. They accomplished this expansion through outright military power and aggression, aided by subversion from within. Continual threats to the independence of many countries culminated in open warfare in a number of instances. Our persistent attempts to arrive at peaceful solutions were rebuffed on countless occasions.

During Stalin's regime, it was repeatedly announced that the communist objective was the ultimate domination of the world. Khrushchev has subsequently reiterated this aim several times.

As a result of these actions, the free world drew together many nations for self-defense. Reacting to military aggression and threats to the peace of the world, 45 countries joined together in the Rio Pact, North Atlantic Treaty Organization; Australia, New Zealand, United States Pact; Southeast Asia Treaty Organization, the Balkan Alliance, and the Baghdad Pact. Thus the free world became stronger and more resolved than ever to resist communist threats of violence and subversion.

Although it had been obvious for some years that the old Russian policies were no longer succeeding, it was not until after Stalin's death that the Kremlin could adopt new tactics and a new approach. This they have now done, and peace and competitive coexistence have become the order of the day in this new policy. While the ultimate communist objectives have remained the same, the problems for the free world have taken on new aspects.

THE AMERICAN WAY

I have outlined here, in only the broadest terms, the problems that we face today. Let us turn for a moment to the American economic system, and evaluate our own ability to cope with this change in tactics.

We know that the Soviets regard our American economic system of free competitive enterprise as a vastly greater impediment to their own designs of world domination than that of any other country. It is upon us, therefore, that they concentrate their efforts and their strategy.

It is strange how unfamiliar our system is to many people abroad. As a matter of fact, one of the major efforts of the communists is to spread an image of the American system as one which embodies the most extreme form of exploitation.

During the past fifty years our system has evolved in ways which were totally unforeseen when Marx and Engels were belaboring capitalism a century ago. Not only does it bear little resemblance to the classical Marxist concept of capitalism, it differs significantly from the systems which prevail in other countries and are conventionally regarded as capitalistic.

When we talk about individual liberty in the United States, we have in mind something which goes beyond the freedom expressed in political institutions. A representative form of government, the right to vote, the secret ballot—these are all part of our heritage. But in this country individual freedom has assumed new and significant dimensions which can be found in few other places in the world.

One such attribute has aptly been called "the freedom of opportunity"—the opportunity to choose one's job or profession and to rise to one's fullest capabilities. Furthermore, there is no other country in the world where educational opportunities are as accessible as they are in the United States or equal opportunities for economic success so readily available.

It is no accident that this system, with its freedom and incentive for the individual and its stress on individual worth, has attained the highest standard of living for its people. Moral and spiritual values have provided the driving force for this achievement. And it is *all* our people who are the beneficiaries of this progress—not a chosen few. In fact, the difference in income between factory workers on the one hand and management personnel on the other is smaller in the United States than in any other major industrial nation in the world, even including the Soviet Union.

I should like to cite a few figures which illustrate clearly the difference between the American system of today and the outmoded Marxist image of capitalism as a ruthless exploiter of the individual:

> In recent years the average American family income has increased over 50% in real terms. But the lowest fifth of income recipients have experienced an even larger increase than the average: their incomes rose 125% in the same period. Of all the great industrial nations, the one that relies most heavily on individual initiative and private enterprise has come the closest to providing abundance for all.
>
> There are other dimensions of individual freedom in the United States which have grown in importance as this country has matured. The worker's freedom to organize is traditional in our system, and responsible trade unions hold an accepted place in our national life.
>
> Property ownership in America is widely diffused. About 8 million people are stockholders in American corporations; 4 million farmers own their own farms; and more than 3 million small business enterprises belong to individual owners. No small clique owns America. The responsibilities and the profits are widely shared.

There are many essential ingredients in our environment. One above all is relevant to our discussion, and that is the tradition of independence and free competition in America. It is a tradition that goes far back over our history. It is the very foundation upon which our system has been built.

How has this tradition of independence and individual responsibility affected our approach to foreign economic relations? I think the answer is that we instinctively conduct our relations with other countries in a way which will strengthen their integrity, their sovereignty, and their independence. We want other countries to be strong, independent, and free; and the more they are so, the better we like to do business with them.

Under our system, international trade and investment are commercial operations carried on by widely dispersed interests, competing against each other as well as against those from other countries. With us, political control is irrelevant to normal commercial relationships. There are no political strings attached to American business operating abroad.

THE FACTS OF LIFE

What are the economic facts of life that face American business in this world today?

> World trade, as measured by exports, was at an all-time high in 1955—$92 billion. Trade between the Free World countries in 1955 was $80 billion, or 86% of the total. Trade between the Soviet bloc and the Free World was $4.4 billion, or less than 5% of the total. In addition, trade among countries inside the bloc accounted for $7.8 billion, or about 9% of the total.
>
> The United States alone generates almost 20% of all international trade. A substantial portion of this trade, amounting to $11 billion in imports and exports, was with Latin America, Asia, and Africa. These are the newly developing areas which are among the prime targets of the Soviet economic drive. By contrast, the trade of the communist countries with these same areas amounted to about $1 billion in the same period.

The significant point of these figures is the great preponderance of world trade which is taking place among the noncommunist countries. The low level of communist trade with the rest of the world is due mainly to their deliberate policy of self-sufficiency. The leaders in the Kremlin want to build a self-contained economic unit. Their recent offers of trade to the newly developing countries are politically inspired. Khrushchev himself said: "We value trade least for economic reasons and most for political purposes."

But the United States does not direct its trade for political ends. It is important that other countries should understand this fundamental difference between the American and the Soviet reasons for international trade. Our approach carries substantial advantages in dealing with other nations. Under our system, companies and industries are constantly vying with one another to create new products, new processes, and new services. Furthermore, we offer relative stability of markets. Demand cannot be turned on and off for political purposes. This is particularly important for the newly developing countries which depend largely on a few export products to earn the foreign exchange they need to finance the items they require from abroad.

To date, the Soviet trade offensive consists mainly of offers to buy or sell raw materials or to deliver specified types and quantities of capital goods, often on a direct barter basis. This is necessarily a cumbersome and limited method of trading, and provides no assurance of large or continuous markets. Soviet trade practices are unpredictable. They may be a large buyer or seller one year, and disappear from the market the next. Such in-and-out behavior may be related to their domestic difficulties, to the needs of satellite countries, or to political objectives elsewhere. Moreover, the history of Soviet trade suggests that the renewal of a transaction may well be attended by political demands, even though the first deal did not appear to be based upon any such considerations.

Sustained economic progress must come from stable trade conditions, from expanding and diversified markets, and from trade activated by commercial and not political considerations. This is the kind of trade that our system has to offer.

GOVERNMENT MUST PARTICIPATE

While American business must shoulder the largest part of the responsibility for our own economic activity abroad, it cannot be expected to do so without adequate support and encouragement from our government. To illustrate:

> Physical security is indispensable to economic progress. Hence the need for our collective security arrangements and our military assistance programs.
>
> Certain types of investment, such as roads and port facilities, cannot be financed on a wholly private basis. Hence the role of the International Bank and the Export-Import Bank in helping to finance basic development projects abroad.
>
> Many types of technical assistance, such as education and public health, require government organization to recruit and channel skilled personnel. Hence the various technical assistance programs.
>
> Nations that have recently achieved their independence and newly developing countries need assistance to strengthen their economies and maintain their liberty. Hence our programs of economic aid. Such programs are vital and indispensable if the challenge of communism is to be met and we are to preserve freedom in many areas of the world.

These governmental programs are complementary to normal commercial activity, which is potentially far larger and more important. United States industry, with its many centers of initiative and ingenuity, its ability to combine capital, technical know-how, and managerial skill, is eminently qualified to play a major role in accelerating economic development overseas.

Although a great deal of attention has been given to the problem of private investment abroad, especially in newly developed countries, the need for foreign capital still remains great. There are a variety of reasons why private capital has not moved abroad in even larger volume than at present. Political conditions overseas, inadequate knowledge of opportunities, and the fact that the major interests of the American business community have traditionally been at home—all are contributing factors.

The government has taken a variety of steps to encourage a larger flow of capital abroad. Commercial and tax treaty programs have long been an integral part of the effort of our government to develop standards of fair treatment on a reciprocal basis. Since World

War II, 15 commercial treaties with modernized provisions relating to investments have been negotiated. Similar treaty proposals are under negotiation or consideration with more than half a dozen other governments. At home and abroad, our Department of Commerce and our foreign missions perform a variety of services for American business interested in foreign trade and investment. These services are largely in the fields of information and trade promotion.

American investors can insure themselves against restrictions on the transfer of profits and capital, and against expropriation, in countries with which we have negotiated the necessary agreements. The problem of more favorable tax treatment for income earned from foreign investment has also been the subject of much attention. As a matter of fact, measures in this field have been presented to the Congress.

In cooperation with other Free World countries, we are continuing our efforts to encourage the expansion of private investment. If we succeed, the American system can play its full role in making the world a better place in which to live—both here and abroad.

OPPORTUNITIES—AND RESPONSIBILITIES

Let us take a closer look at the opportunities that exist abroad and the responsibilities of the United States businessman in the present world situation.

American business today may easily be affected by what happens in any or all of the far corners of the globe. The fact that direct private American investment abroad now exceeds $18 billion, and that the value of our merchandise exports and imports in 1955 alone was over $25 billion are a measure of our foreign interests.

Today, science and technology promise ever new attainments in human satisfactions and welfare for our people. At the same time, however, the greater part of mankind is still living in areas where industrial production and living standards are extremely low. Most of these people are now making great efforts to speed up their industrial development and raise their standards of living. In fact, this effort constitutes one of the most far-reaching economic and social changes in history. In this setting, American business abroad faces great opportunities and heavy responsibilities.

The opportunities exist both in a strictly business sense and in terms of the general interests of our country. With production and incomes increasing in many areas and with a steady reduction of restrictions hampering international trade, new opportunities constantly present themselves for developing foreign markets. As American industry becomes more dependent on basic materials from abroad, it is constantly developing new sources of supply. Foreign investment opportunities of all kinds will increase on an expanding scale as newly developing countries move rapidly into the mainstream of the world economy.

I know from many years of personal experience that one area of American business activity abroad of great potential importance is engineering, construction, and other services. These services are required on a large scale by countries in Asia, Latin America, and the Middle East, which are just beginning to develop modern industries. Their impact often goes far beyond the immediate projects that may be involved.

In purely individual terms, too, there will be many challenging occasions for Americans to participate in the world-wide process of constructive change and to foster healthy economic growth abroad that is complementary to our own.

The opportunities for the exercise of business initiative in these situations are, I am sure, appreciated by all. The relationship between such actions and the national interest may be less evident, however.

Through increased trade and expanded investment abroad, American business can support not only the continued growth of our own economy but also the accelerated development of other Free World countries. By helping to impart to other peoples a sense of progress, achievement, and purpose in life, the American businessman will be helping to guarantee that their aspirations and strivings are channeled along sound and constructive lines.

As I have already indicated, while American business is faced with challenging opportunities abroad, it must also be prepared to shoulder corresponding responsibilities. After all, the American businessman abroad is the representative of our system to many people who have no other basis on which to judge it. His constant aim should be to carry with him the spirit of responsibility that is the hallmark of industry at home.

Our effective businessman abroad respects the attitudes of other nations. He takes an interest in training his foreign personnel with a view to raising them to positions of responsibility. He makes them feel an integral part of the enterprise. He is alert to represent the true image of our system. In short, he strives to develop a mutuality of interest with the country in which his enterprise is located. In the largest sense of the word, the American businessman is an ambassador of his country.

WILL THEY BE FREE?

I have discussed some of the elements which account for the strength of our system, the challenge it faces from the communist economic offensive, and the way it is responding to this challenge. I have also touched on the great opportunities that exist for American business to make increasing contributions toward strengthening the Free World.

Great as is our faith in our system, we do not content ourselves with a belief in it that is merely passive. The initiative and resourcefulness which we have concentrated on solving our own problems are now serving the broader interests of the Free World. Thus we are taking a long step toward solving the overriding question of this century—whether millions of people in vast areas of the earth will continue to enjoy the opportunities of freedom.

QUESTIONS AND ANSWERS *

From the floor: How can the businessman operating abroad figure out what his national responsibilities are and how to meet them?

* At a later meeting, Mr. Hoover answered questions pertaining to his formal presentation; these paragraphs are drawn, more or less verbatim, from the discussion that took place at this meeting. George P. Baker, James J. Hill Professor of Transportation, Harvard Business School, acted as moderator.

Mr. Hoover: I think most American businessmen overseas know pretty well what is in our national interest and what is not. Good common sense, business honesty, and the mutuality that must be a part of any sound business deal are the essential elements. Both sides have to make a profit and receive a return, either tangible or intangible.

In the Department of State we find that we have close relations with almost all types of business, and industrial executives constantly come in to talk over their problems. Furthermore, in most cases our embassies abroad, our ambassadors, and our commercial attachés are delighted to discuss specific problems that arise in foreign countries.

From the floor: Oftentimes we Americans accomplish things for our friends overseas, but do not receive full credit for them in the eyes of the recipient countries. It appears that some of the communist nations promote their lesser activities so skillfully that they overshadow our efforts. Why is this so?

Mr. Hoover: Most Americans are primarily interested in going out and getting a job done. They don't seem to be as eager to talk about it. This is an American characteristic which might be admirable in most situations but which works against us in this case. Furthermore, when the communists do something for somebody, that's news!

However, when you go abroad you cannot help but notice the accomplishments of United States business. Our exports come to about $15 billion annually, about 20% of the total trade of the Free World. Together with our investments and our foreign aid, this adds up to a sizable volume of overseas activity, and it can hardly be overlooked. Also, we should not forget the recognition we get in the form of advertising—wherever you go, you see the names of American cigarettes, soft drinks, trucks, and machinery. We are receiving quite a bit of promotion and publicity in this form.

In other words, though I agree that we have a problem in this area, I do not believe it is as serious as we sometimes think.

OVERSEAS BUSINESS AND NATIONAL RESPONSIBILITIES

Lincoln Gordon, John C. McClintock, and James Terry Duce

THIS CHAPTER will focus on two principal questions: "How can United States business interests best be harmonized with the desires of un-underdeveloped countries for rapid development?" and "What role can United States overseas business play in the competitive struggle with the Soviets in neutral and uncommitted areas?"

For nearly a decade now, programs encouraging progress in under-developed parts of the world have been an accepted part of our national policy. This type of assistance, which had been provided to Latin America since 1940, was formally launched by President Tru-

Note: Mr. Gordon, who makes the introductory observations is William Ziegler Professor of International Economic Relations, Harvard Business School; Mr. McClintock is Assistant Vice President, United Fruit Company; and Mr. Duce is Vice President, Arabian American Oil Company.

man in his 1948 Inaugural Address. It rapidly became known as
"Point 4." Adopted by Congress in 1949, it remains on the statute
books in substantially its original form. Unlike other parts of the
foreign aid program, it was not supposed to have any terminal point;
it was planned as permanent policy.

In all the discussions of public loans and grants, we often lose
sight of the fact that the Point 4 idea stresses two things:

- Governmentally financed assistance in certain fields like public
  health, education, and agriculture, carried out either bilaterally or
  through the United Nations.
- Stimulus to the expanded development of business abroad, with
  the combination of both capital and technical skills that accompa-
  nies private investment.

The fact is, however, that we have not had much private investment overseas in the years since the law was passed, except for the
oil and minerals industries. There are many reasons for this, some of
which are explored in this book. But the point is that the idea of
stimulating private investment was fundamental to the original
Point 4 concept.

We are prone to assume that private investment is automatically
a good thing for us and for the recipient country. If so, why is there
not more of it? This leads us to wonder if private business does, in
fact, necessarily contribute to the accelerated progress of underdeveloped areas. Does it really promote a climate that is favorable to
rapid development? Does it foster favorable relations between
other countries and the United States? What are the difficulties in
private investment overseas? As a constructive effort, where does it
tend to boomerang? How can a sense of mutuality of interest best
be brought home to the underdeveloped country? We can recall cases
in which private business operating abroad has had a destructive
rather than a constructive effect. How does this happen—and why?

The whole problem is given new urgency by the developing competition—on all fronts—from the Soviet Union. The impact of the

Kremlin's programs is already being felt in Southeast Asia, the Middle East, Africa, and Latin America. The effect of this Russian activity can only be to complicate our problem. We need to re-examine both our attitudes and our practices—and do it quickly—if we are to meet this challenge and work out constructive policies of our own.

UNITED FRUIT COMPANY ABROAD*

In Washington, they customarily lump Asia, Africa, and Latin America together in one big category, which they label underdeveloped. But the fact is that Latin America does not belong in this grouping at all.

For example, the areas in which the United Fruit Company operates—Middle America, Ecuador and Colombia—are certainly not underdeveloped. It is true, I think, that the term "underdeveloped" was applicable when we first arrived. The United Fruit Company literally started from scratch in a very wild part of the world; in many areas in which we are now operating there were no people at all. Disease and poor living conditions had driven them out; most of the areas were virgin jungle.

But things are changing. We have cleared jungles and drained swamps, eradicated such diseases as malaria and yellow fever; we have built harbors, towns, railroads, schools, and hospitals. Increasingly, the situation is improving and the future looks brighter.

Our emphasis, of course, has been on farming. During the last 56 years, we have developed what amounts to dragline agriculture. (The modern dragline is the present-day equivalent of the old-fashioned steam shovel.) We have moved more earth since the inception of this dragline agriculture than was excavated in putting through the Panama Canal. This has proved most expensive and highly technical, but it has made it possible to transform remote and unhealthy jungle regions into productive land.

* By Mr. McClintock.

Rapidly Growing Area

This kind of change—and opportunity—is typical of the continent as a whole. The most important thing to bear in mind is that Latin America is growing more rapidly than any other area in the world today, in both population and economic activity. As General Soares points out in his chapter, there are now 171 million people living in these countries. The total is expected to reach 275 million by 1975, an increase of over 60%.

Latin America now produces goods and services worth over $40 billion; by 1975 this figure is expected to top $100 billion, or two and one half times the present amount. These statistics speak for themselves, but Henry Holland, United States Assistant Secretary of State for Latin American Affairs, recently presented some other figures which are even more bullish. For instance:

- Trade investments, loans, and other commercial activity in Latin America during the last three years had a value of over $14 billion; the equivalent figure for Western Europe came to nearly $300 million less.
- Of all new private investments abroad, 60% are in Latin America—the amount is now $6.5 billion, increasing at the rate of $6 million annually. At the present 37% of all United States investment abroad is in Latin America.
- Of all United States imports, 30% come from Latin America; conversely, those countries absorb 25% of our exports. This two-way trade amounts to $7 billion a year, and might conceivably increase to $10 billion in a few years. Incidentally, prices of Latin American exports to the United States have increased twice as much as those of imports from the United States.

Obstacles of Nationalism

Such rapid growth, which is accelerating and bids fair to continue, has created certain problems that make it difficult for foreigners to operate in Latin America.

Nationalism, for example, is more vigorous than ever in this area, as it is elsewhere in the world. In Brazil, this powerful force is working, in some cases, to the detriment of the country. Take petroleum as an illustration:

- The development of this industry is almost completely blocked by one slogan—"O petroleo e nosso," or "Petroleum is ours." When General Soares remarks in his chapter of this book about the shortage of dollar exchange, he does not mention that the Brazilians have been importing some $300 million worth of petroleum products per year but have not seen fit to permit outside help in developing their own supply.

- Iron ore is another resource which the Brazilians are neglecting. For reasons of national pride, little has been done to secure outside know-how in the development of this substantial resource.

- In contrast with the Brazilians, Venezuela has adopted a more progressive policy on oil: they call it "sowing petroleum." By this they mean plowing their oil earnings back into the economy of the country. It is true that some of the money has been spent on impressive structures such as expensive hotels and apartment houses. But on the other hand, a fair portion of the money received from oil exports is being utilized for the continued development of the country. When the oil wells dry up, Venezuela should have an integrated economy that will carry on despite the loss of petroleum revenues.

The rather advanced state of socialism and extremely modern ideas in the field of labor codes and social legislation constitute a second problem for United States businessmen in Latin America. To give you one very minor example, in Colombia my company pays 51%—on top of the payroll—for social benefits. Requirements like these make the task of the United States enterprise a more difficult one. The popularity of a "share the wealth" philosophy that could well lead to expropriation and loss of management control in many cases is another example of this same nationalistic tendency.

Finally, the Latin is a hard bargainer. In this country it is customary to look upon him as a rather impractical individual, a

dreamy-eyed singer of romantic ballads. But nothing could be further
from reality, for he is, in fact, a pragmatist and a most hard-headed
fellow. When you remember that many of our Latin American
neighbors are a mixture of the Spaniard and the Indian, you can
appreciate that they are hardy, realistic individuals.

From Concessions to Participation

What are the characteristics of United States business procedures
in this general situation?

The first fact to be noted is that our practices have changed considerably in the last fifty years. In the old days, the United Fruit
Company—and others like us—never considered operating in any
of these countries without a concession. The word was especially
appropriate; there were practically no import duties, no income
taxes, and, in most cases, a very small export duty. In many instances,
these concessions, although approved by decree of the legislative
authority, were secured from countries that were ruled by so-called
dictators, and did not meet the test of true popular approval. I am
not criticizing the ways and means by which these concessions were
obtained, because they must be viewed in light of the times, and the
mores at the beginning of the century were certainly different from
those of today.

These changing mores have brought with them a new business
philosophy, based on participation. Under this program, the Latin
American nation shares the profits of a venture with the United
States companies involved. This sharing is achieved through increased income taxes under amended contracts between the government and the private companies whereby previous contractual
exemptions are eliminated. In all instances, the contracts are approved by the national congress to avoid the old problems of popular disapproval and misunderstanding.

Until about eight years ago, the United Fruit Company paid no
income taxes of any kind in many of the countries where we operated. Our duties on imports and exports were either very minor
or were waived entirely. Now, as a general rule, we pay a 30% in-

come tax to the local governments. I should note that this arrangement is more equitable for all concerned.

Incidentally, we have been working with the Internal Revenue Department in Washington for many years on this question of foreign income. Administrative rulings have held that 35% of our consolidated profit on bananas was considered as earned abroad and 65% was attributed to operations within the United States. This meant that the countries in which we operate could only tax 35% of our total income from the banana business. We have succeeded in having the United States government liberalize the formula, so it now stands at 50-50. In our opinion, this is a very good deal for the Latin American countries, considering the 30% income tax paid by the United Fruit Company. For example:

> Strictly speaking, we pay a 30% income tax to Costa Rica. Actually, when we compute our export duties, various taxes, and other levies, we come up with a figure of over 40% of our net income before taxes. This 40% which goes to the government of Costa Rica represents over 35% of the total Costa Rican government income per year.

Community of Self-Interest

The change from concessions to participation—or partnership—should have a salutary effect on one of the problems involved in Latin American business: the prevalence of "share the wealth" schemes and socialism generally. Basically, I think that the development of a "community of self-interest" is the most promising approach to the problem and, at the same time, the soundest way of doing business in Latin America.

We think we are building such a community of interest in our business. From the standpoint of the countries where we operate, the following benefits flow from our activities:

> In 1955, the United Fruit Company paid about $23 million to the Central American governments in taxes and duties. The total payments made to individuals—with the largest amount in wages and salaries—came to nearly $107 million. As a matter of fact, a recent

Twentieth Century Fund survey proved that the banana business is the largest income producer in Costa Rica. Surpassing the coffee crop in Panama, the banana industry contributes more to the national income than revenues from the Canal Zone.

Since its organization in 1899, the United Fruit Company has spent over $500 million in tropical betterment projects. We have reclaimed land which others in the banana business were forced to abandon, and we have endeavored to put in new crops that would benefit the national economies. We do not try to compete in other lines of activity—we are primarily in the banana business—but we have introduced complementary crops such as African oil, palm, and cacao on abandoned farms. In Costa Rica alone we spent $2 million on such reclamation projects; we hope they will become self-sustaining enterprises within the next three years.

We employ over 81,000 Latin Americans. If the size of the average family is set at five—and that is a conservative estimate—over 400,000 men, women, and children are dependent on the United Fruit Company for their livelihood. In 1955, our payrolls were something over $73 million, and we were the largest single employer in the Central American countries and in Ecuador. In the same period we spent over $1 million on schools, $3¼ million on hospitals, $1 million for sanitation, and $10 million in other social benefits.

We operate an agricultural school at Zamorano, Honduras. This institution, which has been endowed with $5 million by the United Fruit Company, is designed not only to promote good will but to help in the strengthening of the agricultural economies of the area. There is a student body of 175 boys; they follow a three-year curriculum. Tuition, room and board, and such items as clothing and text books are free. We make only one proviso: none of these boys may work for the United Fruit Company when he finishes his schooling. What they learn at this school, they take back to their own families and homes and communities. One of the most gratifying results of the endeavor is that practically all the ministries of agriculture in the area are increasingly staffed with graduates of this school.

Such activities serve to publicize the change in business philosophy to the country at large, but they cannot do the whole job. We have found that we need to take people right to the plantations and show them what is going on. Many governmental officials and influential private citizens in Central America have never seen a banana plantation. They have all sorts of strange ideas about our operations—they think we are often attacked by tigers and bitten by snakes—and they really know very little about the banana business.

We have a program of organized airplane tours for key people from all walks of life—with the emphasis on government officials, journalists, and local civic leaders. There are student tours as well, so that the young people may know what is being done.

Public relations and education are a continuing concern of ours. We sponsor a press seminar every year in New Orleans under the auspices of International House, inviting representatives of the press from the countries where we conduct our operations and from other countries. These people are not filled with the gospel according to the United Fruit Company, but attend a practical seminar on journalism, emphasizing honest reporting and the importance of freedom of the press.

Building up good public relations is a slow process at best. It will take years to get our story across, but we are making headway.

Good Neighbors and Allies

In conclusion, I want to comment briefly on the role of United States business in the competitive struggle with the Soviets. Here again, the picture in Latin America is considerably different from other areas of the world. In the first place, these countries are neither neutral nor uncommitted; they are definitely and officially on our side. We are bound together in a strong political alliance within the United Nations. Known as the Organization of American States, it is the political outgrowth of the Pan-American Union.

After a series of conferences held over many years, the OAS has taken on authority and proved workable. Its anticommunist structure was formalized in 1948 at Bogota, Colombia, in a resolution against communism, with most of the Latin American countries adhering to it. Argentina was perhaps the only important nation abstaining. In Caracas in 1954, Guatemala alone voted against the anticommunistic resolution, and there were only two abstentions—Argentina and Mexico. I think we are safe in assuming that Latin America as a whole is officially on record as against communism in any form.

In the minds of most Americans, the most important bulwark of our mutual defense was the Monroe Doctrine. For many years, this policy was unilateral; in its infancy it was backed up by the sea power of Great Britain. Now it is a multilateral commitment of all the American republics.

The Soviet economic, not ideological, influence in Latin America has been so minimal so far; I do not think we should be too concerned about any real difficulties in this regard. The ideological threat is still there, however. In some countries, the communists have gone underground; they are still active in Guatemala, and they are infiltrating Brazil and other countries as well. Generally, such activities should be classed as political rather than economic threats to the security of the hemisphere and a definite part of Russia's imperialistic campaign.

The example of fair and honest treatment that has been set by American businessmen for the years that they have worked in cooperation and collaboration with Latin Americans is the best defense —and offense—against any Soviet economic or political threat. We have an expression in Spanish: "Cuentas claras hacen buenos amigos," or "clear accounts make good friends." By keeping clear accounts and acting in a fair and decent manner, by making sure that a community of mutual self-interest is maintained, we should be able to counteract any Soviet moves in Latin America.

DOING BUSINESS IN SAUDI ARABIA*

Mr. McClintock, in his part of this chapter, used the term "community of self-interest" and went on to describe the contributions

* By Mr. Duce.

which the United Fruit Company has made in the areas where it does business. The Arabian American Oil Company represents a case example of the same sort in another part of the world, where its operations have brought massive changes in Saudi Arabia during the past twenty years.

The possibilities of finding oil in Arabia at the time the concession was negotiated were highly speculative, and, with the developments over the succeeding four years, they looked even more speculative. Sometimes there was open question whether the venture should be abandoned and the approximately $10 million spent written off as a total loss. Deeper drilling, however, revised the outlook and Aramco is now one of the most successful of United States foreign ventures.

When the company entered Saudi Arabia, it found a patriarchal government, dependent on the fees connected with the pilgrimage to Mecca for its foreign exchange. Such money as there was in the country was in hard currency—gold and silver of all sorts and descriptions. Savings were in the form of hoards of coin. The total income of the government in 1932 has been estimated at $2.5 million. Of this, less than $2 million was in foreign exchange. There was practically no local industry except for a few small enterprises engaged in the manufacture of ornamental knives and swords and some weaving of rugs and tent cloths and simple leather fabrication. In one or two places salt was mined. There had been some subventions paid by the British.

This was really an ancient civilization which had been barely affected by the progress of several centuries. Prior to 1940 a large proportion of the population existed on the edge of starvation, and famines were not unknown. The main occupation of the inhabitants was guarding the flocks and herds, the camels, sheep, and goats which followed the rains in the desert country. Occasionally, as at Hofuf, there were oases where the date was raised, but in the main the population was nomadic. It was, however, a civilized community with history and traditions running far into the past, with elaborate folk mores and a stern and all-embracing religion. Its people were competent and able as far as their environment was concerned. They learned readily and adapted themselves quickly, under training, to modern techniques. I might add that in Saudi Arabia in the early thirties there were practically no doctors and no hospitals. The schools were mainly religious institutions, and there were very few of them. Thus the impact of industrial developments in eastern Saudi Arabia was immediate and sometimes disturbing.

Impact of Industrialization

Let us look for instance at the income of the Saudi Government (Table I). In 1938 it was believed to be less than $7 million. In 1955 it was between $350 and $400 million, or 50 times as large as in 1938. The main increase in this revenue was from oil, but the general growth of the economy brought more revenue from other sources as well. This, of course, immediately affected the quantity of imports for consumption, excluding those of the oil company (Table II).

In addition, discovery of oil increased the minimum wage in the country from less than 1 riyal a day to 6 riyals—or from about 27 cents a day to $1.62. The general wage scale throughout the country has roughly followed this pattern (Table III).

Because of these developments, higher wages are now paid by farmers, contractors, and employers generally. Such general wage adjustments create real problems for farmers and others, which cannot be avoided. But such adjustments will continue to spread gradually throughout the kingdom until all workers enjoy the same improved standards of living as those in the oil industry.

But there are ways in which some of the rise in prices which normally accompany rising wages can be alleviated:

> During a visit to one of our Arabian installations in 1944 I talked to one of the executives about the effect of wage raises. When I asked how our people were getting along, he replied, "They don't seem to be able to eat any better than they did before. As soon as

Table I

SAUDI ARABIA

CRUDE OIL PRODUCTION

MILLIONS OF BARRELS

ESTIMATED GOVERNMENT INCOME

MILLIONS OF DOLLARS

Table II

ESTIMATED SAUDI ARABIAN MERCHANDISE IMPORTS*
1937 - 1955

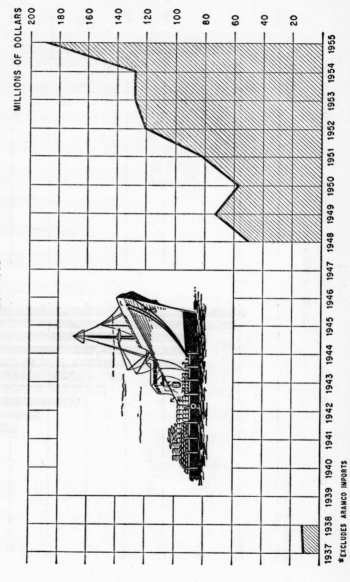

MILLIONS OF DOLLARS

*EXCLUDES ARAMCO IMPORTS

44

Table III

SAUDI ARABS EMPLOYED IN ARAMCO OPERATIONS
(INCLUDES CONTRACTORS' EMPLOYEES)

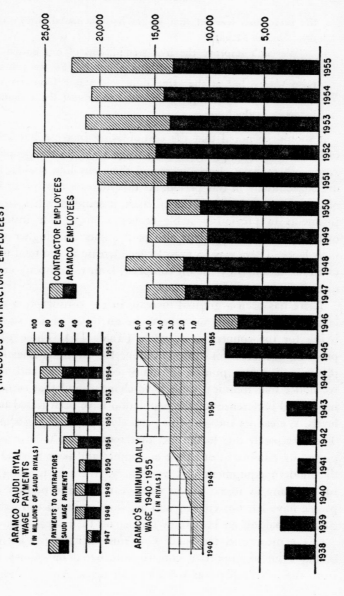

CONTRACTOR EMPLOYEES
ARAMCO EMPLOYEES

ARAMCO SAUDI RIYAL WAGE PAYMENTS
(IN MILLIONS OF SAUDI RIYALS)

PAYMENTS TO CONTRACTORS
SAUDI WAGE PAYMENTS

ARAMCO'S MINIMUM DAILY WAGE 1940 - 1955
(IN RIYALS)

the merchants learned that wages had increased, they raised the prices in the bazaar!"

"We can't improve the living conditions of our employees that way," I said. "Let's do something about it." So we continued to raise wages, but at the same time sold staple food items to our workers at reasonable prices in order to protect them against price increases in the bazaar.

It should be noted that the cost-of-living increase has been held to less than 6% despite the rising wage scale. So the people in the Aramco area have clearly increased their absolute standard of living substantially in this period. As this increase has spread to areas of the country other than the oil coast, it sometimes has created adjustments in previously stable economic areas. For instance, the owners of the date gardens also paid higher and higher wages to their labor. There was an even larger increase in the total payments to Saudi nationals by the oil company, both to company employees directly and to local contractors.

There has been a gradual increase in the consumption of petroleum products, which we take to be an index of the standard of living for the country as a whole (Table IV). These petroleum products are used for transportation, for running Diesel electric plants and water pumps in many communities, and for heat. we notice that technical skills have changed and that consumption habits and preferences of the population have been raised to higher levels. We cannot measure this precisely, but the changes are great. They are partly due to the fact that 100,000 Saudis have been employed by Aramco at one time or another and have learned to handle modern equipment and machinery. We run training schools for as many as 10,000 Saudis each year. A large portion of these people have left our employ and are now scattered throughout the country, making an important impact on their local communities.

In the meantime, the Saudi Government itself has been undertaking a lot of important construction, based on money received from the oil company as royalties and taxes. Among the projects

Table IV

ARAMCO SALES OF CRUDE OIL AND REFINED PRODUCTS
IN SAUDI ARABIA 1938-1955

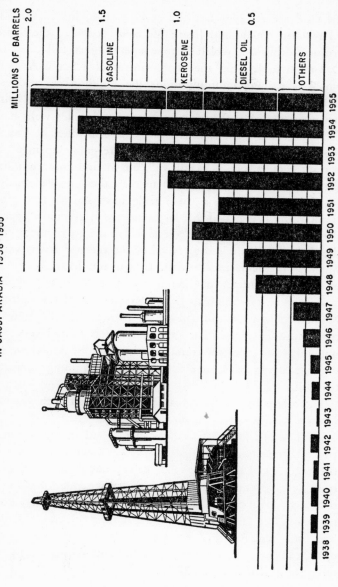

included are the port facilities at Dammam, Jiddah, Ras Tanura, Al Khobar, Yenbo and Jizan; the construction of the Saudi Government Railroad, which is now operating at full capacity from Dammam to Riyadh; the establishment of a Saudi Arab Airline, which is easing communication; the building of roads such as those to Medina and Mecca. Water supply systems are being constructed in most of the important cities and water wells have been drilled in many places, thus easing the difficulties of travel along the desert road. Schools and hospitals are going up in all the important centers, but it is still difficult to find competent teachers, doctors, technicians and nurses to man these institutions.

Local industries on a small scale have started throughout the country and it is hoped that larger ones will gradually appear since they will be badly needed. Projects which the government has under detailed study include the revival of the railroad from Ammam to Medina—the American firm of Brown and Blauvelt was recently awarded the contract for the renovation of this section of the line— and its extension South to Jiddah. Extensions of the railroad from Medina to join the railroad which runs to Riyadh from the east coast is also planned. The government has started surveys of the mineral resources of the country, to be made by American and German geologists with an eye to developing mining ventures other than oil.

There are, I think, real reasons to hope that such ventures may ultimately turn out to be successful.

With regard to social changes in the nation, the distinction between tribes is disappearing. Twenty years ago a man always mentioned his tribal affiliation; today he is proud to say he is a Saudi. A traveler can go anywhere in the country without trouble—although if he gets down on the borders some of the British may arrest him for trespassing on what they regard as their preserves. Walled cities like Jidda and Riyadh have destroyed their battlements, as a part of the efficient administration of justice and the police system which the government has established.

Demands on Government

One of the difficulties in Saudi Arabia has been the fact that the government had a rather simple administrative system and no bureaucracy competent to run its increasingly complex daily affairs. Considering the history of the country, the government's business has been pretty well run, but planning the spending of the great quantities of money now flowing into the country is a mammoth and difficult job. It demands new administrative machinery and better trained personnel—and, happily, great strides are being made in that direction.

For a long time, many of the tribes existed on a dole system which supplied food and clothing to them when the rains failed. Indeed, some of the criticisms that have been leveled against Saudi Arabia, including references to the building of new palaces, overlook the fact that the government must still take steps to see that the large Bedouin population is either assisted or furnished with gainful employment. Construction work—on palaces or other buildings—is an effective means of putting surplus labor to work.

Some of the money received by the government probably is misspent, but that occurrence is not unknown even in the United States! The Saudis admit that there is wastage; personally, I suspect that they do not waste any more than other similar economies in transition from a patriarchal system to a modern state. As the nation's revenues increase—and they are bound to go up if the production of oil continues to rise—the money will be spent in a better and more efficient fashion.

Saudi Arabia has lent money to several Middle Eastern governments, including Syria, in addition to taking care of its own expenditures. Repayment of these loans is to be made largely in surplus products of these countries. Such economic arrangements are, in principle, mutually beneficial and will play a role in the development of a sound economy.

Oil and the Nation's Future

Most of the recent changes in the ancient country of Saudi Arabia
developed as a result of a simple contract for the production of oil.
At the time the contract was signed, Arabia was known as a singu-
larly inhospitable land. But as we began to carry out our operations,
we found that the people were easy to get along with if we respected their traditions. We have conceived our task to be the
coupling of such consideration with the training of these people
to take their place in a modern industrial operation. For that reason
we have had as many as 10,000 Arabs at one time undergoing education in the skills necessary for their jobs and in language as well.
On the reverse side, we try to teach Arabic to our American employees.

We have introduced new ideas of sanitation by precept and are
developing new standards of housing by practice. But we have not
forced these changes on anyone. One interesting example of this
policy of consideration plus education is the matter of clothing:

> The uniform of the Bedouin has always been the aba and thaub,
> but these are unsuitable for work in industrial plants because they
> tend to catch in machinery. The Arabs have not given up their
> traditional costume; it has merely become their Sunday dress,
> while their workaday attire consists of the shirt and trousers worn
> by the average American.

These many changes have been to the benefit of the country and
the people concerned. Some of these advances have, I must admit,
been unexpected. At the beginning of this chapter I pointed out that
the only foreign exchange the Saudis had when we arrived came
from pilgrimage fees. Despite a reduction in these fees, the total
income from this source has multiplied because of the new and
modern facilities now available to greater numbers of pilgrims.

As to the future—I do not like to forecast the amount of income
which the government of Saudi Arabia will receive from the oil

industry and from other sources, but it is rapidly rising and will continue to do so for a number of years to come. The Saudi Government's problem is to strengthen its own internal organization; to build schools, hospitals, and other public services; to develop training systems which will result in Saudis equipped to man these new public services; to upgrade the large supply of labor now in the nomadic population; to develop its limited water resources; and to explore its unknown and unused mineral deposits. I believe that with the development of better government techniques, and more confidence on the part of the business community, many industrial institutions making materials for the Eastern Hemisphere will grow up in the Persian Gulf because of its supply of fuel. The combination of unskilled—but easily trainable—labor, fuel, and a good government should result in great changes in the situation.

All in all, we have had problems, but with mutual confidence they have proved soluble. For this I must pay tribute to the Saudis and to my American associates.

Promoting United States Interests

Needless to say, whatever Aramco does abroad is done with an awareness of its national responsibility. In all of our efforts, we have the prosperity and security of the United States in the back of our minds. When we go abroad, we have to consider the interests of American foreign policy. Our commercial objectives must not conflict with the policies which the United States Government has adopted. Furthermore, there are changes from time to time in the international situation, and we have to adapt ourselves constantly to the realities of the moment. We have learned from the last World War, for instance, that today's enemies are often tomorrow's friends!

As a matter of fact, the impetus for our original foreign explorations came from a sense of national responsibility. In the early days, the petroleum industry was mainly concerned with producing kerosene for lamps and stoves. With the advent of the Diesel and the gas engine, the country had to begin to think about its resources and about how much oil we had for the future. We decided to be pessimistic in our estimate, and so at that time (1918) the American Government suggested to the oil companies that they go abroad and explore for oil.

During the twenty years after 1918, we pretty well explored the world and formed a reasonably good idea of where the oil lay. A great deal of heartbreak followed on the heels of those studies, for there were immense physical difficulties to cope with, and the people in such places as Hungary, Mexico, and Bolivia vigorously questioned our rights to extract the product. When I look back at the casualty lists and the acts of confiscation of that period, I sometimes wonder why we persisted—but we did. Of course, on the other side, we can record our success in the Middle East, Venezuela, and Argentina.

As far as the Soviet development goes, it is interesting to note that the Russians announced they would have plenty of oil to sell in 1960 because they are now producing over a million barrels a day —and will increase the amount to 2 million by 1960. With all due respect to the Russian technicians, any United States oilman would be ashamed to talk about 2 million barrels in 1960. That comes to something less than 187 gallons per person per year, and can mean only one thing: automobiles are not going to be used much in Russia.

I wish I had a formula that would encourage businessmen to go abroad, to take the risks, but I do not. All I can do is testify to our experience, stretching from those bleak first years to the tremendously successful venture we operate today.

QUESTIONS AND ANSWERS *

From the floor: When an American company grants an increase in real wages, don't we make it difficult for the native industries

* Businessmen present at the panel session on which this chapter is based raised certain questions which brought about the discussion reported on these pages.

who can't compete with us? You can't make friends by maintaining a high wage level. In Canada there is an oil boom on, now that the Canadian-American Highway has been put through. American companies have raised their wages to the highest level in the country, so that it is hard for ordinary domestic enterprises—insurance companies and banks, for instance—to get workers because they are drifting into the American-dominated oil industry.

Mr. McClintock: The United Fruit Company pays from two to three times as much as anybody else for labor. For example, we pay a minimum wage of $1.80 in Guatemala for year-round employment, but the average daily earnings in 1955 were $3.02. On top of that, we provide free schools, hospitals, housing, and so forth. Guatemalan employers pay 85¢ a day for labor on the coffee farms and then they only hire most workers during the coffee harvest season.

However, this differential presents no serious problems in the country, because we operate in such remote areas that we are not actually an integral part of the agricultural picture. In other parts of the country our jungle plantations were initially unattractive places to work—even unhealthy—so that we had to pay high wages to get anybody to work there at all. Even after towns were established and sanitation was installed, we had to maintain our higher wage rate because the people in the highlands erroneously believed —and still believe—that there is malaria and yellow fever to contend with in these areas, even though they have been stamped out.

Mr. Gordon: United Fruit's situation is a unique one, but, generally speaking, wouldn't you actually expect a wage differential? It probably does cause a disruption, but if you are interested in the economic development of the country above and beyond your immediate industry, there must be a spread of this kind. If the wage level of the American company were equal to—or barely above— that of local enterprises, there would be no impetus for an increase in living standards. Furthermore, you would be exposed to violent accusations of "exploitation." It is much better that a wage increase be started with the people employed in a new industry, and then spread gradually, nudging the entire economy upwards.

From the floor: It is sometimes said that the British Government is much more responsive to private British needs in foreign countries than is the United States Department of State. To what extent does our government help in business negotiations with foreign governments?

Mr. McClintock: Speaking for the United Fruit Company, there is really no reason for the United States Government to intervene in any of our dealings. This would be considered an infringement of sovereignty by the Latin Americans.

From the floor: How can the United States protect your interests abroad if they have nothing to do with the negotiations?

Mr. McClintock: It is the duty of the State Department to protect U.S. interests abroad, whether they have been in on the contract or not. The excellent piece of work done by the State Department in Guatemala is an example of their responsibility and action.

Mr. Duce: We must remember that the British Government is a stockholder in a good many of the British concessions in the Middle East. Consequently, they have a special interest in private business dealings that the American Government doesn't have. They own about 60% of the British Petroleum Corporation, for example. Furthermore, I think they are a little closer to their companies, though I don't believe that this is necessarily an improvement over the attitude of our government. We keep the State Department informed on what we are doing and if, occasionally, they say they think we should do something else, we usually go along with them. But they don't intervene in our negotiations.

From the floor: It seems to me that when companies of your size go into a country, you become involved in politics whether you like it or not because you are such an important part of their economy. How do you handle this?

Mr. Duce: This is one of the problems you meet in foreign operations. We try to disassociate ourselves as far as possible from the politics of the area, but we do work with the powers that are there.

We try to become a part of the community as a whole, rather than joining any particular political faction. To do this, we have set up an "AID" department—Arabian Industrial Development—headed by a man who works with various local people in building up their own communities. In this way, we hope to become known as good neighbors to everyone, rather than as backers of any one group or individual.

Part Two

MANAGEMENT PROBLEMS AND CASE HISTORIES

AMERICAN BUSINESS GOES ABROAD: A CASE HISTORY

Stanley C. Allyn

THE PURPOSE OF THIS BOOK has been well stated—we are considering here both the *opportunities* and the *responsibilities* of doing business abroad. We cannot discuss one without the other, for the two are inseparable in overseas trade—as in any other business relationship. All too often we discover that efforts to develop business overseas have foundered on the failure to appreciate this fundamental link between opportunity and responsibility.

But in spite of some unprofitable adventures, the country today has a substantial commercial interest overseas. Since this interest is frequently minimized and sometimes completely overlooked, it seems appropriate to take a quick glance at the whole question of overseas business. What does it mean to the United States? What

Note: Mr. Allyn is President of the National Cash Register Company and United States Representative to the Economic Commission for Europe of the United Nations.

does it mean to foreign countries? What are the yardsticks by which its importance should be measured?

I will not attempt to answer these questions in detail, but I believe I can provide a few highlights which may serve to point up the nature and extent of our commerical interests in other countries.

OUR OVERSEAS ACTIVITIES

The total of our exports is the most commonly employed measure of our foreign economic stake. Exports of goods and commodities are currently running at an annual rate of about $14 billion. Now this figure is solid as far as it goes, but it is actually about two-thirds inadequate: it leaves out sales by American plants abroad. These plants —and there are many, including a few which belong to the National Cash Register Company—are selling to the foreign market at an annual rate of $30 billion. Therefore, foreign sales by American industry add up to about $44 billion a year, a sum not even hinted at by mere export figures.

This figure may not look impressive in the full glare of our $400 billion gross national product, but all one has to do is to adjust his focus, and it becomes a rather staggering total:

- It is equivalent to the gross national product of the United Kingdom.
- It is almost twice the gross national product of Canada.
- It is more than the current level of national security spending in the United States.

When one views our sales to foreign customers under that kind of candle power—which is the only logical way to look at them— our foreign business attains the respect it deserves. Thus we see that the United States has a vital interest in the continued economic growth and prosperity of the Free World—an interest far greater than generally estimated.

On the reverse side of the coin, we find that other nations have a substantial stake in our offshore business. American private en-

terprise has been investing $1.5 billion a year overseas. These invest-
ments are not exactly unwelcome in the nations where such funds
are spent, nor are the employment opportunities which they naturally create.

It is rather significant that $500 million of this annual total has
been invested in the underdeveloped areas. This sum equals, almost
dollar for dollar, the amount of our government's proposed economic assistance to these same areas, and it is playing an equally
effective role in bolstering their economies.

NCR ABROAD

With this background on United States private economic interests
overseas, I would like to give the case history of one American
business which went abroad in the 19th century and has maintained
successful outposts overseas ever since. This is the history of my own
company, which made its first journey to foreign shores in 1885.

The National Cash Register Company has been in world trade
for 71 of its 72 years. We are doing business today in some 100 countries. Our overseas sales in the year 1955, for instance, amounted to
over $100 million—or 40% of our total volume—and we anticipate
substantial increases in the future.

In conducting this part of our business, we follow a pattern of
operations which is based on certain definite and proven principles
developed over the years. Except for the inevitable refinements to
meet a rapidly changing world, it has remained constant for a long
time. It is true, of course, that this pattern might not work for other
companies, but it has certainly worked for us—and some elements
of it are so fundamental, in our opinion, that they cannot safely be
omitted from any type of orderly procedure overseas.

The essentials of our program are these:

- When we go into any foreign country, we go in for keeps.
- We believe in a company operation overseas instead of general
  agencies.

- We believe in staffing our overseas operations with nationals of the countries concerned.
- We have learned that—for us at least—*service* comes ahead of *sales*. I am using the word "service" to mean rejuvenation of over-age machines, new parts for old, and skilled repair work.
- We consistently invest part of our profits in the countries where those profits were earned.
- We do not look on our overseas employees as stepchildren. We treat them exactly as we treat our staff at home.
- We try to give the foreign market the product it wants—not the product which we think it ought to have.
- We believe in firsthand contacts with our foreign markets, so we are constantly traveling.
- We are extremely careful to respect the customs, traditions, religions, and sensitivities of other peoples.

These nine principles are the fundamentals of our working pattern, but they do not follow any particular order of precedence. One principle might take priority in one nation, and another be considered the most important one in a different land.

FOR KEEPS

I said that when we go into a country, we go in for keeps. Wherever we hang up our shingle, we plan to stay, regardless of wars, revolutions, and depressions. In many countries the National Cash Register Company has lasted longer than the government. We have, of course, been put out of business in some nations behind the Iron Curtain by the simple process of expropriation, but we have never voluntarily withdrawn.

It has not always been easy to keep our business going, even on this side of the Iron Curtain. The credit for our success under all kinds of bewildering and difficult circumstances belongs to the NCR people in the countries involved—men and women who time and time again have made sacrifices for the business far beyond the call of duty. You could fill a small shelf of books with examples of these sacrifices, but one will suffice to make the point.

Did you ever hear of anyone stealing a factory? That is what happened to us.

Before the war, we had a beautiful factory in Berlin. Somehow it
had escaped being bombed, but when the Russians came in they
virtually rolled it up like a rug and took it home with them. They
ripped out the elevators and the windows and then loaded them
up and dumped loose machine parts on top of the pile in a fantastic
kind of jumble. It must have been quite a sight! I heard all the details from our German employees when I arrived in Berlin in
August 1945, as a guest of the Army. But I also heard what our
German employees had done for us and that's the real point of
this story.

Our Berlin manager, Herr Wilhelm Rohm, began to read between
the lines of Herr Goebbels' optimistic war communiqués some
months before the armistice. He decided that the Russians would
probably occupy the city, and he had a shrewd hunch that his be-
loved factory would be a prize piece of loot for the Soviet Government. Consequently he lined up as many trucks as he could, filled
them with blueprints, tools, parts, and key employees, and moved
115 miles southwest of Berlin to an ancient champagne cellar in
Freyburg. Thus American business abroad sometimes has to go underground if it expects to survive!

But the Freyburg adventure did not last long. Herr Rohm was
tipped off that Thuringia might be labeled for inclusion in the
Soviet zone, so his strange little caravan took to the road again. It
traveled mostly by night because Rohm recognized the possibility
that his tools might be seized by the Russians and that prowling
Soviet troops might imprison him and his men, or even shoot them
on sight.

Eventually, he found a refuge in Gunzehausen, in the American
zone. The owner of a small hotel let him stow his gear in the base-
ment and allowed him to have two little rooms for an office. From
Gunzehausen, Herr Rohm moved to Augsburg where he leased a
small factory, and we were back in business—so to speak.

The war was over by then, but we could not send much help to
Rohm and his men in their miniature enterprise. We could send
CARE parcels, however, so we did that in the thought that he and
his employees might enjoy the provisions they contained. As one

might expect, the parcels included cigarettes. Now cigarettes were a medium of exchange at that time—actually a far better medium than money. So our people traded their CARE cigarettes for tools and equipment and gradually built up a self-sustaining repair business. I suppose you might say that they literally smoked out business where it did not exist! Believe it or not, they even managed to lay aside a little working capital with which to resume manufacturing.

Gradually they lifted the business onto its feet until the first post-war, completely German-manufactured cash register came off the assembly line at Augsburg in March 1949. This matter of a cigarette economy is one hazard which is not usually mentioned when the risks of foreign trade are outlined—but we managed to survive it in great shape!

AGENCIES VS. BRANCH OPERATIONS

Now let us turn to the question of company operation overseas as opposed to the establishment of general agencies.

At the outset of our foreign operations we set up general agencies abroad, but in general this did not work out. Our agents did not plow back sufficient income to expand the scope of their enterprises, nor did they develop a "feeling" for our business. Their attention was divided among a number of different items. This was unfortunate because cash registers, accounting machines, and adding machines are specialty products. They must be sold by specialists who are experts on the machines themselves and understand business systems as well.

There are always exceptions to any rule, and we are, in fact, selling through general sales agents in a number of countries of the world today. Most of these countries are rather small, but two of them are among our most important overseas operations. In these nations, however, the third generation of the families concerned is now in the business. They have held the NCR franchise for more than fifty years and handle nothing but National Cash Register products. It is doubtful if anyone could do a better job than these men have done.

In the main, however, our experience points to company-owned branches as the best method of distribution for a product such as ours. Very obviously, our rule might not apply to many products sold across the counter—for example, it would be difficult to imagine establishing a branch store just to sell fountain pens!

STAFFING WITH NATIONALS

Our overseas business supports an organization of approximately 18,000 employees, only 6 of whom are Americans. It may be that we lean over backwards to staff our operations with nationals, but our experience leads us to believe that it pays off in the long run.

In the first place, when my associates and I visit an overseas facility, we are not insulated from the nationals by layers of Americans who might or might not have adjusted themselves to an understanding of the local scene. We are able to talk directly with the foreign executives because there is no one else to talk to. It is almost that simple, and we propose to keep it that way.

Furthermore, in these turbulent times this policy of avoiding insulation is even more important than it used to be. While the United States has been growing more internationally minded, we are forced to acknowledge that many other countries are growing more nationalistic, and we must recognize this fact in our business policies.

Finally, it is just plain good business. It has been our experience that the local citizens acquire the necessary knowledge of our business with about the same facility as Americans. In addition, they have the advantage of knowing their own people and the problems of their own nations far better than outsiders could ever learn them.

By having so few Americans in our overseas organization, I do not want anyone to think that we do not furnish know-how—which might properly be called our skills and techniques. That is one of the most important and most welcome exports that my company produces. An American boy who knows how to increase production can often be a more valuable ambassador than a lecturer on the fine points of the democratic philosophy. One of the by-products that ensues from doing business abroad is a definite contribution to the mechanical skill of the countries concerned.

EMPHASIS ON SERVICE

In many sectors of the globe, the salesman for American equipment is first asked about the degree of service he can provide and then about the kind of machine he has to sell. This makes sense, for the customer is principally interested in the work the machine will perform. If it breaks down and there are no repair facilities at hand, the owner is left with nothing but so many pounds of useless metal. Our machines contain anywhere from 2,000 to 22,000 precision parts. They cannot go along indefinitely without service, especially since many are in almost continuous use throughout the day. Thus readily available service facilities are most important. When we established a company-owned branch in Baghdad, for instance, we gave first consideration to acquiring quarters for the service department and bringing in the necessary staff of skilled doctors for tired-out and overworked machines.

In times of stress, service has kept our business going when there were no machines to sell and our doors would otherwise have been closed. Our Spanish operations provide one example: During the Civil War, our organization was almost completely disbanded, our premises destroyed, and our stock of machines confiscated. But the manager of our branch happened to be a former repairman—a fine doctor for a sick machine. As soon as the pressure of hostilities had eased a bit, he canvassed around for service, and found enough to keep going. Eventually, he was able to buy a machine in the secondhand market, overhaul it, and sell it. From this nebulous rebirth, our business in Spain was built up again to respectable proportions.

There have been many other cases where service has offered the only means for survival, and not all of them were connected with war. Our policy of putting service ahead of sales results in an almost imperishable business once we have made installations in quantity in any country.

PLOWING BACK PROFITS

Now we come to the important question of reinvestment of profits earned abroad.

I would put reinvestment of earnings—at least in part—very near the top of the list of rules for overseas success. The advantages are twofold. A company acquires necessary facilities, and also demonstrates clearly that it is contributing something worthwhile to a country as well as profiting from it. In other words, the firm is meeting the responsibilities of foreign operations as well as taking advantage of the opportunities.

Our overseas business last year was more than 10 times what it was in 1940. While many factors combined to create this record, one of the most important was this long-established practice. Reinvestment has largely paid for the manufacturing plants we have established since the war and for numerous expansions of our sales and service facilities.

AN APPRECIATIVE GUEST

Our company tries to behave at all times as a guest in other nations—and as a guest who is grateful for the hospitality of his hosts. We not only contribute to the economies of these nations; we do whatever we can for the general well-being of the communities in which we are located. To put it another way, we try to make ourselves welcome enough so that our hosts will want us to stay forever, instead of merely tolerating our presence.

Let me give you an example of this principle in operation:

When World War II was drawing to a close, we could foresee an impending shortage of dollars in practically all the countries in which we hoped to sell machines. This could only lead to increasing difficulty in shipping to those countries from the United States. We had to develop a new source of supply for those nations which would no longer be able to purchase machines from the United States.

Great Britain seemed a natural location for a factory. The British market itself was important to us, and so were the Commonwealth nations. Furthermore, shipment could be made from Britain to many other countries.

A close study of the areas available took us to Scotland and then into Dundee. Since Dundee was a so-called distress area, plagued by unemployment, we were given a hearty welcome. A site was chosen, a factory erected, and production was begun in 1947. As a result of our reinvestment policy, we are following a far more ambitious program of manufacturing in Dundee than we ever visualized in the beginning. The factory, now five times its original size, employs more than 3,000 people. Subsequently, several other American companies built plants in the city, and Dundee is no longer a distress area. On the contrary, there is a shortage of labor today.

In summary, then, the project has been a profitable one for our stockholders and for the British economy. It has been carried through in a spirit of genuine reciprocity. The British government has always been fair with us on the question of remitting royalties and dividends, while we have sought to duplicate in England the practices we have maintained in the United States. You could hold up a mirror to the Dundee plant and see what we do in Dayton, since good working conditions, adequate recreation facilities, and employee benefit programs mean just as much to people overseas as they do here at home. We do everything we can to make sure that our foreign personnel will have no reason to think of themselves as stepchildren—in Dundee and throughout our foreign operations.

THE RIGHT PRODUCT FOR THE MARKET

The next principle really falls into the same category. I am referring to our efforts to adapt the product for the market.

We have learned from experience that it is not enough to say, "What is good for the American market is good for overseas." Though that is often true, there are instances where needs and conditions vary from ours, and the product must be changed accordingly. We would consider it foolish to try to force an American product into a situation where it is not suitable.

To implement this principle, we have established product development committees in every sector of the globe where we do business. We look to these committees for appraisals and reappraisals of the market and accurate information on its requirements. Consequently, our workable ideas do not all originate in Dayton headquarters. Manufacturing for and selling to a foreign market is a two-way street, and we like it that way. A man stationed half the way around the globe from the home office and left without any immediate source of direction is prone to develop a strong trait of resourcefulness. That trait pays off: a number of important developments which were subsequently adopted for the business as a whole have originated abroad.

A brief anecdote from Egypt may serve to point up this principle of gearing the product to the market:

> Egypt, like the other Arab nations, is undergoing a powerful wave of nationalism today. This sense of independence extends right down to the matter of record-keeping. The Egyptians take pride in keeping their books in Arabic and sturdily refuse to adopt a less cumbersome system. Out of respect for this attitude, we are making bookkeeping machines for Egypt which speak mathematical Arabic.
>
> You can imagine the initial difficulties. Like Chinese, the Arabic language reads from right to left, and so do Arabic record-keeping entries. The English alphabet has 26 characters; the Arabic language has 72 characters or variations of characters. If you should ask me how we managed to design a machine that would suit the Egyptian customers, I would only say that our people did not know that it could not be done—and so they went ahead and did it!

PLENTY OF TRAVEL

You cannot sit on the banks of the Miami River in Dayton and get a world viewpoint. It is too easy to say "No" to ideas and suggestions from local managers when your operations are regulated by remote control. Reams of reports and statistics do not tell you about the most important element in any situation, which is simply people—the people in your own organization and the people who are your customers.

That is why our Dayton executives—personnel in sales, engineering, product development, research, finance, manufacturing, and administration—travel thousands of miles a year in visits overseas. Trips to Britain and the Continent are made regularly because of the heavy concentration of sales and manufacturing in Europe. In addition, a flying squadron from the executive office has tried to cover one other section of the foreign field annually in recent years. As a matter of fact, the night of the 26th Harvard Business School Conference I took a plane for Copenhagen, and two days later I was in Leningrad for the beginning of a trip through Russia and several other countries behind the Iron Curtain which I had long wanted to visit.

But we in Dayton are not the only ones who travel. We bring many of our overseas people to the United States, in order to maintain frequent personal contacts between people at the management and supervisory level.

While many of our overseas people are brought to the United States for training, either as salesmen, service people, or managers, we maintain schools for all purposes all over the world. This sort of training is not only in basic techniques, but is often on the postgraduate level. Roughly speaking, we have been running about 2,000 overseas persons through our training program every year.

RESPECT FOR TRADITIONS

The last of NCR's fundamental principles concerns our respect for the traditions of other people. My trips abroad have instilled in me the definite idea that people are much the same the world over in their basic reactions. Their outlooks may vary because of differences in tradition, language, religion, standards of living, and geography, but they all have one common denominator—the desire to be treated like human beings. They all have their sensitivities—and so do we.

Out of many rather quaint experiences abroad, one incident stands out as typical in this connection:

On one trip to the Far East, we spent several days in Singapore. I suggested to some British acquaintances that we ought to have all of our employees get together for a dinner, which is our normal practice on such visits. They were stunned by this idea. They told us that a dinner was out of the question because our employees included Chinese, Mohammedans, and Europeans.

The three groups *worked* together very well, but there was no social mixing whatever. The Mohammedans had their own special rules about food and its preparation. It had to be prepared by Mohammedans and served by Mohammedans. Furthermore, they would not sit at the same table with the Chinese or, for that matter, with Europeans.

The Chinese were only slightly less scrupulous. They did not mind sitting with the Mohammedans, but they had their own very positive preferences about food. Then there were the Europeans. They were willing to sit with almost anyone, but they too had their own ideas about the menu. It seemed only too obvious that we were simply asking for trouble if we pressed the idea of an organization dinner.

But the dinner was held—and appropriately enough, it was held in a dining room in an amusement park called "Happy World." We had three separate tables. Mohammedan food and Mohammedan service prevailed at one table; Chinese food was served at the second table; and there was a separate menu for the Europeans at a third.

The meeting was a great success. There was a considerable amount of visiting among the groups, and by the end of the evening the original lines of demarcation seemed to have been completely forgotten.

BUSINESS MUST COOPERATE

I asked myself more than once on that particular trip, as I have on others, "Why is it that business finds a way to survive and grow in the face of the same obstacles which seem to stifle understanding among nations?"

In my opinion, the basic reason is that business is *forced* to acquire an understanding of the customs of a country and the traditions and preferences of its people and to conduct itself accordingly. You either establish a common meeting ground or you do not do business.

Wherever I have traveled overseas, I have seen American products in use: a Singer sewing machine in a dilapidated hut along the Menam River in Bangkok; Coca-Cola almost every place; signs along the road advertising American automobile tires and the gasoline of American companies. Kodak is a name so universally employed that it must be a word in every language. The *Reader's Digest* is a popular publication in twelve languages. In department stores and smaller shops, American cosmetics are almost always on display. I cannot think of any place where American movies were not being shown. And of course we see to it that there is a fair representation of our own products!

It is something of a paradox that, while American products are universally popular, the same thing cannot be said of American ideas. Perhaps we should re-examine the methods we are using to sell freedom to the rest of the world, for that is the most important sale we have to make. I sincerely believe that world trade—conducted with satisfaction to both sides—can be as important a factor as any in making that sale.

I do know that business relations among men of different nationalities sometimes serve to take the edge off belligerency, and I can testify to it with a little anecdote from World War II:

Our office in Paris was on the line of march when Hitler's Wehrmacht rumbled into the ancient city and along the Champs Élysées. Suddenly, one of the tanks swerved out of line and headed straight for it. The tank came to a halt and disgorged a German soldier who thundered on the door and made it plain he wanted to come in. Come in he did, and there he stood in that enemy uniform, with a gun on his hip and a grim look on his face.

Our French employees had a bad moment—until the German soldier suddenly smiled and said:

"I'm from the National Cash Register Company in Berlin. I'm sorry I can't stay very long, but I was wondering—did you make your quota last year?"

So ends my story of one American company's experiences abroad. In giving you this case history, I hope I have portrayed something of both the opportunities and the responsibilities inherent in overseas trade. I remember saying once upon a time that doing business overseas was largely a matter of learning to live with the complexities and to roll with the punches. I still agree with that statement, but I would like to add to it now by saying that the rewards—if you succeed—are worth the effort, many, many times over. They are worth it in terms of your own business—and worth it in the contribution that your success can make to a better understanding among the peoples of the world.

SMALL BUSINESS GOES ABROAD

*George E. Gregory, E. W. Meyers, Jr., and
John MacGregor*

LICENSING ABROAD °

GREGORY INDUSTRIES WAS ORGANIZED IN EARLY 1948 with a total capitalization of $556,250 in order to purchase the Nelson Stud Welding business from the original inventor and owner, Mr. Ted Nelson. The process itself, created during the war, involves the joining of a metal stud to a metal plate by means of arc welding. Mr. Nelson developed some crude stud-welding equipment, for which he received a citation from the United States Navy, while he was working

Note: Mr. Gregory is President, Gregory Industries, Inc., Michigan, Mr. Meyers is President, Trion, Inc., McKees Rocks, Pennsylvania; Mr. MacGregor is President, MacGregor Instrument Company, Needham, Massachusetts. Paul Donham, Associate Professor of Business Administration, Harvard Business School, acted as moderator for the panel session on which this chapter is based.

° By Mr. Gregory.

as a shipyard welder during the years between 1937 and 1940. From 1940 on, he devoted full time to his development. His direct war production for the period from April 1942 to December 1945 amounted to over $11 million. In awarding him an Army-Navy E, the Navy estimated that over 100 million man-hours had been saved during the war years by the use of the Nelson process.

After V-J Day, however, the company's monthly sales volume, which was $500,000 in early 1945, tumbled to less than $100,000. The process had clearly proven its value in shipbuilding during the war years, but its value to industry generally was virtually unknown. But one did not have to be a mental giant to foresee that the method could be used to effect significant cost reductions in many segments of the metalworking industry. It was equally clear, however, that a tremendous amount of engineering, advertising, and sales effort would be required to develop peacetime markets for the process.

Engineers and mechanics were thoroughly familiar with established welding and fastening methods. For many years studs had been attached to metal plates by drilling holes, threading and tapping, hand welding, or resistance welding. When we acquired the business, we had to educate and convince the metalworking industry at all levels that the Nelson Stud Welding process would do a job that no other method could do as effectively; that it would result in a better product and cleaner design; and that it would substantially reduce costs.

The foregoing has, I fear, been something of a commercial for Nelson Stud Welding, but this background is necessary for a discussion of our experience in licensing foreign manufacturers to make and sell under the Nelson Stud Welding patents. We had to have something that people would buy before we could get markets— either at home or abroad!

Agreements Overseas

Our licensing program was like many projects that we businessmen develop "as we go." We are all guilty of taking off without a clear statement of our objectives and policies. I must admit that I stumbled onto our licensing program, but I feel that it has been profitable to our company in many ways. Furthermore, I can now draw some conclusions which may have value to others in similar circumstances.

The shipbuilding industry is very important in many European countries. The prevalent low labor rates, coupled with many years of experience in the industry, have enabled these nations to build a strong competitive position. Europeans had become generally familiar with the Nelson Stud Welding process through the welding and shipbuilding literature. Consequently, Mr. Nelson had received many requests for licensing arrangements from practically every country in Europe before we took over the business. Some of these people—particularly the English—had made trips to the United States after the war and tried to persuade our predecessor to make license arrangements so that the process might be introduced in their countries. In fact, a tentative agreement had been concluded with an English firm a few months before we acquired the business.

Because of this tangible evidence of interest on the part of worthwhile foreign people, I made a trip to Europe in the fall of 1948 with our vice president in charge of sales. License agreements were completed during 1948 in Belgium, Switzerland, Norway, Sweden, France, Italy, and Australia, and the British contract was firmed up. Because of the soft currencies in these nations, it was essential that the monetary authorities of each government approve the agreements so as to permit exports in dollars. Their approval depended on our ability to show that the process would be beneficial to the economy of the country in question.

Under the formal license agreements, our company had the following responsibilities:

> • We were to give each licensee the right to manufacture and sell under our patents and to use our trade-mark if he chose.
> • We were to provide each licensee with all possible manufacturing, engineering, and sales know-how.
> • We were to visit the overseas plants and maintain correspond-

ence with them, in order to keep licensees continuously informed as to our current engineering, sales, and manufacturing programs. We were to provide these people with the same kind of sales literature and engineering data that we disseminated to the general trade in the United States.

The agreement also specified the obligations of our overseas licensees:

• They were to establish a stud-welding manufacturing, engineering, and sales organization at the earliest possible date with a fairly substantial capital investment. We obviously wished assurance that they intended to build a business, in order to forestall the possibility that our patents might be placed on the shelf.

• They were to pay us royalty and engineering fees on their sales volume.

• They were to mantain certain minimum payments (on an ascending scale) in order to hold the patent license.

• They were to permit our representatives to have the full facts on their business at all times, and allow us to visit plants, review engineering work, and audit their books, if necessary. Happily, we never felt compelled to do the latter.

I am glad to report that all the groups, with the possible exception of one, demonstrated that they had negotiated with us in good faith and have since advised us that the relationship has been profitable for them. Representatives of our company have visited these licensees at least once a year since the agreements were consummated—except for our Australian associate—and similarly the foreign companies have sent representatives to the United States. While from 1948 to 1955 the Nelson Stud Welding business has grown at the average annual rate of 15% in the United States, the growth in Europe has been considerably in excess of that amount, though it started at a much lower base level.

In spite of profitable royalty operations, on April 30, 1954, our company sold most of its foreign patents to our former English licensee for a fixed sum. We determined the price by capitalizing and projecting the royalty fees that were then current. The English company, in turn, granted new license agreements to most of the previous Gregory or Nelson licensees. Under this arrangement, Gregory Industries will still receive an engineering fee based on the total sales of the English company and its licensees when these sales exceed the established sales rates for the year 1954.

When we sold to the English associate, we were granted some nonexclusive licenses on certain English patents which they owned. We felt these would prove valuable if used in connection with our patents in the United States. We agreed to pay the English an engineering fee based on the increase which was effected in our sales rate over the sales level established in 1954.

A Profitable Venture

Our patent licensing operations between 1948 and 1954 brought us an annual profit from royalties and greatly increased our own engineering and sales knowledge about the Nelson process. In addition, we worked out a sale of the patents in 1954 on a favorable financial basis, thus transferring the administration of them—which was becoming time-consuming and costly—to the new patent owners.

But the most important benefit we received was the addition of new brains and facilities to our research and development operation. A company prospers in relation to its know-how. A research-minded approach, in its broadest sense, is an indispensable characteristic of a business that is to grow. Through these foreign relationships, we have created a world-wide research and engineering laboratory working in the stud-welding field. We know that this world-wide laboratory will enable us to provide a better engineering service to our customers in the United States and Canada.

In this connection, we found the Europeans to be particularly resourceful. Though the cost of labor per hour which they were saving through this process was only a fraction of ours, they uncovered certain applications in manufacturing and engineering which have proven to be very useful in our American markets. This was the real payoff of our foreign licensing program; the monetary benefits were definitely secondary.

Since our sale of the patents in 1954, the English have extended additional patent license agreements, particularly to Germany. Sales have increased at a satisfactory rate. We are still actively participating in formal, semiannual engineering meetings with the English and their licensees. However, we no longer have to devote time to problems of patent administration and monetary exchange. Consequently, we are able to concentrate entirely on improving the exchange of engineering information and making this new knowledge available to our customers in the United States and Canada.

In summary, I would like to suggest that anyone considering a license program should appraise his own situation carefully and answer such questions as these:

1. Is our product or process needed abroad?
2. Are our market research findings equally valid in the foreign markets?

    For example, we found that our product often could be very satisfactorily applied in the United States and yet had no application at all in the same situation in Europe, because of the lower wage rates prevailing overseas.

3. Are there European products or processes which are competitive with ours? If there are, it will be difficult to obtain payment in dollars from soft currency countries.
4. Do we have a patent position which will command respect?
5. What compensation do we expect to receive from our efforts in foreign markets?

    As I have pointed out, you can receive both financial and nonfinancial compensation. If you have a growth situation at home and are unable to develop any specific engineering objectives abroad, your time and money can be spent to better advantage in United States and Canadian markets than it can in foreign countries. On the other hand, you can obtain a very fine financial return from a foreign licensing program, if you are prepared to spend the necessary time in the creation and maintenance of it.

6. Are we certain that our position under American antitrust laws will not be adversely affected?

Before you start planning a foreign licensing program it is wise to get the advice of a good attorney who has a comprehensive knowledge of the legal implications.

7. Finally, have we an all-round executive who can be spared to do the job overseas?

Such a man must know his product and its applications, and be equally versed in manufacturing and sales problems. He must be a good negotiator—patient, understanding, discerning, and sometimes tough. Incidentally, if he has a wife who enjoys traveling with him and is generally interested in her husband's business problems, she can be most helpful in the all-important job of getting to know his foreign associates on a personal basis. The social amenities are extremely important in consummating lasting and mutually rewarding relationships with Europeans— and this is, of course, the objective of any overseas program.

EXPORTING OPPORTUNITIES*

A great deal of material has been printed on the subject of the small manufacturer in foreign markets. From my point of view, most of it is about as useless as it is diffuse. So, rather than refer to this material, I want to describe our experience, and then draw some conclusions from it.

A Business Goes Abroad

MacGregor Instrument Company, makers of surgical equipment, has been involved in international projects for about twenty years. During this period we have made many mistakes, of course, but I think we have now developed a plan that is both practical and profitable.

Perhaps rather unfortunately, we first got into the foreign field in that period between the two world wars when everything seemed

* By Mr. MacGregor.

peaceful and calm. We did not quite realize what that fellow in Germany with the black mustache was up to! Our first step was to go to England to find out what type of equipment their surgeons were using—whether it was domestically produced, imported from Germany or Japan, or came from some other source. We spent a lot of time visiting hospitals, attending hospital and surgical conventions and medical meetings, and reading the British medical journals. In those prewar days the Germans were the great makers of surgical instruments, not only for Great Britain but for the United States and the rest of the world as well. They were—and still are—skilled instrument manufacturers.

After many interviews with medical men, hospital administrators, and others, we were convinced that there was a field in Britain for high-quality American-made instruments of our type. Armed with firsthand information, we began calling on the more important distributors or dealers in surgical instruments. After outlining our experience to them and convincing them that a small stock of our more popular instruments would be a good investment, we agreed to furnish catalogues and circulars in generous quantities. In addition, we offered to imprint the dealer's name on the sales literature and provide a limited number of free samples, based on the size of the order they placed with us.

We realized, of course, that putting the goods on the dealers' shelves was not enough. We had to help move them from the stores into the hands of the doctors who were to use them. In order to accomplish this, we started an advertising campaign in the British medical journals. Our typical American copy had to be carefully revised so as to match the very precise language used by the British medical profession, and our statements had to be exceedingly accurate and exact.

After a few months, we were able to call on British dealers and write substantial orders for our instruments. From that time on we had a British agent who called regularly on the dealers, got their orders, paid the import duty, and saw to it that the dealers' stocks were replenished from time to time.

After a two-year period, during which our goods were well re-received, we felt we were in a sound position to approach an English manufacturer and ask him to furnish the necessary capital to manufacture our line. We offered to supply the necessary know-how, which included such items as technical data, models, and gauges. The whole program was to be carried out under an exclusive arrangement which would require a license arrangement under a royalty agreement.

We made this approach in 1938. By 1939 we had the first plant all set up, and I returned to England to break in the first of their employees. But the very day I arrived home in Boston, Hitler went into Poland. There is a moral in this: when you do business overseas, you have to look out for sudden political changes that can alter the whole situation!

The Admiralty stepped in at the outbreak of the war, and for four years we were not able to send any of our instruments to England. Meanwhile, the Admiralty took everything our English associates could produce—and without any profit to the manufacturer.

In the first election after the war, Mr. Churchill was voted out of power and the Labor Government came in. The new administration refused to recognize the contract that we had made with the British manufacturers. This action was very unusual—my experience has been that the word of a British gentleman is as good as any document he ever signed. When the Conservatives got back into power, they did everything that the law would allow in order to make good on the losses we had sustained in the Labor interim. Ultimately our British arrangement was changed into a royalty license agreement, which is working out most satisfactorily for us.

Careful Research

Let me now set forth some general thoughts on foreign business that have grown out of our twenty years of background.

In the event that a company decides to copy the pattern that we used—going abroad with the idea of selling products to the local distributors—careful investigation is absolutely necessary. This research should be undertaken by the head of the firm, unless he has a foreign sales manager or somebody else who knows his way around. To illustrate:

> One company I know of decided to investigate the foreign market and sent its superintendent to do the job because he knew the product line and had been with the firm for twenty years. But this man did not know a single thing about either foreign business or the international economic and political situation. He came back with a three months' expense account and a report which read, in sum and substance: "These fellows do things differently in Europe. Let's stay where we are"!

The firm had spent a lot of money to get no information at all, and this can easily happen unless a company makes sure that its investigators are capable, thorough, and on their toes.

It must be remembered that, while most countries welcome American investment and some have gone out of their way to attract it, all of them have rules and regulations which vary from nation to nation. These laws must be studied very carefully, and on the basis of each individual country.

Any research study must make sure, first of all, that American-made goods can be sold in the country involved. Then a firm ought to find out whether or not it can produce a popular and salable product, given a little lower wage scale and American methods and technical knowledge. Once this has been proved to distributors, a business is in an excellent position to go to the foreign manufacturers and get them to set up a plant with their money, if the American firm agrees to furnish the necessary know-how.

A Ready Welcome

There is no set formula for doing business abroad; each company has to work one out for itself. But the opportunities are there, and American manufacturers are welcome, so arrangements can be

made. This is especially true if you are prepared to make an investment in production equipment. Only recently I received a letter from
a chap in Holland, who wrote:

> "What on earth is keeping you? Why don't you get over here?
> Our excess labor is going to be all used up unless you get busy!
> In my town within the past year Remington-Rand, Nicholson File,
> and Aircraft-Marine have come in and set up individual plants."

This Dutch town of 35,000 people made room for three United
States manufacturers within a single year. The Department of
Commerce recently stated that there are now 3,000 United States
firms with plants in foreign countries. These include almost every
field: General Electric Company; Cluett, Peabody & Company;
Continental Can Company, Inc.; Westinghouse Electric Corporation; Helena Rubinstein, Inc.; Life Savers Corporation; and many
others. They are both large and small, though most of them are
branches of big business.

By way of a hint to would-be investors, I might mention that a
number of our British associates have come over to the United States.
When my wife and I have entertained them at home, we have been
really astonished at the interest shown by both men and women in
all the gadgets we have in our house. They just don't have such
things over there. The average European housewife has no idea
what a modern can opener looks like; she still opens tin cans the old
manual way. Several of our British friends, while here, have had to
buy an extra suitcase in order to take home the gadgets they bought
for their wives. Anyone who manufactures goods of this kind will
find a ready welcome for his products in Great Britain!

It is important to remember, though, that your product has to relate to the needs of the area. Let me give an illustration:

> I had a conversation recently with an eminent engineer who was
> sent over to Italy by the United States Government, and had just
> returned from an eighteen months' stay. He was trying to find out
> why so much of the money we had loaned to Italy for the develop-
> ment of a plastics business was apparently being wasted. During

the time he was there, he worked very closely with our Ambassador, Mrs. Luce, to try to improve the manufacturing facilities.

I asked him, "Would American small manufacturers be welcome in Italy?"

He told me the answer would be a most emphatic "No," if they planned to go over and install labor saving machinery. He said, further, "In one plant where I did some work, we designed a machine that would produce three pieces, where only one had been made before. The development of this machine put five men out of work and I was nearly lynched"!

On the other hand, he pointed out, if an American can bring in ideas for machinery that will *create* labor, he will be most welcome in Italy—and in Spain and France as well.

Quality Counts

The crux of the matter is this: my company would have made very little progress in England if it were not for the fact that our product had something that the domestic and other imported products lacked. We had a high degree of quality that the other manufacturers could not equal, and the British surgeons were willing to pay a high price for it.

Japan is now trying hard to get into the export field with surgical instruments, which they are seeking to sell in the United States. The Germans, too, are very active and are doing a superb job. But both of these countries are missing essential ingredients:

• During the war, the German industry remained stagnant and made no technical improvements. Surgery has changed greatly in ten years—even in five years. The instruments the Germans are making now are the same design they turned out before the war, and they are outdated.

• The Japanese figured that the way to get into the market would be to cut the price. However, they failed to realize that surgeons are dealing with human lives, and price is not an important factor. Therefore, the Japanese are missing the boat by producing cheap instruments which are not popular abroad.

Product quality, then, is an essential feature in our success—and this holds true for other small business firms such as ours. Once a company finds a manufacturer overseas who is ready to do business and sees eye-to-eye with the American company on quality control, it should give the manufacturer all the help it possibly can—tools, drawings, blueprints, gauges, and complete technical information. The temptation to keep any idea secret *must* be resisted. Here is a place to apply the Rotary Club motto, "He profits most who serves best." By giving every assistance to its overseas associates, a company paves the way for a successful business and assures the security of future profits and royalties.

There are a few more suggestions I might make to businessmen interested in the foreign field. If you decide to establish a license royalty agreement, you must make sure that it is submitted to the Foreign Exchange Control Commission and approved by them, or you may find it impossible for your licensor or licensee to send his money to you. All he could do in this case would be to deposit it to your credit in a bank over there, and all you could do would be to wait until you could take your wife over and have a grand and glorious time!

Foreign investments can now be insured. Though existing investments cannot be covered, a new one can be. The International Cooperation Administration in Washington will send you a bulletin on this for the asking.

Finally, it should be mentioned that certain foreign royalties, along with some domestic, received by a patentee will hereafter be treated by the government as capital gain and not as regular profits. This change will make quite a difference in your tax situation.

MANUFACTURING OVERSEAS *

Trion, Inc., produces electronic air cleaning equipment, which is used in conjunction with heating, cooling, and ventilating buildings.

* By Mr. Meyers.

Polluted air is everywhere, so it follows logically that our markets are everywhere—here and abroad.

While our business is new and is still classified as "small," our ambitions are large. To become a big business, we realized that we must build on a strong, broad foundation. There appeared to be no reason why we should not lay our cornerstones in London and Tokyo, as well as in Pittsburgh and Los Angeles. The sooner we took the "foreign trade plunge," the sooner we would become established in the foreign markets.

Consequently, in 1953 we decided to enter the foreign field. Our experience since has validated our judgment: the venture is not only profitable in itself, but it has provided us with a three-year lead on our competition.

The decision to go abroad must be made decisively, and preferably by the chief executive officer. Too often the top executive prefers not to become personally involved in the alleged difficulties of distant travel and unfamiliar customs. However, many people do not realize that it is quicker and easier to get to Hong Kong or Hamburg from Boston today than it was for our fathers, when they were our age, to get to California. Furthermore, when our company went abroad, supposed barriers such as language, money differences, and the need for high-priced experts vanished like mirages. Actually the English language and the American dollar seem to work very well in foreign countries.

When we first considered participating in an overseas venture, we had three possibilities open to us: (1) exporting, (2) licensing, and (3) manufacturing. Exporting we quickly eliminated because of the shortage of American dollars overseas and the difficulty in securing import permits for our particular product. Licensing did not seem advisable since the basic patents were protected in only a small number of foreign countries, and some of them were about to expire. For our product, world-wide patent maintenance would be both costly and complicated. By the process of elimination, manufacturing abroad appeared to be the logical approach.

The Operating Plan

Through an arrangement with a German, a Swiss, and a Japanese businessman, we formed a separate Swiss corporation, known as Trion A.G. This corporation has only four stockholders. The American parent, Trion, Inc., owns two-fifths of the outstanding shares, while each of the other three members holds one-fifth. Thus, we have effective control when our shares and those of any one of the other three members are combined. This mechanism has worked well. Frankly, if we cannot sell a specific idea to at least one of our three associates, it probably is not a very sound thought anyway. Our interest is further protected by detailed corporate bylaws which can be amended only by a two-thirds vote. Thus, with 40% control, we have effective veto power over changes in the bylaws. Too often American businessmen ruin their chances to make advantageous deals by demanding too large a percentage of control.

We have been convinced by experience that it is important to have a national of each country actively participating in the policy making of the company when it affects his nation. We have found that no matter how cosmopolitan an associate may appear, he usually is acutely nationalistic and congenitally fearful of American domination in both business and politics. Our basic plan was designed to ease this problem by insuring that each foreign associate had a substantial financial interest. Such an interest, we reasoned, would give him more incentive to function as a team member rather than primarily in terms of his own and his country's self-interest. But touchiness still exists and must always be taken into account—just as it would be if the roles were reversed and we were participating in a foreign concern.

By contract, the Swiss corporation is responsible for manufacture and sales in the Eastern Hemisphere. The Swiss associate is specifically responsible for administration and sales functions, and he has established representatives all over Europe and Asia.

The European manufacturing facilities are in Germany, and have been personally financed by the German associate. His entire production is sold on a cost-plus basis to Trion A.G., which in turn resells the equipment in the Eastern Hemisphere. Likewise, the manufacturing facilities in Japan are personally provided by the Japanese associate, and all his production is sold exclusively to Trion A.G. In addition to providing manufacturing facilities, both the German and Japanese members function as Trion A.G. sales representatives in their particular countries, which, incidentally, are the two largest foreign markets for our products.

An important element in the plan was the fact that Trion, Inc., purchased its interest in Trion A.G. with stock of Trion, Inc., whereas the other three stockholders purchased their stock for cash. As a result, the stockholders of the Swiss corporation indirectly became stockholders of the United States corporation, and this improved the incentive for cooperation and teamwork.

This cooperation is reflected in an agreement to establish a research laboratory in Germany. Fortunately, the stockholders of Trion A.G. are more interested in long-range income than in quick profits, and are willing to reinvest the corporation's earnings in research. Thus technical know-how and patents—both of which are more valuable than before-tax dollars—are brought back to America, and stockholders of both companies benefit.

A New Frontier

It is obvious that there are extensive markets abroad, many of them in virgin territory awaiting pioneering manufacturers. Here small business can offset some of the advantages of big business by capitalizing on the energy, aggressiveness, and flexibility which are usually inherent in smaller organizations. Three years of profitable operations overseas have also proved to us that foreign competitors are, in most cases, less formidable than the American industrial giants.

Considering foreign activities from a broader point of view, I firmly believe that the general standard of living in the world must be improved. It probably will not be brought up to American levels during our lifetime, but unless living conditions elsewhere approach ours, or at least start moving in this direction, revolt, war, and perhaps the destruction of our entire economy could result. Many, many people from abroad have seen how we live, and they do not believe they should accept less. Much can be done along these lines through more extensive and freer world trade.

SMALL BUSINESS EXPERIENCES OVERSEAS

An Open Discussion *

From the floor: What percentage of royalties and commissions have you found feasible?

Mr. MacGregor: Naturally it varies, and the governments get in on it. The people that I do business with in Britain, for example, were prepared to pay 4%, but the government absolutely refused to allow it. We were finally told to scale it down to 2½%, and that figure went through with the government's blessing. The officials told us that they had never permitted a royalty of over 4%.

As far as agency commissions go, we set them at the same rate as in this country—50%, which is the maximum. The agents had then to pay duty and transportation charges. They set the price themselves.

Mr. Gregory: If you are going to generate business within the country, royalties may run higher—we received 10%. But that is high; 5% is nearer average.

Mr. Meyers: In our experience, it ran to 4%. On commissions, it is 10% to 15% of a price which we set.

From the floor: What, specifically, are the difficulties involved in patents?

Mr. Meyers: In most countries patents do not mean very much, according to our attorneys. About the only countries where we con-

* Businessmen present at the panel session on which this chapter is based raised certain questions which brought about the discussion reported more or less verbatim in the following pages.

sider patents to be of real value are Sweden, Switzerland, Germany, England, Japan, and Canada.

In France, for example, you can apply for and get a patent on anything. But you would have to fight it through the courts before it would be of any value. On the other hand, in Germany a patent application is published before it is issued. Anyone else in the field can file an objection to the patent, and it is studied very thoroughly. Once it is issued, however, the German government backs it up.

As far as South America is concerned, the patent maintenance fee is exorbitant. Consequently, very few companies ever sustain their rights if somebody wants to challenge them.

Mr. MacGregor: Our experience has been that a trade-mark in foreign countries is much more valuable. We do business with medical men, and they care nothing about patents. To a doctor, a patent is anathema, but he will respect a trade-mark, and he will see to it that his nurse or associate orders your merchandise by your trade-mark. He knows the goods we make by the trade-mark we use. This is protection by use, rather than legal protection.

Mr. Gregory: When you are collecting a royalty from a firm and someone starts to infringe the patent, you have an obligation to take action. That can easily become a very heavy responsibility, and its value all depends upon what your objectives are.

In my case, our objectives were engineering, rather than just financial. I preferred to see us take in a little less income, concentrate on engineering progress, and be free of patent administration. Patent administration of a process such as ours is quite a broad task, and could in the years to come be almost a full-time job.

From the floor: When you set out on a survey of a prospective European market, what kind of help can you get? Where do you look for the entrees, the introductions? Do you go through the Department of Commerce or straight to the European Trade Associations and similar groups?

Mr. Meyers: In my case, the experience of big business was extremely helpful to small business. I went to the big companies in the air conditioning industry, such as Chrysler Airtemp Sales Corp., Carrier Corporation, and General Electric Company. I saw the vice presidents in charge of foreign operations, and asked them what I could do about setting up an international company. All three of those companies wrote to their men abroad and asked them to do any favors they could for me when I arrived in their cities. It was just like having a red carpet rolled out. These men proved to be excellent contacts and made it easy for me to meet the nationals in the country.

Mr. Gregory: I found the New York banks extremely helpful. In my particular case, I made a connection with the National City Bank of New York, and their foreign associations were of tremendous assistance to me. I had a real problem with the French government in getting our royalty agreements approved by exchange authorities. I would never have accomplished it without the help of the banks.

ESTABLISHING AND OPERATING OVERSEAS MANUFACTURING FACILITIES

Arch R. Dooley, C. Leigh Stevens, Donald McMaster, and J. H. Stebbins

I SUPPOSE THAT THE PROBLEMS AND COMPLEXITIES of modern-day manufacturing seem almost without limit for those of us whose primary business interest lies in production, even when they are posed in the familiar setting of the United States. Final answers to the endless variety of production problems always seem to be just over the

Note: Mr. Dooley, who makes the introductory observations, is Assistant Professor of Business Administration, Harvard Business School; Mr. Stevens, the founder of the management consulting firm of C. L. Stevens, is a Visiting Lecturer, Harvard Business School, and was a member of the International Planning Team on Small Industry in India during 1953 and 1954; Mr. McMaster is Vice President and General Manager, Eastman Kodak Company; Mr. Stebbins is Executive Vice President, W. R. Grace & Company.

horizon, though that horizon may be a domestic one. But for many of our colleagues, an additional variable has been added to the basic issues—and increasing numbers of us will be exposed to this distinctive factor in years to come. I refer, of course, to the special circumstances surrounding overseas manufacturing. The environmental characteristics of a foreign country, with all the social, economic, and political implications that flow from them, impose new complexities. In this chapter, men who have actual firsthand knowledge about the establishment and operation of overseas factories share their experiences and the know-how of their corporations with us.

Just what do overseas manufacturing operations involve? Under what circumstances is it advantageous to establish a manufacturing plant abroad? What are the real operating differences between a plant overseas and its counterpart in the United States? What are some of the obvious pitfalls, and how can they be avoided? These matters will be considered in the pages that follow.

CONDITIONS IN SOUTHEAST ASIA *

The most helpful contribution that I can make to this discussion is to supply some background about one vast area of the world. In this way I shall hope to give a picture of the kinds of problems that United States businessmen face in overseas operations. Drawing from my experience and observations on the economic, political, and social conditions of Southeast Asia, I want to describe the kind of thinking which executives must do when they establish new plants in this region.

Unfortunately, most United States businessmen have not proven to be very well oriented to the attitudes and problems of nations which are different from their own. We are prone to believe that the conditions in our narrow part of the world are transportable, or even fully established, elsewhere. But we can make no mistake greater than this. Southeast Asia provides a perfect example of an area so

* By Mr. Stevens.

vastly dissimilar to the United States that entirely new patterns of thought must be followed.

Ambassador Mehta, in his chapter describing the situation in India, more or less slid over a consideration which seems highly important to me. He pointed out that the average Indian farm consists of two and one-half acres and that there are sixty million such farms in the country. But he did not add that there are probably ten to twelve fields in each of those two and one-half acre farms. Fragmentation by inheritance—the practice of dividing each field into several pieces to go to each of several heirs—results in such small and widely separated holdings that efficient farming is impossible.

Ambassador Mehta did remind us that India is 75% to 80% agrarian, but he failed to make clear that the monsoons sometimes keep villages of 600,000 to 700,000 isolated for two, three, and five months at a time.

Conditions like these are not unique to India. All the countries in Southeast Asia present pretty much the same general pattern, although the details are different. Consequently, when a businessman plans to establish a plant in that part of the world, he has to recast his thinking.

Language differences give rise to a whole series of problems. It is true, of course, that Burma, Pakistan, and India were English colonies until very recently—and the British did teach them a common language, although a very small percentage of the highly educated speak English. But few people realize that there are four major tongues in India and probably eight or ten dialects. When the Indian leaders argue among themselves they always laughingly say, "We have to fight in English, whether we have a common language or not, because English is the only tongue we all understand."

Another central factor to be considered is the lack of mechanical understanding among the Southeast Asian people. Techniques of irrigation, which the Ambassador mentioned, are a good example. Again, this applies to Pakistan, Indonesia, and Thailand, as well as to India. The fact is that there is plenty of irrigation, but the water is drawn by 15 million pairs of oxen pulling on Persian wheels.

About half of these wheels are constructed from a design 3,000 years old, with very little development since. The major improvement has been an effort to introduce oil cans instead of earthen buckets as containers. Another ancient device still commonly employed is a steer hide dropped anywhere from ten to forty feet into an open well. A pair of oxen then pull it up and a man standing at the top of the well dumps it into an irrigation ditch.

India suffers from a shortage of the basic commodities which undergird a modern industrial society. Take steel, for instance. Here is a country of 360 million people, more or less, trying to work with a maximum of 2 million tons of steel a year. In the United States, with our population of 160 million, we produce 128 million tons annually.

Southeast Asia's lack of transportation facilities and the impact of that shortage are hard to describe in terms graphic enough to convey the true nature of the difficulty. In India and Pakistan there are four or five primary railroads bisecting the country in two directions. When you get more than seven miles away from one of these railroads, you go back about 3,000 years in history, because all travel is by oxcart. Eight miles represents four hours' travel time by oxcart; it is four hours into town and four hours back.

The power shortage in this region is another critical obstacle. The United States 1955 generating capacity was estimated by the Electrical Institute of Public Utilities at 87 million kilowatts installed capacity; federal power units at 17 million; municipal, state, and district power at 9 million kilowatts; and the co-ops at 790,000. Thus our total installed capacity comes to 114,545,000 kilowatts—and we are adding to that at the rate of 11 to 12 million new installed kilowatts per year. Private power plants, such as those of the paper and steel industries, are not included nor is our gasoline power in the form of tractors and other types of self-contained motors. In contrast to this estimate, the present installed capacity of India, hydroelectric and steam, is 3.4 million kilowatts. The plant capacity at the end of the new Five-Year Plan in 1961 will be only 6.9 million kilowatts as now contemplated.

Let me cite a few examples which point up the facts of life in Southeast Asia—facts which the businessman must consider and adjust to before he lays the cornerstone of his factory:

A fertilizer plant was built for India that would produce 350,000 tons of nitrogen annually. Two years ago it was running less than half-time, and imports from Chile were restricted on the theory that Chilean nitrates were harmful to the soil. On my visit there, one of the Ministers of Agriculture asked me: "Do you use Chilean nitrates?" "Sure," I replied, "that's all we had for a long time, until we got some made from the air." No one has ever demonstrated these fertilizers to the Indian farmer, and he has no idea what nitrogen would do to increase his yields.

In one state in India the Ford Foundation Community Development Program has devoted itself strictly to improving tillage methods and providing better seeds. Though the farmers had only their traditional tools with which to work, their income was doubled in two years by the use of seeds and better tillage which produced a longer cotton staple.

There are about 12 million spindles in the textile industry in India, most of which are pretty badly out of date. But the lack of employment is so great that the industry is maintaining ten employees for every one it really needs. You just fall over people when you go through an Indian mill. The situation is much the same in the rest of Asia. One exception is Japan, where costs are low and production efficiency equals that of the United States. Wages in Japan are low compared to ours but higher than in the rest of Asia. Demands for social legislation are widespread. The people's attitudes toward these problems are conditioned by the fear that those few now working will be put out of work. This fear intensifies the general economic unrest.

The Bata Works, a famous Czechoslovakian shoe company, has established four or five big plants and a large chain of retail stores in India. The founders, Czechs who were run out of their own country by the Russians, became Indian citizens and developed this new shoe industry in their adopted land. The wage level in these plants is three to four times the community wage for the same class of work. The plants are as well organized and equipped as anything in the United States, and, believe it or not, their production per man hour is equal to ours. The Indians are looking with a great deal of interest on this particular accomplishment and are trying to find a way to adapt the Czechs' methods to their own particular problems.

In summary, may I say that there is no danger of Asia's becoming communist unless, as Ambassador Mehta pointed out, it fails to make reasonable progress. My plea is that we come to realize the conditions with which we are working—economies dominated by small industry and small development similar to ours in 1870 or 1875—and that we tailor our activities in these countries to their needs and hopes.

EASTMAN KODAK ABROAD *

Eastman Kodak Company has had an international flavor practically since its origin. George Eastman was one of the earliest internationally minded industrialists in the United States. His first photographic patent, on a plate-coating machine, was obtained in England in 1879 before Kodak, as such, was founded. The parent Kodak company, in which the public held shares, was incorporated in Great Britain from 1898 to 1901. Kodak's publicly owned securities were stated in terms of pounds sterling.

Kodak now has 5 overseas plants, in addition to our Canadian factory in Toronto. We have importing and distribution houses in a total of 44 countries, and our advertising appears in more than 35 languages and dialects. The company's first factory abroad was built at Harrow, England, in 1891. Kodak (Australasia) began operations in Melbourne, Australia, in 1908. In 1927 we purchased a plant near Paris, France, and formed Kodak-Pathé. In the same year a German sensitized goods factory outside Berlin was acquired—and became Kodak A.G. Our German company bought a camera manufacturing plant, the Nagel Works, in 1931. In 1954 Kodak took over the op-

* By Mr. McMaster.

eration of an established photographic paper factory in Sao Paulo, Brazil.

In 1955, Kodak's equity in its overseas companies amounted to about $99 million. Net earnings of our plants and distributing organizations outside the United States reached a record high of $16.8 million in 1955, and dividends totaled $6.2 million.

From this brief summary, it is clear that Kodak's business is world-wide in scope and has been for many years. We have had long experience in a large number of markets. The advantages and disadvantages of overseas manufacturing, which need to be reappraised from time to time as economies change, are consequently much on our minds. I would like to indicate here some of the reasons why an out-of-country manufacturing operation can be extremely profitable. Then I shall discuss some of the problems that one is likely to meet and certain prerequisite conditions that should be established.

The Advantages

In general, the overseas factory affords broader distribution opportunities and greater stability since it can meet the demands of the local situations more effectively than United States installations. Kodak distributing houses, for example, can be supplied from the United States, Britain, France, and Germany, depending on which currency is more practicable at any one moment and which import quotas are the most favorable.

In many countries lower wage and salary rates, which may result in lower production costs, represent one of the most important benefits of overseas manufacturing. Rates may be only half—or even less than half—of those in the United States. This, of course, is an appealing advantage when the product requires much hand labor and the requisite skills can be found—as they frequently can be. Of course, hourly rates can be complicated by burdensome social security benefits, and low productivity levels may result in high unit costs. Furthermore, in many manufacturing situations the expenditures on complex plant equipment for production and quality control are much larger than any savings that might be achieved through lower wage rates. An advantageous wage rate situation overseas would have considerable importance for products in which labor costs are a large proportion of unit costs, but the reverse is true when the labor factor in costs is relatively low. As far as our business is concerned, production costs vary from area to area. Nevertheless, we try to get about the same percentage of return on investment in all our plants. Our prices are fairly standard, and in general we seem to make no more profit in one country than we do in another.

In this age of sensitive nationalism, people in many countries are much more disposed to buy a product that has been largely produced by their own countrymen, within their own borders, from materials purchased from local suppliers. Then, too, a locally manufactured product may be more adaptable to the particular needs of a country or area of export than one made by people far removed from the region in which it will be sold. For example, our photographic paper plants in Europe produce paper with a cream-colored base because consumers there prefer it to the white-colored paper sold in this country.

Overseas companies often develop unique approaches to research and development which might have universal applications. Our large research units located in overseas factories have emphasized certain phases of photography and have pioneered in the development of a number of new products. Efforts are continually being made to adapt photographic materials to conditions and equipment available in Europe, and we learn many new techniques useful to us back in the United States. For instance, a new and more effective method of handling processing solutions came from our laboratories in Australia last year. It has now become a part of our standard processing method.

Certain tax advantages are also available in overseas operations, if the local tax rates fall below the 52% levied by the United States Government on corporate profits, and opportunities exist for the use of retained earnings in overseas plant expansion. Puerto Rico, for instance, has tried to encourage the establishment of factories there by exempting new enterprises from taxation for the first ten years of operation. This provision, however, would not be very helpful to companies planning to remit the bulk of their profits to the United States, where they will be taxed at the normal corporate rate.

Kodak has benefited from lower tax rates abroad by retaining earnings for use in the country in which they were made. The $31 million which we have invested in new and replaced capital assets overseas since 1945 has all come from retained earnings. Generally speaking, tax incentives must be balanced against other factors such as costs, markets, availability of raw materials, distribution, and profit convertibility into dollars.

The Disadvantages

These various advantages of the overseas manufacturing facility are bound up with two factors which may or may not impede the operation of a plant abroad. One of the foremost questions is whether the industry lends itself well to decentralized manufacture. In some businesses, for example, unit costs do not decline appreciably through plant expansion after a certain output has been reached. Under some circumstances, one large factory or a dozen small ones can turn out the same product with equal efficiency.

In photographic enterprises, a single plant can often expand capacity, thus lowering its costs considerably. Multiple plants, on the other hand, tend to increase costs appreciably because of the need for expensive and complicated equipment for production and quality control.

In setting up a factory abroad, the problem of uniform product quality is a basic consideration for us. The manufacture of several hundred types of Kodak films and papers which are sold around the world is an extremely difficult and complex matter. Likewise, the production of our photographic apparatus and optics requires rigid quality controls. At our Kodak Park Works in Rochester we have over 3,000 people engaged in designing and building the highly specialized machinery required to produce film, photographic paper, and other items. We carry this staff because firms doing this type of work generally do not provide the particular kinds of equipment we need. As in the case of quality standards, we have to consider the problems of making, operating, and maintaining this equipment.

For us, therefore, and for many other companies, the question of establishing an overseas factory is complicated by the peculiar conditions demanded in the manufacture of our products and the special requirements of the markets in which they will be sold. We must find such conditions abroad in order to mass produce our complex materials and equipment at uniformly high standards.

Retention of control by United States management is a second factor to be considered before deciding to produce abroad. Countries inclined toward economic nationalism, for example, may not allow outsiders to maintain majority control. In one country, the holdings of the parent concern in a newly formed firm are limited to 25%.

Partnerships with overseas businessmen may not work out harmoniously if complex production and quality control procedures are involved. Such procedures can be somewhat alien to the experience of the foreign partners or minority owners, who may be willing to apply less rigid and less expensive standards in the manufacturing process.

In general, the right to home office management is highly desirable. But substantial market opportunities in countries that restrict majority control may make partnership—or some other cooperative arrangement with interests abroad—worth developing, despite the difficulties that may be incurred.

The Prerequisites

I would like to emphasize the point that the establishment of an overseas factory is not practicable at all unless certain conditions exist before plant construction is begun.

First of all, the United States businessman must make sure of a reasonably stable government in which the danger of nationalization is minimized. The British loss of oil interests in certain areas, the problems of the oil industry in Central America in the not-too-distant past, and certain local actions regarding tin mines—situations like these have made outright seizure seem like a major risk in operating abroad. In some cases where compensation has been made by the overseas government, it has been in the form of depreciated currency or inconvertible government bonds. Also, a few countries have imposed discriminatory fines and retroactive taxes on foreign concerns.

General risks of revolution, war, and invasion very often figure in the picture. Since the beginning of World War II, we have lost our film-manufacturing plant in Copenick, East Germany; our paper-producing plant in Vacz, Hungary; and of course our distribution houses in Rumania, Poland, Czechoslovakia, Yugoslavia, Hungary, and China.

Another prerequisite condition, just as important as a stable government, is the right to remit current profits. Repatriation of earnings is now allowed by all the countries in which Kodak has overseas factories, although there were restrictions in Germany and Brazil during the years right after World War II. Even if profits may be sent home, however, the parent concern should face up to the fact that the capital investment itself may be more difficult to transfer.

In many instances, it is desirable to secure additional working capital and funds for plant expansion by the reinvestment of those earnings that are subject to remittance controls. Sometimes this can be done advantageously because local taxes, as I mentioned before, may be below the United States income tax rate. Dividends remitted from our companies abroad in 1955 were about 39% of the company's equity in their earnings.

The operation of an overseas factory, including transferability of current profits, may be affected by currency devaluations and official exchange rates which are at variance with market conditions. This raises real complications in determining the true dollar value of the assets in the foreign operation.

There are other questions that a United States manufacturer should ask before deciding to set up his plant overseas. For instance: Is there sufficient economic development—are there people who can be trained, adequate roads, sources of power, credit facilities—for a factory abroad to be feasible? What are the added costs of international supervision? Careful selection and development of managerial talent will minimize these costs, but the question must be considered.

Finally, what are the responsibilities entailed in constructing manufacturing facilities abroad? A United States company has direct obligations to its shareholders, customers, and employees; these obligations require us to look closely at projected overseas plants in terms of dollars and cents and return-on-investment. But there are other responsibilities which must be assumed overseas. We must take a vital interest in the welfare of the people affected by our operations. Indeed, this is a responsibility which involves our own self-interest. Failure to maintain good community relations in this era of sensitivity to our wealth and power can mean more than the loss of good will alone; it can mean loss of assets, too.

Building Good Will

How can a firm sell itself effectively to the country in which it is operating and forestall excessive nationalism? This is no simple matter. Even our close neighbor Canada manifested strong nationalistic tendencies recently in the course of fierce Parliamentary debates over the Trans-Canadian pipeline, which is controlled primarily by United States capital.

I would like to divide this issue up into several parts. First of all, you have to convince the government of the country that you are interested in its problems and progress. Kodak has successfully accomplished this over the years by taking a relatively small percentage of profits back to this country. The retained earnings—in most of our overseas plants the figure has been about two-thirds of total earnings—have been put back into enlarging the local manufacturing facilities. When you do this sort of thing for an extended period of time, the government begins to respect you as a good neighbor and grants you its approval, along with certain privileges.

With regard to employee compensation, you have to apply the same practices we use in this country. In Kodak's United States plants, the fringe benefits we provide equal 36% of our total payroll. We do not go quite as high as this in all of our plants overseas, but we come close to it—and we are more liberal in this respect than many of our United States colleagues operating abroad.

We try to maintain good community relationships generally, and we attempt to fit in with local circumstances. We have unions in Australia, for instance, though we do not have them in Britain or the United States. Where labor is organized, we negotiate in a friendly manner with the unions and maintain communications with them. We try to establish attractive buildings, keep the air free from smoke, and drain off disagreeable material that might go into the rivers; we have halls and assembly rooms which we loan to local organizations for their meetings. We try to make ourselves a very real part of every community into which we go.

The new Russian economic offensive gives all this special pertinence. United States business has a great opportunity and a great responsibility, both in taking advantage of the promising possibilities of overseas manufacturing and in its conduct of these operations once they are established. Given proper attention and adequate performance on our part, there is every reason to believe that the system which has brought high living standards and great personal satisfactions to our own people can do the same for the vast millions in the developing areas of the world.

MANUFACTURING IN LATIN AMERICA*

Since World War I, and particularly after World War II, there has been a steady and constantly increasing trend toward greater industrialization in the world. Each country has been keen to take full

* By Mr. Stebbins.

advantage of the growing prosperity; each has been anxious to become industrialized as quickly as possible and thus place itself in a position to produce more and more of the articles which are demanded by increasingly high living standards. To this end, it has welcomed the participation of United States capital. In no area of the world has this been more true than in Latin America.

By and large, when the United States has invested abroad, it has followed traditional lines. We have concentrated on the extractive industries and various miscellaneous manufacturing projects which serve to make life more comfortable. In this connection it is interesting to note that in 1954 total United States investments in Latin American manufacturing activities—and this excludes petroleum—were $1.2 billion as compared to $780 million in 1950, or an increase of more than 50%.

Incentives for Investment

Paralleling the increase in the total volume of investment is the growing number of individual United States firms involved. Why are so many companies interested in investing abroad in the face of such pressure for capital in the United States itself? After all, here at home they are free from such problems as convertibility of foreign exchange, language difficulties, and other adjustments between nationalities. The answer is simple. In spite of foreign exchange difficulties, in spite of fairly frequent revolutions, in spite of different nationalities and, in some cases, strong national feelings, the return on the capital invested is usually higher in foreign investments than it is at home. As a matter of fact, it is generally as much as 50% higher.

There are, of course, other inducements. One is the duty protection which foreign countries frequently impose in order to save foreign exchange or encourage local production. This is an obstacle to the United States manufacturer exporting to that country; it is also an inducement for him to create new manufacturing facilities within the country.

There are still other incentives, perhaps less tangible but no less important. The deep sense of satisfaction which comes from contributing to a higher standard of living in a foreign country—especially one which is seriously underdeveloped—is a real reward. Furthermore, every new United States manufacturing establishment abroad is, in effect, a representative of the United States, and generates much-needed good will if it is properly managed. Finally— and I can testify to this from my own experience—it is most pleasant and agreeable to do business with executives in Latin America.

Curiously enough, none of the reasons which I have just listed were responsible for the fact that W. R. Grace is a manufacturer in Latin America. We started our business in Peru over a century ago, branching out from shipping and foreign trade into an industrial organization. In the years which intervened we have acquired manufacturing knowledge at home and abroad, so that we are in a fairly good position to draw comparisons between domestic and foreign operations. I do not mean to convey the impression that we know all the answers, but our highly diversified experience has led us to certain conclusions about the best way to achieve success abroad. I hope that some of the lessons we have learned may be of benefit to other United States businessmen interested in Latin America.

Joining the Local Community

Anyone wishing to establish manufacturing enterprises abroad finds himself confronted with totally new and different tax laws, customs procedures, monetary regulations, labor laws and labor relations, and in some cases different marketing techniques. Though there is a tendency to adopt more and more United States business practices because they are considered the most modern and efficient in the world, such practices are most effective if they retain a local flavor. My company has an inflexible policy that requires us to work within the traditions—not just the laws—of the country. We abide by the local customs, expectations, and rules of business etiquette. Our doors are open to anybody and everybody, and we remember always that we are guests of the country in which we are operating.

We seek to plant our roots deeply and firmly in the national life of the country and our company participates in the development of its economy. In other words, although we avoid all forms of political activity, we try to immerse ourselves in the economic and social community.

To achieve this objective, we work along two main lines: first, we employ as many nationals in our foreign enterprises as we possibly can, at all levels right up to the top; and, second, wherever practical we cordially welcome national capital participation.

We train local employees and promote them to jobs with better pay and higher responsibility. In this way they do not get the impression that they are mere workhands for foreign managers, but rather they understand that they are members of a team working for a company that is part of their national life—a company which offers them real opportunity for advancement.

In most countries, the law compels a firm to employ at least 85% nationals; we are rather proud of our performance on this score because we employ 98.6% nationals and only 1.4% Americans and Europeans in all of our Latin American operations. I think the actual figures are equally impressive. We have some 30,517 people on our payroll in Latin America. Out of that total, 30,097 are nationals and 420 are non-nationals—100 Americans and the rest Europeans. For example, there are only 20 Americans on the staff of our entire Peruvian organization, which employs some 5,000 persons.

Wherever possible, we develop local managers for our enterprises in Latin America. We pay the national the same amount we would give a United States employee of equivalent ability for the same type of work. In Peru and Chile, the two countries on the west coast of South America where we have our largest investments, we have been particularly fortunate in recent years in being able to develop two outstanding men—each a national of his own country. These executives have qualified to become vice presidents of our parent company, in full charge of our operations in their own lands. Naturally, we do not make this rule an inflexible one. If we are unable to find the right man, our top administrator will not necessarily be a national.

I have placed particular stress on the personal element, because after all that is the only real difference between manufacturing in Latin America and manufacturing in the United States. The spindles and looms in our South American textile mills are made back in New England at Saco-Lowell Shops, at Draper Corporation, and at Crompton & Knowles Loom Works. They are identical with the machines used in our North American textile industry. Both natural and synthetic fibers are the same as those used here. Only the men who manage the plants, the workers who man the machines, and the people who buy the cloth are different. This is true in our paper mill, our flour mill, our cement factory, our paint factory, and our other manufacturing enterprises.

We have learned that it is unwise and unproductive to try to "Yankeefy" Latin American management, labor, and consumers, even with all this Yankee machinery and Yankee know-how. So we adapt ourselves to our habitat. Managing a Latin American enterprise demands creative skill and finesse, but of a different kind from that exercised in New York and Boston. We emphasize the personal element and the dignity of the individual. Latin American management generally is much more personal in its dealings with labor. This may be due to the Latin character or to the prevalence of ownership-management, but the fact is that in most of our enterprises the lowest worker can always talk with the top man when he sets out to do so. While unions do exist and collective bargaining is carried on very much as it is here, matters of pride and personal appreciation are frequently more important to the workers than money or hours—although their standards in this regard are constantly rising.

Another important aspect of our foreign manufacturing enterprises is the degree of participation of national capital. Though we have no fixed rule about majority or minority United States holdings, we usually seek to obtain control, if only by a slight majority. We like to manage our companies ourselves, since we believe that we have something to contribute in this direction, and we are, after all, a United States publicly owned corporation. But the participation of local capital and the advice of local members of our boards of directors are of tremendous value in guiding our policies in Latin America.

Planning for Progress

To aid in setting our policies, we have an industrial planning department. During the past several years it has been an informal operation, but we are now crystallizing it. We have an over-all planning committee, and a subdivision for South America is currently in process of formation. We found the over-all committee to be a little cumbersome and unable to spend the necessary time and thought on Latin American problems. Consequently, we are now assigning some of the ablest and most imaginative of our young men to the South American committee, and backstopping them with a couple of executives from each of our Latin American countries. Though its job is planning only, this committee does work very closely with another department which is charged with implementation of policies—the industrial relations department. The whole planning committee reports to the president of the company, who in turn, of course, works closely with the executive heads responsible for particular areas.

One final point I would like to make concerns the matter of diversification. Ours is a very diversified company, but we are getting to the point where we are trying to decide just how diversified we want to be. Though we prefer to be in a few large industries rather than a host of small ones in order to keep our management problems to a minimum, specific decisions depend on the part of the world under consideration. Small countries like Colombia, Ecuador, Peru, Bolivia, and Chile do not offer opportunities for any large United States investments, except for the extractive industries. Consequently, we have diversified widely, entering a number of small businesses in those countries.

In undertaking these small ventures we have tried to contribute to the country as well as to ourselves. As a matter of fact, opportunities for service are one of the criteria we use in our decisions. In Peru, Colombia, and Chile, we are in the paint business because we believe we can contribute the Glidden know-how to the modernization of paint techniques there. We make biscuits and candy in Colombia and Peru because here, too, we have been able to introduce superior talent and know-how. On the other hand, large countries like Brazil and Argentina do not need our assistance in small businesses, so we prefer to operate in such areas as petrochemicals and paper.

The doors of W. R. Grace & Company in Latin America are always open to American businessmen. Many have come to us for advice or assistance, which we have given freely and gladly. In the future, as more and more Americans become interested in Latin America, we shall continue this century-old policy by making available the full fruit of our experience to any new company. We are delighted to help others get started in Latin America, and we sincerely hope and trust they will find the experience as pleasant, as satisfying, and as rewarding as we have.

The same fascinating challenges exist in the establishment and operation of overseas industry as in domestic production—with the added satisfaction of bringing the world closer together and increasing international good will. Beyond this, it is my hope that we are making a contribution toward the establishment of a more enduring peace.

QUESTIONS ON MANUFACTURING OVERSEAS

An Open Discussion *

From the floor: Assuming equal mechanization, do you find that labor productivity varies in different areas of the world—as among, for instance, Britain, Germany, France, and Latin America?

Mr. Stevens: The inherent ability to produce is constant through-

* Businessmen present at the panel session on which this chapter is based raised certain questions which brought about the interplay of ideas reported more or less verbatim in this section.

out the parts of the world where we have made studies. But this does not mean, necessarily, that this ability is realized everywhere. In Japan, the productivity is very high; in some cases it exceeds our own. On the other hand, in India there are often ten men doing a job that one man could easily do; the situation is hard to improve because a man cannot be fired once he is employed. You will find the same problem in Cuba. However, the labor productivity *potential* is the same so far as we have been able to observe.

Mr. Stebbins: After Latin American workmen have been trained, they are able to get as much, or almost as much, out of their equipment as do workmen in the United States. It should be said, however, that productivity varies from country to country. In some areas more people per machine are employed than in the United States, but there is a gradual tendency toward improving this situation. Employees in Latin America are amazingly intelligent once given the opportunity to learn.

Mr. McMaster: My experience has been similar to that of Mr. Stebbins. When we started a new unit in Sao Paulo, we put in one or two of our own technical people. They trained the local workers as quickly as they could. To strengthen our personnel we drew from the University of Sao Paulo and found the people there very intelligent and sensitive to our needs.

From the floor: How can a concern establish contacts if it has not previously been engaged in overseas activity?

Mr. Stebbins: The first step would be to go to the country (or countries) in which you are interested and talk to the people at the American Embassy there. A visit to one of the leading banks and discussions with a prominent lawyer who has had some experience with United States firms can be most helpful. In this way you can begin to get a feeling of the atmosphere in the country as well as an appreciation of what the area wants and needs in the way of business activity.

Mr. Stevens: India presents a little different kind of problem. National economies in Asia are based on government operations of one sort or another, because the government is about the only institution capable of running a big industrial project. Most of the executives who used to manage the industries were from Western countries. They went home when these nations became independent, leaving behind them a great lack of technical know-how and ability. Consequently, some governmental department is at work in every field, and you almost have to work for the government.

You will find, however, that the government is most willing to cooperate on any intelligent proposition. Your governmental dealings depend a great deal on what you are attempting to do. If you are in the steel or chemical business, for instance, you have to go into a partnership with the government. Not much private capital is permitted in these areas. On the other hand, if you are making consumer goods, you will find government officials anxious—probably too anxious from the viewpoint of their own people—to set up a joint ownership in an American company. It should be pointed out that such an arrangement is not always satisfactory from our point of view. Some United States firms have refused to go in, and Ford and General Motors have pulled out of India.

There is some possibility that the Asian governments will permit United States capital or other foreign capital to go into fields which are largely nationalized, if these outside investors are already operating in related industries. This happened in the case of oil refineries, where the United States had large investments in petroleum products. But generally speaking, the best markets for foreign manufacturers are in small consumer goods.

From the floor: Have incentive and/or suggestion systems proved usable in overseas plants? What about stock options for executives?

Mr. Stebbins: As far as my company is concerned, we have not reached the stock option phase yet! In fact, this practice is not too widely established even in the United States. Extra compensation, however, is very definitely a part of our system in all our operations abroad—as in the United States. Under our system we pay voluntary extra compensation based on profit levels to a large number of our employees. Department heads and up benefit from this program. We do not pay extra compensation to all employees because the laws in practically every country provide for a certain percentage, amounting to at least a month's extra salary, to be paid to every employee at the end of the year. We also use a piecework system in some of our industries in South America, though not in all of them. It depends entirely on the conditions prevailing in the particular country.

Mr. McMaster: We have no stock option plans, either abroad or in this country. Eastman Kodak does pay substantial bonuses to everyone, figured in proportion to his service and wages, and we do have incentive forms of payment. We are inclined toward group incentive schemes in both our domestic and foreign factories.

From the floor: In administering the establishment and operation of overseas activities, do you give the local men extensive autonomy or do you decide all major policy and operating questions at the home office?

Mr. McMaster: We give a very large degree of autonomy to the local people all over the world. Over-all policy related to expansion is determined back in Rochester, but all of the routine implementation is handled by the people themselves. Purchase of major new equipment or new land is referred back to us. All our plants send us their annual budgets, but we seldom, if ever, alter them. It is rather humbling when our overseas people suggest procedures better than those we follow ourselves, but also so rewarding we give them free rein!

Mr. Stebbins: We at W. R. Grace do maintain a certain amount of control from New York, but I must say I believe we permit a very wide degree of latitude to the head men in our different countries. We are constantly aware of this problem, and last year started a decentralizing policy which is leading toward more autonomy for the local managers. As a result, we can make rapid two-day or three-day trips to various overseas plants and accomplish all our business in a very short time, instead of having to be constantly engaged in detailed correspondence and red tape.

To be perfectly frank, we do feel that some areas need a certain amount of nudging from the United States end if they are to move as quickly as we would like. Many people, by nature, like to take life a little easier than we do in the United States. I am not saying we are right in our attitude toward work—but that is just the way we do things! Consequently, we feel that we have to watch each of our units pretty carefully—but we do try not to interfere beyond the extent of asking some rather direct questions if the monthly reports are showing a decline in profits.

In the areas of expansion, diversification, or abandonment of facilities, policy ideas do have to come from headquarters in New York. In short, we try not to be too authoritarian with these countries. We like them to run themselves, and the more the better. Our stateside training programs are designed to reduce the amount of necessary interference and direction still further.

EXECUTIVE PERSONNEL MANAGEMENT IN FOREIGN OPERATIONS

John Fayerweather, George D. Bryson, Bruce Payne, and Joseph C. Sweeten

I DOUBT IF THERE IS ANY NEED to restate the case for management training, selection, and development in modern industry, but these activities do take on special significance in the field of foreign operations, where sound executive personnel practices are vitally important.

Note: Mr. Fayerweather, who makes the introductory remarks, is Assistant Professor of Business Administration, Harvard Business School, and served as moderator for the panel discussion on which this chapter is based; Mr. Bryson is Vice President, International Operations, General Foods Corporation; Mr. Payne is President, Bruce Payne & Associates, Inc.; Mr. Sweeten is Supervisor of Management Training, Socony Mobil Oil Company, and served previously as Assistant Manager, Employee Relations, Mobil Overseas Oil Company.

In the first place, companies are faced with the problem of long-distance management. It is essential to have men on the spot who can do an effective piece of work without frequent direction and guidance. Furthermore, foreign activities are complicated by a variety of conditions and constantly changing circumstances. They demand executives of the highest ability who possess special qualifications fitting them for foreign service.

Qualities of an Executive

I am particularly interested in this field because I am currently undertaking a research project on the relationships between American and foreign executives. While engaged in field work in Mexico, I attempted to isolate and identify those characteristics which enable a man to work effectively with his foreign associates. The definition of these characteristics is especially important in selection and training procedures, and in determining the kind of guidance that superiors give to their subordinates down the line.

Obviously, there are general technical requirements for the job of overseas manager, just as there are for any job, but I am thinking primarily of the personal characteristics and qualifications which make a man particularly fitted for such work. There are three that seem to me especially important.

The first is a capacity for *flexibility*. Practically speaking, it is a willingness to talk to the other fellow in his own terms. One can think in terms of customs, like the backslap and the handshake, but these are only the obvious and superficial forms. There is a wide range of more subtle traits which determine the way in which people work together to elaborate:

> It is quite clear that cultures vary and businessmen operate differently from country to country. To single out just one example, Latin American relationships are characterized by what is called the soft, or indirect management approach. Latin Americans employ much less of the frank give-and-take with which we are familiar. There is a more indirect, diffused communication of ideas.

Suggestions have much more meaning than they have in our culture. Men who can appreciate and adjust to such differences possess this quality of flexibility.

2   The second characteristic is that of *maturity*. Maturity is obviously desirable in any executive position, but in the foreign field it is particularly important. The readjustments that a man must make as he works in a foreign country are substantial. Challenges are constantly posed to his patterns of thought and action—even to his values. If he is uncertain and immature he will be unable to meet these challenges. For instance:

> Bribery is a good example. Most of us do not approve of bribery, and we do our best to eliminate it from business dealings. But in Latin America the bribe is an accepted part of business activity. The United States businessman has to accept this fact and learn to live with it, even while he does his best to change the climate which encourages the practice. The man who can deal with this problem sensibly, who can resist it without being belligerent and self-righteous, who can operate in this atmosphere without surrendering his own moral code, is a mature person.

3   The third quality is the capacity for developing close personal relationships with associates. Even with all the flexibility in the world, it is hard for any man to integrate himself with the life and thinking of others whose backgrounds are different from his own. Some characteristic that goes beyond flexibility is needed to overcome the barriers. That element is the ability to make friends.

As Mr. Allyn said in his chapter, human beings are much the same the world over. There are a few people who want to live in a box, saying, "People are no damn good." But for the most part, we all seek friendship with people whom we can respect and like and with whom we can have social interchange. If executives who go abroad are able to make an effort in this direction, they can build personal bonds which will by-pass the inevitable barriers that arise between differing cultures. They will be able to work harmoniously with a wide variety of people.

Furthermore, the fact is that personal relationships play a major role in all foreign business. Though this is true in the United States as well, it is possible here to maintain relatively impersonal relationships at work and to limit the overlap of work and home associations. But business overseas has not acquired the professional status it has in this country, and businessmen value social activity very highly. Thus a kind of extended family relationship is imposed on whatever formal organizational structure exists.

So much for general comment. Clearly, this is a vast topic which cannot be covered within the pages of a single book, much less in one chapter. But we can touch on a few of the most pressing problems in the field as a means of stimulating the interest—and imagination—of our readers.

PERSONNEL MANAGEMENT POLICY*

The biggest problem in overseas executive personnel policy is not found out in the field—it is here at home.

As I attend various conferences and meet men whose business responsibility falls in this area, I find very, very few who have anything like a sound management viewpoint on personnel. Most United States executives are badly informed and have a minimum of experience. Many of them have never been abroad and have little sympathy for the viewpoint of people in other countries. Fundamentally, they think we ought to make people accept our products and our ways on the theory that what has been successful here will be successful overseas. They are unwilling to see the other man's point of view.

This attitude is not only wrong—it is dangerous to the future of a business. Consequently, personnel policies ought to be designed to screen out these men—or their foreign counterparts who think everything American is bad—and develop broad-minded executives, both here and abroad.

But this is not as easy as it sounds. You cannot be dogmatic about

* By Mr. Bryson.

job assignments with management or anyone else because you can never prove you are right. In spite of all the help available from professionals, the research which has been done, and the psychological studies which are at hand, executive selection is still a high-class guessing game. You just cannot predict whether or not a man is going to be successful and happy in a particular assignment.

A Good Man Is Hard to Find

Furthermore, it is difficult to locate experienced, suitable executives who are even willing to consider foreign service. Once you are lucky enough to find a man who likes it in Bogota—the city is 9,000 feet above sea level, in the clouds all the time—the tendency is just to leave him there. I hope this situation will change as we convince management to look on foreign assignments as a training ground for domestic leadership—but it is certainly true today. To illustrate:

> Recently we transferred our British manager to the United States to be plant manager of one of our largest divisions, and I suspect that this action will do a good deal to dispel the idea that foreign assignments are a "dead end." But when I interviewed six of our best men in the domestic organization in an effort to replace him in England, I found no one who was interested in going. One of them said to me, "George, I have known and worked with you for a long time. You can give me any assignment you want to here in the International Division at White Plains. But my wife and I have never been abroad." So that was that.

We have a rule that we will not take a young man in any capacity— even clerical—in our International Division at White Plains unless he spontaneously answers "yes" when we ask him, "Would you be willing to live abroad for three to five years if the circumstances arose?" Actually, we do not expect that many of them will go overseas, but a negative reply indicates a provincial frame of mind which we do not think we can cure. If a man looks on foreigners as something peculiar, different, and beneath him, we do not want him in our department. We insist on people who are interested in foreign matters and want to find out about them. But such people are hard to find at any management level, and are almost unavailable in the top echelons.

Some General Principles

I recently returned from a trip to Europe, where I discussed contemplated changes in our European executive setup with several of our management people. On my return I wrote a recommendation, which includes a statement that expresses my philosophy of management in the foreign field. I said that I was sure of only one thing: in management personnel decisions it is impossible to be sure. The best we can do is begin by studying and clearly defining each assignment and each candidate. Is the job loaded with technical or marketing problems? Is the particular situation one that calls for handling many people or a lot of money? What's the issue at stake? Often we fail to ask—and answer—such questions.

Secondly, we must remind ourselves to give the greatest weight to the judgment and experience of those nearest to the jobs and the men. Wise managers get down to where the work is and where the men are and then eliminate personal prejudices and preconceived opinions from their judgment. For example:

> Before I left on the visit mentioned above, I am ashamed to say I participated in some detailed discussions in White Plains under the illusion that the matter could be decided at home without the benefit of a firsthand look. I was tempted to think that it could be done because I knew the people, was familiar with the field, and had been there several times during the year. But I learned that general familiarity is not enough. The more I thought about it, the more I realized that I did not know exactly what the people involved thought, and the more certain I was that I could not make a sound recommendation to management without actually meeting the people concerned—both Europeans and Americans.

United States companies are well advised to gamble on youth in the foreign field, even more than in the domestic. The mature man who is a successful and seasoned executive makes too much money to want to go abroad. If he is a successful national in business in his own land, he is not inclined to go to an American company. Very often enthusiasm and energy, if they are hitched to character, will compensate for a lack of brains or experience; and it is prudent to recall that the job often makes the man. Do not be afraid of youth!

Finally, the uncertainties in each decision can be covered by providing strength to back up weakness. This is a kind of insurance against loss in the event of error. Since each assignment must be made with some doubt, precautions are necessary. For instance, I may put a man in a key spot even though he seems weak on marketing. If I do, I back him up with a good marketing man somewhere in his staff. By the same token, when I employ young men and gamble on them, I take out insurance by having another man spotted in the group who could step in if anything went wrong.

These are my general operating principles in a field that is still vague and full of uncertainties.

PERSONNEL POLICY IN ACTION *

In our brief experience—we have been in Latin America only a little more than six years—we have learned one thing about foreign management. It is dangerous to generalize! Valid observations can only be made in terms of a specific company.

But I think it is fair to say that the key to the success of the best United States companies in Latin America can be found in forward planning. These companies have determined where the strengths and weaknesses lie in their type of business. They have set a pattern for growth and development overseas, just as they have in this country, and then have used the type of organization that best fits their plans.

Such planning is vitally necessary, for American companies all over the world have more competition today than they had six years ago. To meet it successfully, operations must be tighter and well man-

* By Mr. Payne.

aged. W. R. Grace & Co. and Radio Corporation of America are two prime examples of this kind of planning, and other firms might do well to study their techniques.

Furthermore, United States executives would be well advised to focus special attention on personnel problems. The basic requirement for executive success—and there are many qualities which are important—is the desire to go into overseas work. Next is a fondness for the country where the operation is located. In our company, for instance, a man is not sent overseas unless he and his wife really want to learn the language, and evince a clear desire to be a part of the country to which they will be assigned.

But a man should not be forced to stay overseas forever. We never ask anyone to go overseas for more than three years at a time, for example. It is true, of course, that not all companies have the type of operation which permits them to bring men back or shift them from one nation to another. But great care should be taken never to lock a person out or even to have him feel that he is prevented from returning to the United States. He may always stay overseas, but he should feel that he is working for the parent company and can come back at any time. Communications are highly difficult at best; without a sense of oneness that connects the overseas executive staff to the parent company, they become well-nigh impossible.

From the standpoint of a rising young executive, overseas service appears to be a sidetrack. But this is not so, and wise managers will set up programs to encourage young men to go into the foreign field. The experience offers many advantages. For one thing, executives achieve an independence of action abroad that they can never get in a large domestic company. Furthermore, they may reach a major management position at thirty or thirty-five—far younger than in this country. With foreign experience behind them, they are in a good position to come back to a significant post at home.

In short, if a man selects the right company and the right position and goes overseas at an early age, he acquires experience that is very difficult to get in any other way.

Thus a company in the foreign field—or one considering the possibility of international investment—should make a special effort to establish sound personnel practices. The first step is a careful study of the particular qualities demanded of overseas executives in its line of business. Attention to the duration of foreign service and its relation to the morale of men assigned to posts abroad is the second. Finally, the company should make a conscious and well-considered effort to attract able young men into its foreign division by stressing the real benefits of overseas experience in building a business career.

PLANNING, HIRING, AND TRAINING EXECUTIVES *

One of the key problems in the development of executives for foreign service—Americans or nationals—is the modification of traditional techniques to fit the particular needs of the company in question *and* the culture of the countries where it is operating. These cultures vary tremendously, and each must be considered in its own right.

A colleague of mine recently caught a taxicab in Cairo that was being driven by a bilingual chauffeur. My friend soon got chatting, and asked him, "What do you folks think about us Americans?" Quick as a wink, the driver pulled over, stopped the car, and turned to talk to him. The point of the conversation came out a few moments later, when the driver said, "Look, Mister, we have known the British for five generations. They have kicked us around and we know how to tolerate them. What we can't understand is why an American comes over here and tries to copy the British. Why don't you just be yourselves?"

His observation is a most significant one. Margaret Mead, the eminent anthropologist, recently completed a volume for the United Nations Economic, Scientific, and Cultural Organization. In it she describes culture as being the "learned behavior" of an individual or an organization. Executives overseas must learn to live with the

* By Mr. Sweeten.

culture of the country where they are stationed—according to its body of learned behavior—or they will be unwelcome and unsuccessful. They must not try to emulate the British or anyone else—but rather understand and cooperate with the national temper as they see it.

Thus there is no set pattern—no formula—on "how to behave abroad." Each area has its own anxieties and aspirations, and United States managers overseas must be trained to understand and operate with them.

This problem was brought into sharp focus for me by an experience I had in 1954. One evening after dinner with a group of Brazilians in Sao Paulo, I joined them in an informal conversation about the economic problems of Brazil. I asked the group why Brazil was so unwilling to permit the entry of foreign capital. My friends hedged and evaded the question, but finally one of them answered, "Well, Joe, we are afraid." "For God's sake, of what?" I asked them. "You know our history," one replied. "It started four hundred years ago with the Conquistadores. They came here and enslaved the native Indian population. Later they brought blacks from Africa, and Portuguese as slaves. They made indentured servants of the poor people. From that experience our population has learned to be very skeptical of Conquistadores."

"But what has that to do with American capital coming down here and investing in your economic system?" I demanded. "Joe, we are afraid that if we permit an American company to come in, all the top jobs and the good jobs in the company will go to Americans. We think it will be the Conquistadores all over again." Though I remonstrated with them, and cited examples, they maintained their position. "We know, we know," they said, "but we are still afraid."

By the same token, foreign nationals have to be trained to understand the ways and ideas of the United States. They must be able to fit into an American company, just as United States executives must have the capacity to work with people in other lands. It is a matter of mutual understanding.

Personnel Planning

With that as background, we can divide the problem of executive development into three major parts: planning, hiring, and training. The preliminary stage is identical with planning for domestic operations, and consists of:

- Organization planning and analysis.
- Identification of key positions in the organization's structure.
- Establishment of requirements for key positions.
- Inventory and appraisal of available manpower.

Unless these steps are accomplished—and the fit between the man and the job is good in every particular—real problems will develop.

Some years ago, we chose a promising young man for a post in Nigeria. We were sure that he was suited for the job. But the man had a family—two small children, and a wife who had been born in Montclair and had never been west of Pittsburgh. When they arrived in Nigeria, that young wife from Montclair discovered how big the insects are in Lagos. Three weeks later, we brought the family home at a cost of almost $15,000. Technically, the man fitted the job requirements; but there are more than technical specifications involved in overseas posts!

Hiring and Training

Once the necessary preliminary steps have been taken, actual hiring processes for foreign nationals are not very different from those at home. My company, for example, has affiliated corporations in many countries—some 108 of them—run by local personnel, with a light sprinkling of Americans. The problem of employment at the local level is handled easily. The affiliates do their own college recruiting, use the local school, advertising, friends, employees and all the various techniques that are needed—and they run into competition as we do here.

Of course, recruiting varies from country to country. In some countries, for instance, a young man hired for a future executive position has to have only two qualifications—he must come from a good family and be a graduate of the right school! But except for a few situations such as this, the mechanics of employment and recruitment are pretty much alike anywhere.

Recruiting Americans to go overseas is another matter, however. Though there are 45,000 people in our domestic organization, we are sometimes unable to find executives who want to go abroad. We have finally come to the conclusion that we are going to have to adopt a rather long-range program of recruitment of young men to satisfy our future needs. We put them on our international payroll, thus earmarking them for foreign service, and turn them over to our domestic side for an optimum period of training. When that is completed, we pick them up again and put them to work.

Our "on the job" training for foreign nationals abroad is pretty much a duplication of our programs at home, and we have seen no real reason to change it. But we have worked out a little different pattern for the United States part of the plan.

First, we analyze the man's individual needs in terms of his present job or a future responsibility. Then we devise a special program for him here at home. Finally, after adjusting the program as we find out more about him during his visit, we send him back to his country and make sure he has some opportunity to apply what he has learned. In this way we can be sure that his training will stay with him throughout his career.

I might also point out that we use many of the accepted United States programs for our foreign executives. For instance, we are sending a promising young man from our British company to Harvard in the Advanced Management Program. I wish, incidentally, that there were formal schools and courses of administration overseas that could match ours. The British Institute of Management, which is the British counterpart of the American Management Association, has been quite active in this area. Other countries are making sincere efforts to develop such educational facilities. We hope they can advance rapidly.

In conclusion, let me repeat the thought in my introductory paragraph: whatever the planning, hiring, and training process may be in a particular firm, it must be based on the specific needs of that company and the culture of the country in which it operates.

QUESTIONS AND ANSWERS[*]

From the floor: What is your opinion on the use of foreign nationals?

Mr. Payne: I think there is too much emphasis in this book on the wisdom of using nationals. My experience with close to 100 companies in Latin America indicates that you can be predominantly successful as a United States executive. Use nationals wherever convenient if they have been developed, but do not make a fetish out of it. After all, training men in fundamental concepts and philosophy is a major problem, and it may take a number of years to develop local people who are as good as the men we can supply from the United States. For example:

> One of the large sugar companies in Puerto Rico is predominantly an American company. Though national thinking is important in the country, this particular firm is the most respected company in Puerto Rico. It has earned that respect because it is so well operated, and its United States management is outstanding. The company uses all the nationals it can, but the top men are mostly United States citizens.

Mr. Bryson: It depends, of course, on the level of management you are discussing, and the time-scale you have in mind. We have found that we cannot yet do what the big, successful foreign operators have been able to accomplish, at least insofar as top management is concerned. Mr. Allyn, for instance, tells us that he has 18,000 people in foreign operations and only six Americans. General Motors has a ratio of something like 85,000 to 160. These firms, and others like

---

[*] Businessmen present at the panel session on which this chapter is based raised certain questions which brought about the interplay of ideas reported more or less verbatim in this section.

them, are way ahead of us. But we do put nationals in at the works-manager level, and are constantly trying to find local people for key spots. By and large, we have not yet been successful in bringing local executives along to the point where we can place them in top positions. But that is our objective, and I believe it is sound.

Mr. Fayerweather: This matter of training nationals to take jobs is not an easy proposition. For example, training foreign executives in the United States has not been thought through in many cases. There are two reasons for bringing people to the United States. One of them Mr. Sweeten has indicated: there may be programs here which are simply unavailable abroad. Second is that a United States visit is the best way to equip nationals with a thorough understanding of our marketing techniques, for instance, or our system of human relations in factories. While this is extremely valuable, many firms try to do it much too fast, without considering the ways in which internalized learning really takes place.

I am especially concerned with the notion that you can bring a man over for three or four months, send him around to several sales offices, let him work with a few salesmen, and expect him to go back with a thorough understanding of United States sales techniques. A year is really too short a time to absorb an attitude or a point of view—and that is what you are after. Furthermore, if a man is simply an observer, he probably learns about as much as I do when I go down to Brazil as a semitourist and look at various things for a short time. Unless he takes on a job and really becomes a part of an operation, it won't become a part of him.

From the floor: If you look to the North instead of to the South, you get a slightly different picture. I am a Canadian, and can say with strong feeling that one of the greatest mistakes being made by some of the important United States companies in Canada is the effort to dominate them with Americans from the top all the way down. The reaction in the country toward this practice has now reached the point where it is an election issue.

Mr. Payne: I left out Canada, because it seems to me it is a unique situation. Canadian companies are so well managed that they don't need much assistance from our side of the border. Certainly it is a clear mistake to dominate firms up there!

Mr. Sweeten: I can add something to this matter of Canadian-United States relations. Several years ago my family and I went to Ontario for a vacation. On the way up to Algonquin Park we stopped overnight at a farmer's cabin. The farmer's daughter came out—incidentally, I should emphasize at this point that I had my wife and family along. I asked her if she would rent the cabin and whether she wanted to be paid then or in the morning. "If you don't mind," she replied, "we would like the money now so you won't be held up tomorrow." "Fine," I said, "do you take American currency?" The look in her eye changed immediately, and she firmly said, "We take *United States* currency. We are Americans too!"

From the floor: What is the relationship in pay which should be maintained between a national and an American doing essentially the same job?

Mr. Sweeten: We believe that the pay of any national should be geared to his home country. That's where we recruit him, and that's where he will retire. The formula, however, for arriving at his ex-patriot pay can be precisely the same as the American formula.

Our company's foreign operation is divided into two major parts—marketing and producing. Each has its own pay formula. In marketing, the pay scale of an American going abroad is set by four factors:

- Base salary, which is identical with the American base pay.
- A tax equation factor, which means a deduction relatively equal to the income tax he would pay in the United States were he here.
- A 30% foreign resident allowance. If he is in West Africa, we add a 10% geographic allowance.
- A cost-of-living allowance based on the State Department formula, which attempts to equate the cost of living between Washington and posts abroad.

We use the same formula if we transfer a British subject to Lagos, starting off with the base salary in pounds. We make up the tax

—in the case of the Londoner, we let him pay the Nigerian tax— but we don't bother with the tax equation. He is then paid an expatriation allowance, a geographic allowance, and a cost-of-living allowance between Lagos and London. Thus the formula is identical for all practical purposes.

Mr. Bryson: It may be comforting to know that a survey we just conducted among companies in the international field indicates that there is no uniformity of compensation practice. While Mr. Sweeten's formula sounds like a good system, it just does not work in our case—but none of the others work either! We are going to have to build our own.

Mr. Payne: I think we have pointed up a moral here! Each company has to approach its own problems very realistically, depending upon the facts of the situation and particularly its type of management. There are some broad principles which indicate that a man overseas should be paid in some relation to the standards in his own country.

Mr. Sweeten: We employ about 2,900 people in one of our affiliates. We have about 300 nationals of that country stationed in another country. If we paid the 300 according to United States pay scale, can you imagine what would happen among our 2,900 when the men from abroad went home to retire?

From the floor: Can you transfer nationals from one country to another?

Mr. Sweeten: If you move carefully, you can transfer a man who is a national of one country to another country successfully. Our present sales manager in Turkey, for example, is a British subject who was formerly sales manager in Morocco. There is one peculiar angle that should be watched, though. It may be unwise to send a man who has become a naturalized American back to his original country. He may not be well received.

From the floor: Do you believe that transfers can be made as easily in Latin America?

Mr. Bryson: Yes. One major firm has actually opened offices in Europe to recruit Europeans for their Latin American operations.

Their manager in Colombia is a very brilliant and capable young man whom they found in Holland. As for us—we have just bought a business in Venezuela which is managed by an Englishman.

Mr. Fayerweather: Of course, it does not always work. I know of a case where a Cuban was brought over to a key job in Mexico and failed miserably. The Mexican attitude toward the Cuban was pretty poor! But another company trained three Mexicans for work in Costa Rica, Venezuela, and Colombia, and did it successfully.

From the floor: I get a little confused between what is ideal and what is true in fact. Mr. Payne says that three years is the maximum practicable tour of overseas duty—yet you all complain that it is difficult to find men. Don't you have to keep a man in a foreign post more or less permanently because there just are no replacements available? Isn't he committing himself to a lifetime overseas if he accepts a foreign assignment in the first place?

Mr. Bryson: It is important to remember that we are in the early stages of overseas operations. Few companies have been involved up to now, and it takes time to develop a philosophy. I think once we get across the idea that foreign service is excellent training, we will find plenty of men willing to go abroad for a few years. Then we will be able to promise tours that don't run any longer than three to five years.

Mr. Sweeten: I am frank to say that Mr. Bryson's viewpoint seems highly theoretical to me. When men go overseas for our company, they go for a career. The only promise we make is this: "If you succeed, you may be promoted back to headquarters as a member of the foreign department. You probably will not join the domestic operations. Except for this possibility, you are embarking on a career abroad until retirement." We make that point very specifically to them, because competition in the oil business forces marketing and other techniques to move at such a rapid pace that men who have been abroad for ten years are lost when they come back to the domestic unit. They just don't know what it is all about, so they have to go down the scale in salary to pick up the needed experience. Most men are unwilling to do that. Personally, I suspect this is always going to be true, and most businesses will move in the direction of a career foreign service, rather than toward an in-and-out policy like that which Mr. Bryson describes.

From the floor: I represent an insurance company which started abroad in Shanghai in 1919. It appears to me that most of us make a major error in talking about selling American products to people that live abroad. This is not the problem at all. We ought to develop local, indigenous businesses which operate in whatever way is appropriate, within the general business area of the parent company.

Applying this specifically, let's look at this tour-of-duty business. Telling a young American that he doesn't have to stay more than four or five years is dead wrong. You are not going to develop a business abroad unless the fellow looks on the business as his baby and wants to build it up. In our organization we have people who have served ten, twenty, or thirty years as the heads of local businesses. This is what they look forward to, and what we expect of them. They cease to be Americans, for they are not just members of a sort of pool which is constantly circulating around the world, always hoping and expecting to come back home again. Home has got to be where they are working.

Then take that matter of pay. I went to a management association meeting recently and asked a lot of people, "What would your reaction be to the proposition that one of our Americans who goes abroad should feel as much at home in Paris or Bogota as he does in New York?" Almost universally they laughed at me—yet that must be so. The men must want to live where they are working, and their pay should be scaled accordingly. I disagree with Mr. Sweeten's formula which pays a man 30% more to work in Paris than in New York. Why? What's so bad about working in Paris? If he is the kind of fellow that has to be paid 30% more to work in Paris, he is not the man you want in Paris.

Then we have the problem of the wife who was born in Montclair and does not want to live in Nigeria or Bogota. But on the other hand, there are wives who were born in Montclair who never had it so good as they did in Nigeria—and you cannot get them off again quickly enough when they come home on leave. Here they cannot possibly have a servant; abroad, they have three or four servants. These people do not want to work in the United States any more, and it does not make any difference where they were born.

To sum up, we have to find people who intend to develop and eventually to run businesses which are purely local, except in that they conform and contribute to the objectives of a major parent organization here in the United States.

Mr. Bryson: I am not going to try to disagree with that viewpoint, because I cannot speak specifically about the insurance business. But I certainly cannot accept a single word of it as far as my business is concerned.

LABOR RELATIONS IN FOREIGN COUNTRIES

*James J. Healy, Sumner M. Rosen, and
Melvin Rothbaum*

FOR THE PAST SEVERAL YEARS, members of the Harvard Business School
Faculty have had a unique opportunity to study the differences between United States and foreign union leaders and between their
conflicting methods of operation. During the academic year, the
School offers two special courses which highlight these contrasts:
an Advanced Management Program for top-level experienced executives, and a Trade Union Program for labor leaders. In addition to
United States trade unionists, the TUP student body includes seven
or eight representatives from various overseas unions.

These two programs meet simultaneously, and hold several classes

Note: Mr. Healy, who makes the introductory observations, is Associate
Professor of Industrial Relations, Harvard Business School; Mr. Rosen is
Professor of Economics and Research Associate, Northeastern University;
Mr. Rothbaum is Research Associate in Labor Economics, Harvard University.

together. In addition, the members of both groups seek each other out for informal conversations. As observers of these various contacts, we have been able to assess some of the contrasting attitudes displayed by our labor leadership and that of other countries. These distinctions are greatly dramatized when the two groups are present in the same classroom or dining hall.

It is no exaggeration to state that normally the degree of controversy between United States and foreign trade unionists is far greater than any of the disagreements between union members and management, here or abroad. The Americans are usually advised by their overseas colleagues that they are not pursuing effective policies. The foreigners, for the most part, rely on political action as a means of securing the various benefits they seek, and they think their American brethren should devote more energy to the formation of a third party or the development of some other type of powerful political influence. The United States union leaders, however, want no part of such a program.

I recall, for example, a debate we scheduled at the Harvard Business School at the time of the English election when Mr. Churchill was seeking to regain power. We wanted to take up the question of the role of the Labor Government in Great Britain. Since we had a man from a British company in the Advanced Management Program as well as a leader of the Maritime Union in Great Britain who was a strong proponent of the Labor Government and a factor in the Bevanite wing of the party, the situation seemed made-to-order.

The debate was planned for four o'clock. At about a quarter of four, I received a call from the Dean's Office asking me if I was scheduling any event that afternoon. When I said, "yes," the Dean's secretary suggested I might want to look outside and see what was going on. I did so—and found the School being picketed, and the entrances to the meeting hall surrounded by men carrying signs. Needless to say, the thought of a casual observer coming upon the Harvard Business School and seeing it picketed was not to the taste of the Dean!

When I approached the line, I found that the men were all members of United States unions. Their signs were bitterly denouncing the British Labor Party. In the debate that followed, the English-man stood very much alone as he tried to present an affirmative position for the Labor Government!

There is real reason for us to take an interest in labor relations problems in other parts of the world and the differences which exist between us. Any company which is actively engaged in operations abroad needs to be conversant with the institutional structures of foreign unions and, more important, with the mores and traditions of other countries. As other authors in this book have pointed out in various connections, it is dangerous to apply American personnel and labor relations methods without regard to the very sharp differ-ences in belief and custom which exist in other societies.

Recently a research report along these lines appeared in *Business Week*. Entitled "Getting Along with Foreigners," the article pointed out that 20 or 30 years ago the major new interest of American business was in matters of psychology and human relations. Now, it continued, those companies which have developed direct or indirect involvements in overseas operations are beginning to concern them-selves with the older fields of ethnology and anthropology in an effort to understand the cultural backgrounds of the countries where they do business. The article offers a number of interesting illustra-tions of the diversity in social customs and values, including this one:

> In Liberia, Firestone Tire & Rubber Company was having costly trouble keeping workers on the rubber plantations. Tribesmen would drift in for a few weeks, earn enough money to buy another wife or some other household convenience, and then disappear into the jungle again. Overseers never knew from week to week just how many men would show up for work.
>
> The company tried building houses on the plantation to attract families to take up permanent residence. The houses stayed empty. Several different colored tiles were used to roof the houses—one color per roof. Then quite by chance the builders ran short of tiles of one color and mixed several colors in a geometrical pattern on one house. The natives scrambled to occupy that one. Patterns were

introduced on the other roofs and soon all the houses were filled
with proud native families. It seems decorative houses traditionally
have been symbols of prestige in the tribal culture.*

There is another angle to this matter which should not be overlooked. In addition to the inherent benefits for overseas operations
which accrue from an understanding of foreign unions, I think a
knowledge of overseas labor organizations, their objectives and
methods, might serve to give us all a better appreciation of the in-
herently conservative nature of our own trade unions.

ADAPTING U. S. METHODS
TO THE NEAR EAST†

Many underdeveloped nations have bet their future on industrialization. These nations want and need western capital. Some of them
have made an effort to provide legal and financial protection for
foreign business as an inducement to western investment, despite
their bitter memories of "colonialism" or "imperialism."

When a United States company establishes itself abroad in response to such inducements, not only is our ability to produce on
exhibit; our version of private enterprise is also on trial. Its accomplishments or its failures will affect both the political and the economic development of these countries. Consequently, it is important
to devote careful consideration to the problems of labor and industrial relations in a book of this sort. Where traditions of political
democracy are weak and modern capitalism is misunderstood, totalitarian methods for achieving economic growth may exert a powerful
attraction, to the detriment of our stake in world affairs.

My comments will be along two lines. Initially, I want to outline
those conditions which are peculiar to overseas operations and have
an impact on the general performance and the labor relations of
foreign branches and activities; secondly, I will consider three specific

* "Getting Along with Foreigners," *Business Week,* June 9, 1955, pp. 82, 84.
† By Mr. Rosen.

problems of labor and industrial relations which present particular challenges, and suggest methods of approach which may prove helpful. Although some of my observations apply equally well to industrial nations and to underdeveloped areas, they are drawn almost exclusively from United States experience in the latter—particularly in Turkey and other countries of the Middle East.

Labor Conditions Abroad

Political Orientation. It is a rare labor movement abroad which does not devote much, if not most, of its energy to the promotion of broad goals of social justice and the achievement of its aims through political action. These aims may have an explicit socialist or Marxist orientation, or they may reflect no specific ideology. They may involve acceptance of the prevailing political and economic order, or they may advocate its abolition by peaceful or by violent means. They may focus on pragmatic issues or be devoted to abolishing private property.

United States businessmen may not always enjoy dealing with domestic labor unions, but they have never had any real reason to fear that labor would lead a social revolution in this country and change the basic nature of our society. On the other hand, this possibility is very often a real one overseas, and must be faced.

Centralization of Authority. Unless a nation is simply too vast to make centralized government and administration possible—as is the case in India—politics tend to cluster around the middle, and pressures will focus there. Parallels to our dual, federal-state system are rare, so it is difficult for different areas and industries to work out solutions based on their local needs and experience.

For this reason—among others—the familiar American device of collective bargaining at the plant or local level does not tend to develop abroad. Union leaders overseas must spend all their energy on making things happen at the center, where the power is concentrated; they consider their local efforts as a means of facilitating this process, rather than full-time responsibilities in themselves.

This centralized activity tends to increase the pervasiveness of politics. It tends to rear its head everywhere, in areas where an American would least expect to find it, and political jockeying dictates both union and management tactics. Trivial decisions must often be referred to national government departments in Cairo or Ankara, and ministers and members of parliament will frequently intervene in local disputes when it serves their political interests. Consequently, men at the top are terribly rushed and overworked, unable to give the major problems their due attention.

In many countries, wages, hours, and overtime regulations are uniform everywhere. Sometimes this uniformity extends to relatively minor matters which are settled by local contracts in the United States. Examples include the frequency at which wages must be paid, the day of payment, layoff and discharge payments required, and methods for handling grievances. Incidentally, the latter often involve governmental participation, even in the early stages.

Labor law tends to be all-embracing, complicated, legalistic, and detailed. It is administered by men without special training, accustomed to reading and applying the fine print rather than analyzing problems on their merits and suggesting realistic solutions.

Labor Turnover. Unless an employer operates in one of the few areas where industry is concentrated and a labor force has been created, he is likely to be faced with the elementary and staggering problems of transforming masses of untrained men into industrial workers.

In countries like Turkey, where new industries are growing up rapidly and agriculture is in a state of upheaval and transition, today's workers are often yesterday's peasants. These people have never seen the inside of a city apartment, let alone the inside of a factory. They have lived simple lives, according to the traditional village patterns, and have never had to come and go by the clock or subject themselves to the discipline of a stranger. Such men need more than instruction in machine-tending to become productive workers. They must, with help, create an entirely new way of life for themselves.

When villagers first go to work in factories, they are usually under economic pressure and consider it a short-term expedient—a way to raise sufficient cash to go home again. Often they do just that, so bewildered managers and foremen find their best efforts rewarded by a substantial disintegration of their labor force. Even in cases where great efforts are made to hold on to employees by providing housing, setting up mosques, stores, and recreational facilities, and by similar measures, the results can be disappointing.

Psychologically, industrial life has not yet become a long-term proposition for many people in the underdeveloped countries. Even though it may be new and strange—perhaps exciting as well as materially rewarding—the fundamental adjustment is slow and painful, while the ties to the village remain and the possibility of returning still exists.

Conspicuousness. United States firms establishing themselves in new nations must expect their every action, however minute, to be the subject of relentless scrutiny by all segments of the society. Their sharpest critics will undoubtedly be the local communist groups where they exist. Life overseas is really lived in a goldfish bowl. This can have some desirable aspects, of course, but for the most part it accentuates the difficulties faced by American managers and technicians who are trying to build up an industry. Furthermore, it means that personnel selection procedures for overseas positions must examine qualities beyond a man's technical skill.

Coping with the Problems

Given this background of the situation overseas, what are the areas in which United States business can work toward improving its labor relations?

Wage Administration. In the United States, management pays workers the value of their work. This may be determined scientifically, by job evaluation; it may be negotiated through collective bargaining; or it may be set unilaterally by management, after a study of the labor market. Whatever the method, the goal is the same: a particular job pays a particular wage.

United States executives overseas are often surprised to discover that the worker is paid in relation to his circumstances rather than the work he does in some foreign nations. Seniority and family size, for example, are two factors which determine the pay of many industrial employees, despite great differences in the job performed and the skill required.

Efforts to change this custom have been and can be made successfully, but in many cases resistance must be expected. Traditional systems of wage payment are based on the great desire for security on the part of workers deprived of their village and family insurance systems and on the kind of economic egalitarianism which village life tends to foster. Primitive agriculture is a cooperative enterprise and the whole family must work together; thus a bias develops in favor of equal sharing of the rewards. Naturally enough, this attitude carries over into the industrial environment.

Although I would support efforts to change this wage philosophy in United States plants abroad, I would urge gradual change. The wholesale importation and application of fancy methods of time-study and job evaluation is inadvisable. These methods may work beautifully in the United States, but it is only because they rest on a cultural and economic foundation which has yet to be constructed abroad. All the job-evaluation experiments which I know in Turkey —even the most successful—have been forced to extend the anticipated time for completion and reduce the thoroughness of application. The flattened wage curve which management resists at home tends to appear abroad, though for different reasons, and sometimes it makes sense to leave it alone.

Personnel Administration. The concept of personnel administration is one of the most effective ideas we can take abroad, but it needs and deserves careful adaptation. In particular, it often has to be far more personalized than in the United States.

Our society has become atomized, and the relationship between worker and boss is relatively impersonal. This has not happened in other societies. In areas like the Near East, a tradition of paternalism plays a significant role in determining the character of labor-management relations. A clear pattern of behavior has been established, which requires loyalty and deference from workers, concern and protection from the employer. This pattern extends beyond the factory gates and helps explain the profusion of fringe benefits paid out by many firms. These extras include death, maternity, birth, sickness, marriage, and other allowances, as well as free or nominal-cost meals and work clothes. Such symbols of the employer-employee relationship are often embodied in the law. The stringent terms of in-plant discipline and the status consciousness of both workers and managers also carry over into off-the-job community life.

Personnel administration in this climate demands a departure from the United States norm, which emphasizes policies rather than persons, insists on uniform standards of behavior and judgment, and is preoccupied with creating an enlightened in-plant atmosphere and high morale. Such a system, if transplanted without modification into other societies, could arouse great resistance and antagonism. It would seem to the nationals that we were discrediting their time-honored ideas and subverting traditional moral standards of behavior. Its connection with concrete problems of production may not be obvious to local engineers and technicians, and they would resent being forced to acquire and use new, nonscientific skills and approaches.

For these reasons, the United States personnel administrator abroad must proceed with infinite caution and only after the most thorough preparation. Unless he does, he will soon find himself standing on one side of a semantic gulf, with his foreign colleagues or subordinates on the other. Furthermore, he will stir up a storm of controversy and distrust in the work force.

This does not mean that the situation cannot be changed. I favor the gradual introduction of modern personnel methods, with particular attention to the training of line supervisors and executives so that they will understand the problems and goals of good personnel practice and assume the responsibilities it involves. In the long run, such practices seem to me infinitely better suited to the needs of industrial life than do the older, indigenous methods which are characteristic of a nonindustrial economy. The question here is partly one of *timing*. If we push too fast, we are very likely to fail alto-gether.

Personnel administration overseas must cover many areas which do not have to be considered in the United States. Management has taken on a great social responsibility in training the new workers and accommodating them to industrial life. The needs of the people are great, and the adequate fulfillment of these needs is crucial to the success of the enterprise.

Industrial Relations. We often assume that unions abroad can be disregarded because they are weak, naive, or ineffective. Thus we are inclined to postpone attention to sound labor-management relations until the far-distant day when the unions will finally have reached such a position of strength that they cannot be put off.

In my view, no single attitude can be more of a threat to our long-term interests abroad, both as managers and as citizens, than this one. When we accept such a line of reasoning, we forget that bitter memories of yesterday in the United States have a great deal to do with the labor-management difficulties of today. Because we ignored our unions when they were weak, we are forced to do penance now that they are strong. To make the same mistake again is not only stupid but dangerous as well.

American management abroad faces a golden opportunity. We have a wealth of experience in the solution of social conflict, and a chance to help other peoples to benefit from our knowledge. When United States management abroad behaves toward unions the way it did fifty years ago in this country—and it does happen—we need only ask ourselves what will be going on in that nation or community fifty years from now. And half a century is not a long time, as cor-porations and nations calculate.

We have been fortunate that the discontents have never been mobilized under one banner for any length of time in the United States. The unions here have had to win their own way without the support of farmers or other impoverished, bitter, and vengeful groups. Abroad just the opposite is likely to be the case. A militant labor movement, appearing when inflation and shortages arising from industrialization are at their height and, denied the opportunity to play a constructive role, can become the catalyst uniting all the elements of protest into a potent and destructive force.

Often the local managers abroad, deprived of the advantages of our experience, fail to see this possibility. Too often American executives overseas follow the local ways and neglect the desires of the unions. A better course, though a more difficult one, is to lay the groundwork for constructive relations and good feeling at the beginning of the industrialization process. This means taking the long-run view in personnel and labor relations matters as we do in finance, marketing, and other management areas.

I would emphasize, therefore, that the best policy abroad is for management to welcome unionization and work toward realizing its long-term possibilities, despite the short-term difficulties which are bound to arise.

LABOR RELATIONS IN EUROPE*

In discussing labor relations in Europe, I want to divide the problem into three parts:

- The process of adaptation to a new value system.
- The question of existing restrictions on management's freedom of decision.
- The political aspects of the situation.

As general background, I might first point out a major difference between doing labor relations research in Europe and in the Near East. Far from being unwilling to talk, trade unions, business groups, and government people in Europe are more than anxious to present their views. They have highly individualized beliefs, so the observer must constantly try to distinguish the personal view of the man with whom he is talking from the general policies of the government, the union, or the business. This is not always an easy proposition!

Social attitudes of trade unions and employer groups vary greatly

* By Mr. Rothbaum.

throughout Europe. Each country presents a sharp contrast with every other one. Consequently, an outline of the labor situation in one particular country would not be very valuable to businessmen interested in locating a plant in another part of Europe. Therefore, I want to set up a general analytical approach which can be used in each country. What are the types of questions a United States executive would want to ask? What are the most significant aspects about a country's value system that he should consider? I have arbitrarily chosen three such questions which seem to me especially important.

The Employer and the Corporation

First of all, what is the attitude of the population in general toward the employer and toward the business corporation? What, specifically, does the worker believe? What are the unions' attitudes?

Employer-employee relations in the history of Europe differ from nation to nation:

> In France, for example, there has been bitterness and strife between management and workers. The French trade unions have a long history of economic ineffectiveness behind them. Ideology and frustration have driven them into political activity, usually with unsuccessful results. The lack of a common meeting ground between employer and employee partly explains the radicalism of the Confédération Générale du Travail and the successful control of this organization by the communists. An extreme social stratification characterizes French society. The employer and the worker do not mix; indeed, the two groups are mutually and outrightly antagonistic.

On the other hand, there is a very different atmosphere in the Scandinavian countries. In Norway, the early part of the century witnessed a socialist movement that was undoubtedly one of the most radical of its time; today, this group could hardly be called radical. Association bargaining was developed in Norway in the early days. Employer and worker groups participated, and many of the workers' ideas were gradually assimilated into management policy. Because employers were willing to recognize the importance of the unions' position, organized labor was never forced into violent measures for achieving its goals. In general, the labor movement in Norway today could be described as conservative, as compared to trade union organizations in many other European countries. Its policies are pragmatic rather than dogmatic, and union leaders are not afraid to suggest economic policies that may involve high profits or deflation or islands of unemployment if these seem to fit the current economic needs.

Thus in every country historical factors condition the attitude of the worker and his organization toward the economy in general and the employer in particular. Now, how do they feel about the modern corporate form of business organization?

Today, the general feeling in the United States is that the corporation brings about public gain in pursuing its private benefit. Generally, we feel that the private enterprise system produces advantages for all. It is true that we place certain restrictions on it when we feel it has gone too far, but basically we believe it is sound.

But this view is not typical of the European countries. There are many reasons for this:

For one thing, many corporations are family-owned. Their purpose is to maintain and increase the prestige of the family that runs them. Therefore the owners will decide against further expansion at some point because any further growth would require professional management and deprive the family of control. The corporation may not consider the benefits which expansion could bring to its employees and the community—the decision is based entirely on the private interests of its management. Even some of the most progressive firms in Italy have taken this course of action to protect family control.

In these family concerns, there is an inherent tendency toward conservatism which leaves a sour taste in the mouth of the worker. Furthermore, the ladder of promotion is a short one: a worker may be able to rise to the position of engineer, but the engineer ordinarily cannot hope to move into the managerial class because he has not gone to the right school and was not born into the right family. These limitations, based on class affiliation rather than ability, also embitter the worker.

The middle management people in European corporations—the nontechnical personnel who *have* gone to the right schools—are in a sort of never-never land so far as advancement is concerned. There is no clear line of responsibility from the family at the top to the middle managers underneath, so these men rarely know where they are going or what their next step should be. In this sort of situation, favoritism on the part of particular members in the family that owns the business may be more important in the career of an employee than his own capabilities.

The local European attitudes toward the corporation and the employer in general constitute an important aspect of the social and industrial value system of this area—a system to which United States businessmen must adapt their ideas on labor policy.

Attitude Toward Work

The attitude toward work itself is another factor to be considered. Ideas vary from place to place. The ancient Calvinistic view prevails in Switzerland, where work is deemed the highest virtue and prestige adheres to the person who works hardest and longest. In other areas people have the opposite idea—the less work and effort you can get away with, the better.

To many Europeans work still means following a specific trade or craft. Americans may run into real difficulties trying to convert the craftsman into a production-line laborer. The skilled artisan has little respect for the wonders of mass production—he considers the new methods a degradation of standards. He tends to become cynical and deprecative about his job, and he has difficulty switching over to a role as an efficient participant in a mass-production system.

The tempo of the work pace is often much slower overseas than it is in the United States, and this is another factor to be reckoned with. A Danish productivity team which recently visited the United States reported that the tempo was about the same here as in Denmark, except for the automobile plants. They felt the work pace at the Ford factory, for instance, was most excessive. In general, foreign workmen are conscientious and punctual about their working hours, but they resent being hurried on the job and they are accustomed to taking longer midday breaks.

Feelings Toward Americans

The attitude of workers toward American managers is colored by their feeling that we are "materialistic." Again and again we hear this thought expressed. I might mention that I have spent a considerable amount of time in Switzerland, and in my opinion Switzerland is at least as materialistic as the United States, if not more so. However, because of the tremendous gap between the material welfare of the United States and that of other countries, this theme seems to be repeated all the time.

The real point, though, is not the question of whether the criticism is justified or not; the feeling exists, and we must reckon with it. An American manager must step softly, making sure he does not downgrade the nonmaterialistic values of these societies, recognizing their worth, and expressing appreciation of them. He should keep the picture which his colleagues hold of him in the back of his mind and try to counteract it.

Also, foreign employees feel a need for a more personal relationship in the work environment than we maintain in the United States. In this desire they are similar to the people in underdeveloped countries. They do not feel at home with the style of personnel relations that we have developed in American corporations overseas, though our patterns are, at least, an improvement over the family favoritism in the traditional companies.

So much for the significant economic attitudes and values in Europe. Let me try to summarize the problems faced by a United States firm entering an area where this different value system persists. It starts off with two handicaps: (1) the general unreceptiveness of workers to our way of doing things, and (2) the traditional attitudes toward the employer, the corporation, work, regimentation, and other requirements of industry.

On the more hopeful side, the United States company going into another country will eventually be able to capitalize on some of the corporate policies characterizing business in this nation. The gradual introduction of a good promotional system would be very well received in European countries, for current policies are the source of a great deal of unrest. The general efficiency of a United States factory, with the consequent reduction of drudgery, together with the high wages paid by American firms should help in establishing satisfactory labor relations overseas.

Legal Restrictions on Management

What are the restrictions on United States executives in the labor relations field in Europe? The manager is limited on the one hand by legal regulations and on the other by the standards set through collective bargaining between employers' associations and trade unions.

We are familiar with some of the legal limitations. These are protective in nature: minimum wages, maximum hours, and so on. We are not as familiar with a second group of government regulations that affect the freedom to hire and fire. For example, there may be an attempt to build national unemployment policy into the structure of private business organizations. Thus a plant may be required to have a certain ratio of veterans among its work force or to shoulder heavy severance payments to laid-off workers or contribute to retraining expenses for them. One effect of such laws is to lead a firm to carry an excessive labor supply. Also one may be required to hire workers through public labor exchanges.

Social insurance represents a large part of total labor costs in Europe; it may run to 40%, 50%, or even 60% of the payroll. In setting up these benefits, the governments are not really making an attempt to provide people with the same security in factory work that they had in the villages; rather, this insurance is a device used by industrialized countries which are trying to raise the minimum standard of living right across the board. They are trying to match the levels in other countries which have a higher per capita income, like the United States, Great Britain, and Switzerland. The only way they can force the scale upwards is to pay a man according to his needs instead of his production. If his base pay is not high enough, special systems of family allowances, maternity benefits, and so forth, are inserted. Political and religious beliefs reinforce these economic pressures.

A third category of legal restrictions on management is in the area of collective bargaining. Here governmental regulations are much more extensive than in the United States. First, full collective bargaining agreements (as distinguished from simple wage accords) must meet certain legal requirements, including a long list of obligatory clauses on such issues as trade union rights, conditions of hiring and firing, shop stewards, plant committees, conciliation, and apprenticeships. Associations are often required to meet certain registration requirements. Furthermore, the provisions arrived at in one collective bargaining agreement can be extended to people who had nothing to do with the original contract, a practice unheard of in this country:

> By way of illustration, if a number of unions in a particular area of France concluded an agreement, the government could extend the principles of that settlement to all other employers in the same industry, regardless of whether or not they belonged to the management association which agreed to the contract or dealt with the union that put forward the demands. This means, of course, that decisions made by a small group can be made applicable to everybody by law.

Power of the Unions

The second type of restrictions that United States employers come up against in Europe are imposed by the labor organizations. The scope of union influence often extends to matters of production, pricing, market scheduling, and the purchase of raw materials, as well as labor policy. When it comes to wage issues, the trade associations can determine minimum levels, set actual wages, and bring about wage changes completely outside formal bargaining sessions at the plant level with management. For example:

> In Italy, a primary contract decides how wages in most industries in the country will rise with the cost of living. An escalator clause provides wage changes across the board when prices go up. These increases are not bargained for with employers as the need arises; they take place automatically. Worker benefits are standardized in this contract—there are set provisions applying to all industry regarding vacations, holidays, special Christmas bonuses, and the like. Some nonmonetary issues, which are decided through the plant level collective bargaining process in the United States, are also standardized in this manner.

The government's job-classification system is often based on trade association recommendations and marks out grades into which employers fit their workers. Highly skilled workers are separated from the semiskilled, and firms then adjust their wages accordingly. Thus the plant-level prerogative of job evaluation is often subordinate to the trade association and the government.

The scope of association bargaining power differs greatly from nation to nation. In some, all the employers get together with all the unions and sign the major contracts. Such confederal bargaining would be equivalent to the National Association of Manufacturers sitting down with the American Federation of Labor. This major agreement ordinarily sets minimum wages, and further bargaining settles the pay scales for individual industries.

In addition, regional bargaining occurs from time to time. In France, the employers have managed to secure a regional bargaining setup, although the unions would prefer a national approach. Actually, these regional agreements come pretty close to national bargaining, but they do allow a little more variation than would the central contract.

United States businessmen must, of course, always distinguish between what actually happens and what seems to happen. From what I have said here, it would appear that an American employer in a European country is under almost impossible restrictions and has no freedom of decision at all. Actually he has a much greater degree of autonomy than appears on paper.

Let us see how this works:

- Since settlements are often made on an industry basis, individual problems can be, and are, taken into account. Such matters as the type of product, the market, and the kind of worker employed are considered.
- Wage rates are often proclaimed merely as a basis for further collective bargaining. If you look at the actual figures from firm to firm, they turn out to vary just as they do in the United States.
- Most United States firms overseas have a high capital ratio and so pay wages higher than the level set for them. Thus the agreements have little impact on them. This is similar to the situation in the domestic steel industry—minimum wage legislation does not have much effect on the pay scales of these companies.
- In the field of welfare benefits, a firm can give about what it pleases without the government intervening.

Employers' associations pose a difficult problem for the United States businessman. Should he join one and go along with whatever they determine? There are certain advantages in doing this. Joining the employers' association in a new country is the best way to become accustomed and adapted to the new pattern of labor relations, and minimizes the problem of social adjustment for the company's managerial personnel. They will be accepted by the local management because they are meeting the local management standards. Furthermore, such membership permits the American firm to exercise some influence on the political decisions that are made by the association without sticking its own particular neck out. It can express views within the confines of the employers' association and, perhaps, will have some influence in directions which it might not dare take by itself.

On the other hand, I think the attitude of the employers' associa-

tions in countries such as France and Italy may not be one with
which most United States businessmen would care to identify themselves. Also, by pledging oneself to observe certain labor relations
practices, one is likely to find himself committed in other areas as
well, since these associations do not limit themselves to bargaining
agreements; they also have certain cartel implications.

Keeping Out of Politics

The last major area I want to cover is the political. Should you
be active in this field? What is the right course to follow with regard
to European politics?

My own feeling is that the survival of a United States corporation
depends on the art of being useful in a modest and quiet way. If a
firm can make a contribution to the economy and to the welfare
of the nation as a whole, while at the same time accomplishing its
own immediate production objectives, it is best to let it go at that.
By and large, it is good policy to stay out of political strife. Nothing
is to be gained; certainly if any dissatisfaction develops, the American is more likely to take the brunt of it than anyone else.

In summary, it is clear that the position of an American corporation in Europe is far better than that of one in the Middle East or
Asia. Nationalism is less explosive and sensitive. Europeans do not
have feelings of inferiority, because they have a political history
longer than ours and the gap between their standard of living and
ours is not so great. The area is already highly industrialized, so
there is no danger of an American firm coming in and becoming the
dominant enterprise in the nation. Nevertheless, it is highly important that United States firms adapt their policies to the attitudes
and values of the country in which they are operating and send
over management personnel who are sensitive to these attitudes.
Americans should be able to operate and develop within a different
value system, while at the same time educating the people in a new
philosophy more in tune with today's needs.

QUESTIONS AND ANSWERS*

From the floor: Would an American firm that is planning to establish operations either in Europe or the Middle East be wise to secure a personnel administrator from that country, or should they import one from the United States?

Mr. Rothbaum: In Europe, you would do better to start off with one of your own men, although this depends, of course, on the individual situation. If you could get someone locally who was basically in sympathy with the policy of the corporation, he would help you to adapt to that particular country's value system. But ordinarily such a man would have to have a history of association with the company.

Mr. Rosen: I would recommend an American for Turkey—and for the Arab countries as well. I would add that he should spend a great deal of time soaking up the atmosphere before he made his first move, but that first move should come from him. He ought not to depend on the nationals of the country to make it.

From the floor: How about supervisory personnel? Are they unionized?

Mr. Rothbaum: Yes, in Europe they are often unionized.

Mr. Rosen: This is a most interesting situation. The supervisor in the Middle East is really cut off from top management, and there is no foreman's class as we know it here. Actually, the supervisor is often equivalent to the head man in the village, and is often elected to local union office. As a member and an officer of the union, he is among the most militant defenders of the workers' rights, although his job is in theory that of a foreman.

* Businessmen present at the panel session on which this chapter is based raised certain questions which brought about the discussion reported more or less verbatim on this page.

PROBLEMS IN REMOTE CONTROL OF OVERSEAS OPERATIONS

Pearson Hunt, Willem Holst, W. C. Meyer, Frank Collinge, and Ralph Waller

THE TOPIC OF THIS CHAPTER might be restated as the problem of establishing satisfactory relationships between the head office and the field in order to define policies and observe and control the results. In essence, we are concerned here with communication between various members of an organization.

Note: Mr. Hunt, who makes the introductory observations, is Professor of Business Administration, Harvard Business School, and served as moderator for the panel discussion on which this chapter is based; Mr. Holst is Manager, Economic Coordination, Standard-Vacuum Oil Company; Mr. Meyer is General Division Accountant, Procter & Gamble Company; both Mr. Collinge and Mr. Waller are with Arthur Andersen & Co., where Mr. Collinge is Partner in charge of Foreign Operations and Mr. Waller supervises European operations from an office in Paris.

This communication goes beyond formal, systematic reporting. It involves the ever-present, informal interactions which take place in a group and the organizational machinery for coordination of those relations. The four men who have prepared this part of the book have stressed these aspects of communication as they relate to the administration of foreign business.

There are, of course, many ways to approach this matter. The one we have chosen concentrates on the appraisal of field performance in relation to home office objectives in both short-range and long-range planning. The authors have examined this question from the standpoint of the man in the field as well as that of the administrator in the central office.

Needless to say, similar control problems face an executive with a decentralized operation located strictly within the continental limits of the United States. But there are some special aspects to communication in the context of international business, and it is to these that we will turn our attention.

LONG-RANGE OBJECTIVES °

One of several aspects of control—remote or otherwise—is the establishment of targets, or objectives, by the top management of a company. In overseas operations such targets may be arrived at in a number of ways—for example, on the basis of American experience, or by a comparative analysis of a number of overseas units, or by an individual analysis of conditions applying to a single operation in a particular country. Frequently a combination of these approaches is used. But whatever route is taken, whether past performance or some other criteria is employed, these two conditions must be met if the goals are to be set successfully and if subsequent control is to be maintained:

- There must be a continuous flow of information between the field and the central office.

° By Mr. Holst.

- The information must be consolidated and analyzed in reference to given standards of performance.

I will limit my discussion in the following pages to the longer-range aspects of remote control, concentrating on the planning and coordination of supply and demand for five to ten years ahead, and the associated financial problems. Long-range planning is just as dependent on a continuous flow of information between the fields and the central office as is short-range planning. But the type of information and the relationships between the overseas units and headquarters are likely to be somewhat different in short-range planning, where an appraisal of past performance is usually involved. Before describing Standard-Vacuum's control system in this context, however, I would like to digress briefly to describe the company's operations.

Scope of Activity

From the 1890's to 1933, the Standard Oil Company (New Jersey) and the Socony Mobil Oil Company had been operating as separate firms in the Eastern Hemisphere. Jersey Standard had only producing and refining facilities there, while Socony Mobil was limited to a marketing organization. The two companies felt that they could achieve better service and greater operating efficiencies by combining operations. So in 1933 they formed the Standard-Vacuum Oil Company, which was to operate in the Asian and African countries east and southwest of the Persian Gulf. This portion of the world includes more than 50 separate political entities and has a population of almost 900 million, exclusive of the mainland of China.

Today, Standard-Vacuum operates as a fully integrated, separate oil company. It has its own officers and directors, and formulates and administers its own policies. It has just completed a new headquarters office in White Plains, New York, which houses the 700 employees who comprise the company's headquarters staff.

Overseas, Standard-Vacuum has 40,000 employees. About 95% of them are nationals of the countries in which they work. The company has established 21 wholly owned subsidiaries and 14 branches abroad; in addition, it has one affiliate in which it owns a majority interest, and seven in which its interest is less than 50%. These operating units cover all phases of the oil industry—exploration, production, pipeline transportation, refining, marine transportation, and marketing. At present, the company's principal exploration activity is in Indonesia, India, Pakistan, Western New Guinea, Papua, British Somaliland, and the Philippines. Standard-Vacuum currently operates refineries in Indonesia, India, South Africa, Australia, and Japan. Marketing activity throughout the so-called "Stanvac Area" is conducted through 22 branches and subsidiaries. In addition to its own production, Stanvac is a purchaser of both crude oil and products in the Middle East, where its parent companies have a share in petroleum operations in Iran, Iraq, Saudi Arabia, and Qatar. For transporting the petroleum, the company owns and operates 23 vessels totaling about 340,000 dead-weight tons. In addition, it usually has another 30 to 40 ships under period charter.

Stanvac's branch and subsidiary offices are located at points as far apart as Capetown, South Africa, and Yokohama, Japan, and Karachi, Pakistan, and Wellington, New Zealand. Some 10,000 miles separate these locations. Singapore, close to the center of the Stanvac area, is 180° both east and west of New York, where the company has its headquarters; hence the adjective "remote" is particularly applicable to Standard-Vacuum's operations.

The company's rapid postwar growth, combined with the vastness of distance and variety of activities it embraces, has made the problem of remote control an exceedingly complex one for us. Our volume of business increased from about 70,000 barrels per day in 1938 to 200,000 barrels per day in 1955. Consequently, the topic of this chapter represents an operating problem which demands our continuing attention.

Planning Agencies

Standard-Vacuum's long-range planning is done through the cooperation of several agencies in the central office, which consolidate field information and translate it into company-wide plans for the future:

> The functional departments—exploration, producing, manufacturing, marketing, and marine transportation—act as technical liaison agents between their field counterparts and other central office control agencies.

> The economic coordination department provides the supply-and-demand framework for the company's long-range logistical planning, evaluates possible alternatives of supply through the preparation of economic studies, and establishes the basis for a long-term capital investment program.

> The treasurer's department translates the investment program into its financial implications. Included in its reports are a consolidated forecast of cash available from profit and depreciation, a breakdown by currencies, and a statement of sources for additional funds, if such are needed to arrive at a balance with the company's over-all capital requirements.

> The coordination committee is responsible for reviewing all forward plans, associated budgets, and appropriation requests before recommending action by the board of directors.

The Control Mechanisms

We can now look at Standard-Vacuum's machinery for long-range planning and control in somewhat greater detail. There are four main mechanisms:

> 1. The establishment of definite objectives with regard to areas of operation, degree of integration, product quality improvement, and similar matters.

> 2. A forecast of petroleum consumption five to ten years ahead on an area-wide basis, with an estimate of the company's sales opportunities based on that probable consumption.

> 3. The determination of an optimum supply and demand balance by individual years.

> 4. The preparation of a cash and currency forecast, taking into account capital investment requirements, crude and product pric-

ing, freight rates, and the profitability of each phase of the company's operations.

The long-range objectives are established at two levels—the policy level, where the political stability and economic climate of particular regions determine their acceptability as areas of large-scale future investment; and the operational or budgetary level, where the long-range logistical and financial framework determines how much each phase should be expanded or contracted, or what degree of integration should be sought, taking into account parent company supplies of crude and product in the Persian Gulf.

The determination of the economic climate is accomplished in various ways. Many governments publish pamphlets describing incentives for foreign investment, and these are most helpful. Also, agencies of our own government prepare excellent material on foreign industrial opportunities through local embassies and consulates. Stanvac's own field offices periodically submit pertinent data to guide the central office in matters affecting both the economic and political climate. In addition, when a large new investment is contemplated, direct contact is established between directors of the company and high government officials to explore the economic conditions further and to discuss terms.

Forecasting Demand

The second planning mechanism is one which I am sure is familiar to all readers: the forecasting of future business volume. Standard-Vacuum has continuously modified its forecasting techniques over the past ten years. In the process we have markedly changed the character of our relationships with the field, especially in this matter of appraising future outlook.

Prior to 1947 forecasting of demand was almost exclusively the responsibility of overseas marketing units and was confined to Stanvac sales as opposed to industry-wide prospects. The New York office did little reviewing or revising beyond the consolidation of individual field forecasts, which were largely based on local knowledge of sales contracts for the near future, combined with an attempt at simple projection of past sales trends for individual petroleum products. While this method yielded reasonably good over-all results for the two or three years immediately ahead—with errors averaging only 2% to 5% for aggregate demand—estimates for five to ten years into the future were always far too low. For example, a projection made in 1946 for the year 1955 proved to be 40% below the actual tenth, or terminal year, of the forecast period.

In order to improve such forecasts—particularly those for individual products—and to permit a more careful New York review, the field units were given new instructions. These programs suggested the preparation of forecasts by an "end-use" technique—that is, an estimate of the number of passenger cars, buses, trucks, and tractors that would be in operation and the average amount of petroleum each would consume. Such forecasts, prepared on an industry-wide basis for two to four years ahead, made possible a more careful New York appraisal of field estimates and provided a good basis for a reasoned exchange of views when New York felt the estimates required revision. However, longer-range estimates for over four years continued to be made largely on the basis of the simple projection technique, a device with limitations which readily became apparent.

More recently, therefore, the New York staff has adopted a technique which is coming into ever more widespread use: the determination of long-range trends in petroleum demand by an analysis of the entire energy balance of an area. This means forecasting the *total* demand for all forms of energy from primary sources such as coal, hydro-power, natural gas, petroleum, and, eventually, nuclear sources. Then an estimate is made of the part that petroleum is likely to play in meeting that total demand. This requires an appraisal of the probable rate of industrialization and economic development generally, of future balance of payments problems, and of the availability and rate of exploitation of competing energy sources. With New York's encouragement, a few of our major field units are beginning to adopt this technique; smaller units, however, simply do not have an adequate staff to carry through such a relatively sophisticated approach.

Japan provides an illustration of the operation of this energy-balance method of forecasting demand:

> About five years ago, when we first tried this approach, we looked at the Japanese government's estimates of future coal production. Their figure was something like 55 million tons a year. As time went by, Japan's actual coal production dropped from a level of 48 million tons down to 43 million. At that point, of course, we became quite worried about our balances. We made a local survey and discovered that the coal situation seemed to be getting even worse, indicating that the government's higher coal production forecast was likely to be nowhere near correct. Consequently, we turned our plans around completely, basing them on the more realistic figure of 43 million tons of coal. The difference in consumption of fuel oil was enormous and we had to make drastic changes in our expansion plans for the next five years.

Balancing Supply and Demand

The determination of supply and demand is a complex problem, involving an infinite number of permutations and combinations. We have more than a dozen crude oils available, at least 8 refinery sources of supply including the Persian Gulf, and over 20 marketing entities to satisfy with products covering a wide range of quality specifications.

Our third control mechanism, designed to balance supply and demand, is based generally on estimates of product output by overseas operational units, but any plan extending beyond three years can be modified if necessary by selection and construction of appropriate refinery equipment. The final determination of what may be regarded as an optimum over-all balance for the company as a whole is therefore essentially an economic problem, involving a comparison of major alternatives. By its very nature, this is a centralized

New York office function. In large measure, the staff work is carried out by the economic coordination department which works in close collaboration with the New York functional departments. Of course some trial and error is involved in arriving at optimum solutions, but a new supply-and-demand balance must be prepared once every six months because of the ever-changing aspects of the petroleum industry as a whole.

The fourth and final mechanism of long-range planning is the translation of the supply-and-demand balance into financial terms, and the reappraisal of various major alternatives in the light of over-all financial feasibility. Costs, requirements for investment in fixed capital and working capital, and cash generation through profits, depreciation, self-insurance, and other reserves must be projected by major functions.

Standard-Vacuum's overseas units are responsible for the initial preparation of such cash forecasts for periods up to four years into the future. However, these estimates are subject to general guidance from the New York office, which determines the assumptions that should be used with regard to prices, freight rates, and so on. Some New York adjustments usually prove to be necessary. Generally we have found that these modifications suggested by the central office and based on its comparative analysis of past field forecasts are helpful in improving future field accuracy.

The New York staff tends to assume primary responsibility for the preparation of longer-range financial forecasts—that is, forecasts extending beyond four years. Individual field units are not in a good position to determine the size and location of needed new refineries, or to judge the relative priorities to be assigned to various regions in terms of their comparative political stability or investment climate. As in the case of demand forecasting, however, it is hoped that the larger field units can make an increasing contribution to such longer-range financial projections.

In closing, I would like to make a few general observations, based on Stanvac's experience, about the relationships between field and central office with respect to long-range forward planning:

Standard-Vacuum's system of remote control is not static, but is subject to constant development, experimentation, and change.

What appears to be a highly centralized long-range planning control function belies the fact that in many other respects, and even in short-range planning, Standard-Vacuum encourages an ever-increasing degree of decentralization in order to free top management for major policy issues.

Because of the complexity of the company's operations, certain appraisals and decisions can be made only in New York; nevertheless, here too an attempt is made to keep information flowing in both directions between the field and the central office. A continuous interchange is essential for improving the accuracy of longer-range forecasting and for logistical coordination.

In planning a sound program for the future, Stanvac feels that the central office agencies should always have the courage to look as far into the future as is necessary to discern the major trends. Because it may well take up to five years to negotiate, plan, and build a new refinery from scratch—and even longer to develop a new producing field—Stanvac believes that forecasting and planning should extend up to ten years ahead.

SHORT-TERM CONTROL*

The general business of the Procter & Gamble Company is the manufacture and sale of soap, soap products, synthetic and other detergents, shampoos, dentifrices, home permanents, shortening, cooking and other refined vegetable oils, peanuts and peanut butter, and by-products such as glycerine. We are doing business in an important way in 15 countries all over the world—in Latin America, Europe, Africa, and the Far East. Our foreign subsidiaries follow our general business pattern, although in certain countries selling, or packaging and selling, are the only activities. Not all product lines are carried in each country.

The same objectives we have developed for our business in the United States are usually applicable to an overseas operation, so our

* By Mr. Meyer.

thinking and planning are directed toward instituting those objectives and practices in each country where we are doing business.

This is not, of course, an iron clad rule. If there is a special reason why we should not carry out some general practice in a particular country, we do not do so. Thus we combine flexibility with a well-defined framework for control.

The few men who compose the overseas division of our home office have all had experience in overseas subsidiaries, and most of them have had major responsibilities in those operations.

Overseas we try to have nationals in all positions up to and including management. We maintain about 65 Americans as compared with 8,000 foreign employees.

Removing the "Remote"

The problem of remote control in foreign operations comes down to the matter of communication between the home office group and the overseas people. For some reason or other, a Biblical injunction comes to mind at this point. To paraphrase a little: "If you would control the beam in your subsidiary's eye, you must first remove the 'remote' from your own eye!" We try hard to do this. Our associate directors travel over 100,000 miles a year apiece, and other members of the organization do the same. We are in continuous contact with our overseas subsidiaries.

The people on the subsidiaries' end of this process have to be carefully chosen. Selection begins in the personnel offices in the United States and overseas, with the emphasis on recruiting abroad. We screen the applicants as precisely as possible. They are interviewed by executives, their references are checked, and we find out everything that we can about them. In addition, we use a general intelligence test and a specific-area-of-interest test, the latter for correlation with the individual's particular specialty. Although United States tests translated into foreign languages do have limitations, we have found them very useful. The men who are hired participate in training programs which include visits to this country that may last anywhere from a few days to several months or even as long as a year.

Once these people are on the job, we have to make sure that they perform as we think they should. This involves keeping in close touch with them, no matter how far away they may be.

The Communicating Process

To start with, we have a basic operating understanding which is reduced to writing. Each general manager has a copy. This statement is divided into two types of policy decisions: those on which mutual agreement will be reached before action is taken by the subsidiary, and those which will be reported to the home office after the fact.

Mutual agreements on significant policy matters involving expenditure of funds are achieved largely on the basis of the forecast "Statement of Source and Application of Funds." This simply means an estimate of where the money is coming from and where it is going. These forecasting procedures are standard throughout the company, and constitute the hub of our reporting system. When the controllers of our overseas subsidiaries are not Americans, they come to Cincinnati to be trained.

Incidentally, this is an area where we find American ideas need selling abroad. They will be accepted, but it takes some persuading! The best argument we can make for these methods is to point out their usefulness to local managers as tools of administration.

The periodic forecasts—which are converted from foreign currencies into American dollars by the subsidiaries—enable management on both sides of the ocean to think together about the business. We do not ask foreign executives to pinpoint a specific target three or four years away, but we do ask them to project broad plans into the future and to express these plans in monetary terms. At this point the communicating process begins. Each subsidiary annually forecasts for three years ahead. Every month it forecasts the balance of the current quarter by months and the next four quarters by quarters. Thus the home office maintains continual communication with the overseas units, and is informed well in advance of any important matter.

The "Statement of Source and Application of Funds" is a technical accounting document, and would not be very useful to management by itself. The hub needs spokes to support it, and the spokes are the detailed explanations which back up each of the items on the document.

> For instance, take the profit item. All of our subsidiaries prepare what we call a V.P.A. sheet—physical volume, profit, and advertising—which is designed for a three-year period. It shows the projected physical shipment volume by brands for each individual year, the profit by brands per unit and in total, and the advertising per unit and in total. Here are the necessary spokes supporting the profit item.

Suppose one of the items on the V.P.A. sheet was a new brand coming into the picture three years from now. It would be listed simply as "Brand A," and would appear in 1959 for the first time. It would be identified in a broad way only—maybe it would be a heavy-duty synthetic detergent. The profit target for that type of product would be set up on the V.P.A. sheet, as well as the planned advertising support. The moment this V.P.A. sheet containing Brand A showed up in Cincinnati—presuming that it had not previously been discussed—it would come to the attention of one of our associate directors of marketing. That director and the overseas subsidiary would consult about it on the director's next trip abroad. They would discuss the feasibility of introducing such a brand, the probable effect on the company's existing brands, and the possibility of making our target profit after the introductory period. The required capital expenditure would be estimated by the engineering division of the subsidiary, and this would be checked by a parallel unit in the home office. Finally, the potential profit would be related to the capital investment or to turnover to see whether the brand would prove sufficiently profitable.

In my experience, the first time something like Brand A appears in a forecast the absolute amount of money involved is not of prime importance. What is important is getting the item into the forecast early so that everyone can start thinking about it. The planning will be refined and clarified as time goes by.

This conferring, planning, and forecasting process is a continuous one. Market research tests and studies on raw material availability and manufacturing capacity are undertaken. Advertising plans are detailed, sales plans developed, profit probabilities reassessed, and financing arranged.

Each of these steps has a definite financial impact on the "Statement of Source and Application of Funds." These impacts are reflected in the "Statement" in one of two phases:

> In the first phase, the expenditure of money is involved. Any such action requires authorization from the people in the subsidiary and the concurrence of the home office. These authorizations are termed appropriations, and precisely specify both the money amount and the purpose for which it is to be used.
>
> In the second phase, the expected profits resulting from new operations such as Brand A are taken into account. Again, authority for actually placing the brand on the market is required.

We have found that no purely financial forecast, however detailed and thorough, can maintain effective control of overseas operations by itself. We must always take the personnel in our subsidiaries into account—the people who develop and carry out the plan for the future. Consequently, personnel forecasts are set up. Each subsidiary has organization charts indicating every position in the company, the man who is currently filling it, and contemplated and possible transfers. Furthermore, two or more individuals who could, if necessary, take over various important jobs are listed, together with the training time these men would need before they would be ready to step in. We find that this type of forecast insures against personnel crises— there is a better chance that you will have the people when you need them. These charts are sent to the home office each six months.

Appraising the Results

Once a communication and control system is set up, how can management appraise the results? In an operating pattern such as I have described, responsibility for the outcome is shared. The home office works right along with the subsidiaries, rather than throwing the entire responsibility onto overseas management.

To figure out how we are doing, we compare the actual facts with the plans as finally approved.

Thus "three years beyond the current year" have been devoted to preparation. They have been years of communicating, planning, and modifying. Specific appropriations have been authorized, and specific actions have been timed to occur at the right moment. By setting actual performance as it occurs against the targets, considering both expenditure and accomplishment, we have a sound basis for appraising the effectiveness of our control.

As operations enter the current phase, specific appropriation control is tightened. Departmental operating budgets are presented, as are market research and advertising appropriations. Profit control during current operations is vital, and reporting on profit is stepped up. The subsidiary now reports physical volume and profit and advertising costs by unit and total each month. These figures for the month and current year to date are compared with the targets established during the communicating process. Explanations are furnished if there are differences.

Physical volume and profit and advertising in total and per unit are forecast for the balance of the fiscal year, and explanations are made of any differences between the previous month's estimate and the latest figures. We compare the target with the actual inventory and the forecast cash position with the cash actually on hand. The required explanations of any discrepancies bring out and spotlight any weakness in control and define any area where remedial action may be needed.

In summary, our overseas operation draws on a world-wide pool of experience. There are excellent lines of communication keeping information flowing in both directions. To make sure that the system stays fast on its feet, any general manager overseas has complete authority to act in an emergency. Our experience is that this authority is seldom used, because good planning obviates the necessity for it.

Our company's policy is to make a careful choice of the countries in which we operate, maintain clear objectives, and select and train local personnel for management positions. We have established a communications system through which plans that present the best company thinking can be made and compared with the final results. In the competitive field in which we operate, we can testify that this system has produced very good results so far.

HOME OFFICE LEADERSHIP *

My thoughts on the problem of controlling overseas operations are built on observations of a large number of business firms—old and new, large and small. This experience covers a broad area, so brief treatment of any single topic should not be taken to mean that I think it is unimportant or less significant than others.

In both foreign and domestic operations, control is maintained basically by people working together as a team. It requires mutual understanding and sharing of responsibilities, and is sustained through forward planning, the reporting of results, and systematic checkups. In these essentials, there is no difference between doing business at home and running a subsidiary abroad. The overseas operation, however, is formed to integrate United States capital, methods, and policies with foreign identities and resources, and consequently presents additional difficulties that are inherent in its foreignness and its remoteness.

Guidance and Understanding

The job of the home office in overseas operations is to furnish leadership. This requires a general familiarity with the workings of the parent company and specialized knowledge of the problems

* By Mr. Collinge.

peculiar to each of the foreign nations. The latter point is especially important. We should not oversimplify international operations by assuming that every company and every country are the same.

Top management abroad is naturally chosen by the home office. There is no universal rule that says these key executives should be American or foreign citizens. Other things being equal, the companies which have been the most successful in foreign operations for the longest time employ the largest number of nationals, but this of course depends on local conditions. One point is clear: if top executives are American, they have to demonstrate the same qualities that make for success in the home office. Conversely, if top management is foreign, it must have a sympathetic understanding of our principles and ideals.

It is also obvious that any management which is ignorant or contemptuous of the laws, traditions, customs, and national sentiments of the country in which it proposes to operate cannot control foreign operations and should not engage in them. Furthermore—and this does not bear directly on control but is nevertheless most important —high-grade Americans in business abroad are the most effective answer to any criticism from the communists or other unfriendly sources. By and large, I think our businessmen are doing a good job in this department.

Personal Contact

One theme which is stressed by every person who has participated in foreign operations is the importance of personal contact. This repetition is not a coincidence, nor is the idea a mere platitude. It is the most significant single factor in conducting an enterprise abroad. I admit that "personal contact" is difficult to define, but nonetheless it is necessary. The only effective way to work together is to get together and work!

There are elements in the idea which we can identify. Social contacts, of course, are part of it, but should not be overstressed. Foreign executives realize that there is a holiday aspect to some of the trips

American businessmen make overseas, but basically they consider them as business visits, and we too should regard them as such.

Another element in personal contact is mutual confidence. You have to respect your opposite members in the foreign operation. They are members of management, and should be treated that way. Most companies require training periods in the United States for their overseas employees. Such training helps the foreigner to know his United States associates and gives him a familiarity with the parent company's aims and policies. Some firms have a regular planned program to accomplish this. They bring their top foreign managers over here for two or three months every year. Almost all companies arrange to invite the more promising younger men.

Even forward planning—surely an important means of communication—in the final analysis is only a supplement to personal contact. You need the reports, to be sure, but they should not be set up in such a way as to damage the interpersonal relationships between the home office and the overseas branch. Unless local executives understand the purpose of the report and the uses to which it will be put, they are likely to prepare it in a perfunctory fashion and the finished product may be well nigh unintelligible.

Foreign associates ought to report to the home office on local business and political conditions. Of course, you can get such information from other sources, but your own people have a view which relates to your particular situation. Also, such reports will give you a good idea as to whether they are on the job and whether they understand what is going on.

Checking the Books

Policing—or making systematic checkups—is actually nothing more than a process of securing coordination. Traveling auditors are used by nearly every company. These men extend their activities beyond the mere books to physical inspection of the plant, surveys of the inventory balance, and evaluation of personnel. Incidentally, many companies require their independent auditors to assume a great many of the traveling auditor's functions, either as a recheck on their own man or as a supplement to his activities.

The last point I want to mention deals with the control of cash. By and large, this chapter is on a rather high level. No one really discusses the matter of making a profit! Yet, after all, that is what we are all interested in, and that is why we go abroad. Strangely enough, many companies go through this business of forward planning, reporting, and whatnot—but do not control the remittance of cash.

A large cash balance abroad, in my opinion, is unnecessary. It should be either reinvested or brought home. We have no reason to assume that we are at the end of a period of currency devaluation. Generally speaking, cash and receivables ought to be covered by obligations—accounts payable and other obligations—payable in local currency. Such a balance will protect a firm from loss by devaluation because devaluation abroad is followed by an increase in the local currency value of fixed plant and inventory.

I hope this quick summary of some keystones in foreign control will serve to highlight the important areas.

THE FIELD OFFICE *

In describing the problem of control from the viewpoint of the field associate, I draw on my experience in nearly all parts of Europe and my contacts over the course of many years with both the home offices and the local personnel of many United States companies.

I am not an American, and perhaps for that reason I hear things which Americans in the head office will never hear. I get a chance to find out from non-Americans what they really think of their American associates! They also tend to talk freely about the policies they are carrying out and the measures and procedures imposed on them by their home offices.

Foreign associates are more than just *willing* to be a part of the

* By Mr. Waller.

whole organization—they really *want* to be identified with it and implement its policies in their own territories. Naturally, at all levels there is dissatisfaction and resentment of too rigorous controls, too onerous reporting of what seems to be unnecessary information, insufficient definition of instructions, and failure of the head office to answer letters. As a matter of fact, the latter complaint is perhaps the most frequent. Maybe the head office feels the same way about the field! But such conflicts are inevitable, and their resolution is one of the major problems—or challenges—of doing business overseas.

These difficulties arise because the form of the foreign organization and the over-all division of responsibilities within that operation are generally determined by the parent group. This is unavoidable, but its impact can be tempered if local customs and regulations are taken into account. For instance, I have heard of a United States firm, operating in Latin America, which was losing out on a lot of good business because the community felt *it* was being "Americanized" instead of the *company* being "Brazilianized."

One aspect of this problem, incidentally, is the matter of language. It would be desirable if all the home office people who are dealing with foreigners could speak their language, but this is hardly practical. However, it is desirable—necessary, actually—for the local managers overseas to be able to understand and converse in English. It is extremely difficult to find professional interpreters who are proficient in technical and accounting methods.

The Local Manager

The first responsibility of the head office is the selection of a person to head up the foreign operation. Success or failure depends on that choice. My experience, as I noted before, has been largely in Europe. At least in that part of the world, I am convinced it is best to have a citizen of the country of operation—or, at any rate, a European— as the person in charge.

American companies starting out in Europe often fail to find competent management for their local operations until after they have suffered several costly setbacks through unfortunate choices. There are plenty of able, honest people abroad, but unfortunately they are not the ones that United States companies on the lookout would usually meet. The good managers are usually in important positions already and are not searching for a change. There are certain agencies abroad which can be helpful in personnel matters, like the branches or correspondents of American banks, American Chambers of Commerce, and United States government agencies. However, their knowledge of the particular needs of the United States company and of the ability and integrity of the candidates they recommend is necessarily incomplete.

American companies which are launching operations abroad for the first time should not appoint a field manager until they have worked with him in the United States for a period of time. It would seem most unwise for a company to trust its name and reputation to somebody hired "off the street," no matter how good his references might be. The problem of choosing top personnel is not so great in an established subsidiary because there are—or should be—men available who are being groomed for succession.

Levels of compensation, as we all know, vary from country to country, but in many areas they are much lower than in the United States. American companies are foolish to take advantage of this, as they often do, and try to get men cheap for their field management. Levels of compensation for the same degree of responsibility and performance within an organization should not vary. This does not necessarily mean that the same number of dollars should be offered—compensation can, perhaps, be better coordinated with purchasing power. But there should be equal recognition for similar functions. When an American is replaced by a national, the latter must receive the same pay.

Training Programs

Training in the field should be a constant preoccupation of the head office, and a continuous process. Field organizations ought to have the benefit of the parent company's experience in training matters. Training material and reports of educational activities can be circulated, and functional and technical experts from the head office or from other parts of the organization should make visits to the field. Traveling internal auditors can form a valuable training link in organizational and accounting matters by interpreting home office instructions and policies.

Training programs should not only offer technical information but should provide education in American philosophies of business and business conduct as well. American companies should try to overcome local patterns of excessive subservience to authority when such tendencies exist in their foreign personnel. They may well instill the spirit of cooperation and mutual respect which is a hallmark of modern American business and one of the dynamics of its successful growth.

As a corollary, local personnel should not be constantly criticized by the head office. Praise is often merited and should be given; daily reprimands can be most discouraging.

Visits from Home

It is true, as many others have stressed in this book, that home office executives should make a point of traveling extensively. But leaving it at that is not enough. A wild merry-go-round of trips by unprepared personnel is not likely to do much good, and may even do some harm.

> There is the story of a company president who was always running around the world at the drop of a hat. One morning he was working feverishly in his office to get the one o'clock plane for the Far East. He finished his letters and dashed to the elevator—only to come running back again to ask his secretary, "Miss Briggs, where am I going?"

Representatives from the head office should be men who can merit the respect of their colleagues in the field. I know of cases where local officials have laid plots to frustrate visits from the head office because they had no respect for a particular visitor and were convinced that his trip was neither necessary nor useful. And then sometimes the American visitor is wined and dined so well that he doesn't feel like work; or more subtle means are used to evade bumbling interference from the United States! If the visitor from the head office is *persona non grata*, there are many ways of circumventing him. I know that some of these methods are used, and I have often wondered how the stateside emissaries account for their frustrated missions once they get home.

Conclusion

My final observation is that the home office should not require unnecessary reporting. Local officials are resentful of head office requirements if they believe them to be exaggerated or unreasonable. I have known personnel in the field who set traps to see whether the reports they were obliged to prepare were ever used back in the United States or just filed away as soon as they came in. They found out!

Personnel who prepare the reports should understand why they are needed and what happens to them back home. The few companies who are aware of this do not require any reports from the field that are not necessary for maintaining effective control by the local management. I commend this policy. It is not very often followed, unfortunately.

In conclusion, I believe that American companies who operate abroad have a responsibility, over and above the needs of their own businesses, to represent American principles and ways of living and working. They should set high standards of business conduct and relationships. They should not approve or connive in tax evasions or any acts or policies which are contrary to local laws or regulations or harmful to national interests, even though the local management may often urge such conduct and find plausible reasons for it.

QUESTIONS AND ANSWERS*

From the floor: Mr. Collinge, you emphasized the need for both personal contacts and a good reporting system. Do you feel that reporting systems can reduce the need for personal contacts between the home office and the foreign office?

Mr. Collinge: I think the answer to your question is "yes." But I believe that the aim should be to have the personal contacts reduce the need for reporting.

From the floor: What is done about the problem of class distinction within foreign corporations? Is there any program which will discourage it?

Mr. Waller: Such class division is very undesirable and completely unnecessary. Through a soundly conceived training program, American companies can replace this attitude with a better atmosphere of working together, much as people do in the United States.

A lot of such training is done and, generally speaking, the atmosphere of an American-owned or American-controlled company in a foreign country is better than that in a firm owned by nationals. The community respects this new climate of cooperation, by and large, and considers it an improvement. Ultimately, I think American practices will affect the general living habits throughout the area, whether the people involved are company employees or not.

From the floor: Are interest rates in local banks normally higher than in this country?

Mr. Holst: Rates of interest vary greatly all over the world, and they are unstable within individual countries. Japan is an example of this: two years ago they were offering an interest rate of 10% at least, but now they are down to about 8.8%. In spite of such fluctuations, our Treasury Department keeps a close watch over the varia-

* Businessmen present at the panel session on which this chapter is based raised certain questions which gave rise to the discussion reported in this chapter section.

tions and tries to encourage local debentures as a hedge against inflation or deflation.

Mr. Collinge: Interest rates, by and large, depend on two things: the supply of money and the risks involved. If any firm thinks it is saving money by borrowing in the States at cheap rates, it may have a bad time, because the risk is inherent in the country where the money is being used. A great many companies found this out in Mexico only recently. They were using American money down there, invested in receivables. The devaluation caused them great and unnecessary losses because they were not using local money.

From the floor: How do local companies feel about the competition they are getting from American firms operating abroad?

Mr. Waller: They don't always like it, of course. But the justification for the American company being there is that it has something better to offer.

From the floor: Maybe, then, we'd be better off from the national public relations standpoint if we didn't have overseas business operations.

Mr. Waller: I think that is a matter for company managements to decide on strictly business grounds. If they think they could succeed without an overseas subsidiary, fine, but I don't think they should give up their operations because of some foreign objections.

Furthermore, if American companies act properly, they can be ambassadors of good will, and this antagonism will ease. Of course, there is bound to be a good deal of friction over the introduction of American products in some cases. In France, for example, there is much objection to Coca-Cola. It is competition. But I do not think that such protests are a valid reason for not going into foreign operations, nor do I think that staying out is the way to solve the public relations problem.

MARKETING OPPORTUNITIES AND PROBLEMS OVERSEAS

Harry R. Tosdal, Rowland Burnstan, A. S. Hart, and Albert F. Watters

ONE OF THE TOUGHEST OVERSEAS MARKETING PROBLEMS which United States executives encounter today is the failure of foreigners—particularly non-Westerners—to understand our marketing procedures, based as they are on our unique cultural pattern. Two of the most misunderstood elements of our merchandising system, for example, are the role of advertising and selling and the concept of teamwork.

"Why do you waste so much time and money in advertising and selling?" foreign businessmen want to know. "Why don't you elim-

Note: Mr. Tosdal who acted as moderator, is Professor of Business Administration, Harvard Business School; Mr. Hart is Vice President, Export and South American Operations, Quaker Oats Company; Mr. Watters is Vice President, Radio Corporation of America; Mr. Burnstan is President, Borg-Warner International Corp.

inate all that extra expense and cut prices?" To clarify the point, United States executives have to start at the beginning and explain the leadership impact of advertising and selling, which provides the impetus for a rising standard of living. Marketing specialists have to describe the many-faceted motivations of consumers and show that price alone is not enough to stimulate sales. In other words, the whole role of marketing in our economy has to be laid out clearly. Such an undertaking involves a discussion of our whole way of life and value structure.

Teamwork, to most foreign businessmen, means a competent leader backed by a group of subordinates who obey him implicitly. These underlings do not—and should not—deviate from his instructions, nor are they individually responsible for injecting ideas and opinions.

This concept is a far cry from the informal kind of teamwork which is so characteristic of administration in the United States— in marketing or in any other area. It is true, of course, that groups of foreign visitors observe our teamwork process in action, listen to lectures about it, and think they understand it. But when they hear a subordinate engaging in the relaxed give-and-take conversation that makes up the teamwork process, their automatic reaction is to charge him with disrespect and a lack of discipline. Thus their limited acquaintance with our culture has prevented them from gaining a clear understanding of what teamwork really means to us and how it works.

Despite these difficulties, however, the future appears promising. Nationals of countries where United States firms operate are increasingly willing to accept our merchandising techniques. This change is partly due to the leadership of Americans who are on the spot in executive posts; it is also the result of intensive training programs which include formal sessions overseas and special visits to the United States.

To back up this training, many companies are now attempting to standardize overseas and domestic advertising practices. Of course, this cannot be done completely—take the differences between English and American medical advertising, for example. But the tendency is there. The self-service idea and the principle of display as opposed to storage of goods in the back room are being extended to overseas markets by a number of firms. Needless to say, these techniques have to be adapted to suit differing circumstances; but in essence they are American.

The authors in this chapter point out, for instance, that market research is now being undertaken by very competent people, though their frame of reference may be quite different from ours. One German manufacturer is making an electronic flash which is being sold in this country. He has established his business strictly on a mail-order basis, selling directly from the factory to the retailers. Before he got under way, he did some pretesting which stood up well when compared with his actual experience. But by and large it is true that our techniques are more advanced and will probably continue to dominate foreign operations.

As the pattern of merchandising overseas becomes more similar to that in this country, comparisons of distribution costs are increasingly meaningful. In some cases costs are lower, partly because there is less competition in the field of branded consumer items. Businessmen do not need to lay out such large sums for trade markups and selling and advertising expenses. On the other hand, some companies have found that their costs are higher on consumer goods because of special circumstances with which they are faced, while technical products may net them larger margins than they realize in this country. No general rules can be laid down, and each company must study its own particular situation, but rough approximations are becoming feasible now whereas a few years ago they were not particularly reliable.

By way of summary, and of warning too, I would like to cite the experiences of two flour companies that entered the foreign field. Though not directly competitive, their cases can be compared:

> Both firms decided to move into Canada at about the same time. Frequently we consider our neighbors to the north as part of our domestic market, because they are clearly more like us than any

other country, but the sales manager of Company A was not taken in by the myth that their needs and problems are just the same as ours. He spent three months finding out how retailers and wholesalers operated in his line, what terms they wanted, how advertising should be handled, and so on. But the men at Company B had more confidence that they knew their way around. Consequently, they charged ahead and got under way in a hurry without any special preparation. They sold just the way they wanted to, and tended to duplicate the procedures they used at home.

Company A now has a substantial slice of the market, and it did not take them long to get it. But the other company is in bad shape, and has had to start all over again in order to build a sound sales position.

CONTROLLING FOREIGN OPERATIONS*

The history of Borg-Warner is quite different from the backgrounds of the other two companies discussed in this chapter. We started in the 1920's as a combination of relatively small companies that were primarily interested in supplying parts for the automotive industry. Gradually we expanded into other fields until we have become somewhat of a giant today.

The international company came into being in the early 1930's when our central management realized we were missing out on many opportunities. Some divisions were reporting overseas inquiries of various types which they had neither the staff nor the know-how to handle. These divisions have always operated as separate entities, coming together only at a high financial level, with limited supervision from the top. Consequently, their consent was required for the establishment of the new company, Borg-Warner International, which was set up to meet their needs in the foreign field. A separate concern, its stock is owned entirely by the Borg-Warner Corporation, which in turn owns the various manufacturing divisions here in the United States.

The new company's first assignment was to sell abroad, so it was

* By Mr. Burnstan.

designed primarily as a sales organization with headquarters in Chicago. Replacement parts were originally its chief sales item, but as time passed it took on additional activities, paralleling the expansion of the domestic company. Ultimately it supplemented or complemented Borg-Warner lines with those of other manufacturers who were receiving inquiries from abroad but were unable to capitalize on them. Thus our International Company today represents 20 outside firms in addition to the 35 Borg-Warner divisions.

Sell American

As is the case with many other companies, our activities include selling, licensing, and manufacturing. However, foreign manufacturing and licensing usually result from a failure to make foreign sales. Generally speaking, therefore, we have preferred to sell abroad from United States plants rather than to enter into licensing or manufacturing arrangements.

Our methods of operation overseas depend on the conditions of the specific market. We try to avoid using manufacturers' agents, but our results have occasionally been good where market conditions have led us to use this method. In some places we have our own offices staffed with field men. In others, we own small marketing subsidiaries which do nothing but sell our products through the companies we own abroad. Still others are supervised directly from Chicago.

The last arrangement is becoming increasingly feasible with the growing convenience of transportation. Recently we gave up our offices in Havana and Panama, because we can now leave Chicago in the morning and have dinner in San Juan, the furthest point in the western Caribbean. The men who supervise those areas work out of Chicago and make regular trips into the territory instead of maintaining homes there. I suspect this pattern will become more widespread because we have found that the greatest problems arising between field and home personnel stem from breakdowns of communication. No matter how hard we try, we cannot seem to get our messages straight to the men in the field, and they cannot get their reports clear to those of us in the office. We get straightened out eventually, to be sure, but it is a continuing source of difficulty. Furthermore, a man working in the office is constantly aware of day-to-day company developments, and therefore does a better job of supervision.

Operation of plants abroad is based on anything from a simple license—where we have neither legal nor equitable ownership— to complete ownership. We have acquired plants and developed them in various ways—some of them quite strange! For instance:

> The Morse Chain Company was bought by Borg-Warner. Through it we got Morse Chain Co., Ltd., in Letchworth, England. For many years it was a stepchild, until someone discovered that money could be made there. It was expanded until we now have an automatic transmission and overdrive plant at Letchworth, which was combined with Morse, and another chain plant, all of which form a company called Borg-Warner, Ltd.
>
> In Australia we purchased a controlling interest in a company that makes gears and transmissions. In Brazil we have just in-corporated a company to make clutches—and it will probably make other automotive products later. We have a white goods line and some manufacturing operations abroad, in all of which we are minority stockholders.

Internally, our organization functions with a product executive who serves as a liaison man with all the manufacturing divisions and the other companies with which we are associated. A sales execu-tive supervises all the sales activities in the field, and others are in charge of our licensing activities, our foreign operations, and our administrative and control work in the Chicago office.

Prior to the formation of the International Company we entered into some licensing agreements in response to requests that seemed to promise a little extra income. In some of these deals we gave away too much—and we cannot recoup because the agreements were permanent. But the creation of Borg-Warner International has reduced our percentage of error because we now have specialists to conduct our overseas transactions. Needless to say, this improvement is a real asset. Competition abroad is too sharp today to permit haphazard administration. Foreign operations demand trained experts and special handling, and the incorporation of a company which is carefully designed and staffed to deal with international problems has proven to be a most successful way of operating in our case.

TO MARKET, TO MARKET—WITH CAUTION*

RCA's experience in the foreign field goes back more than fifty years. The RCA of today is the lineal descendant of the Victor Talking Machine Company, which was founded in 1898 in Camden, New Jersey, and of the Marconi Wireless Telegraph Company of America, which was established in 1899. More than fifty years ago, both of these parents of RCA were already actively engaged in business abroad.

In fact, the Marconi Wireless Telegraph Company was owned by the British Marconi Company, Ltd., at the turn of the century. Until its acquisition in 1919 by the newly formed Radio Corporation of America, it was the only commercial wireless link between the United States and the outside world. At about the same time that the American Marconi Company was starting to transmit and receive messages from foreign countries and from ships at sea, the Victor Talking Machine Company was making its debut in the United States and abroad.

The great achievement of Victor was to take the so-called "talking machine" and convert it into a serious musical instrument. It did this not only by investing in the engineering and manufacturing skills which developed the Victrola and the flat-disc type of phonograph record, but also by searching the world for the great musical talent

* By Mr. Watters.

of the day. By 1903, Victor had already signed the great Italian opera star, Caruso, to a recording contract.

Since great music was then, and is today, "the international language," the Victor Talking Machine Company almost immediately found its products in demand abroad as well as at home. It proceeded to sell in foreign markets through independent distributors. The present RCA distributor in Cuba, for example, started with the Victor Talking Machine Company as a vendor of Victrolas and records back in 1904. Incidentally, he has done quite well. I think, at the last count, he was worth about $7.5 million!

Export Growth

Prior to World War I, the sale of Victor products overseas was a United States-based export operation carried on through independent foreign distributors. Starting in the mid-1920's, however, Victor began establishing its own manufacturing and distributing subsidiaries abroad, beginning with the construction of manufacturing facilities in Canada in 1925. In 1928 similar installations were set up in Argentina, Chile, and Brazil.

With the advent of the "talking pictures" in the late 1920's, RCA formed subsidiaries in Great Britain and Australia to distribute and service the RCA sound reproducing and recording systems used by the motion picture industry. In 1936 a company was established in India for the same purpose. We are now in the process of expanding these companies into full-fledged manufacturing and distribution facilities.

To complete the story, manufacturing companies were established in Mexico in 1935, and in Italy and Spain in 1951 and 1952. In 1954 we established an associated company in Germany, and only very recently we set up our newest subsidiary in Venezuela.

To serve independent, foreign electronics manufacturers with whom we have patent licensing and technical aid agreements, we formed subsidiary companies with laboratory facilities and technical staffs in Japan in 1953, and in Switzerland in 1955. Altogether we now have 14 active associated companies in foreign countries, 9 of which are presently engaged in both manufacture and distribution and 5 as service and/or sales operations. The over-all foreign activities of RCA extend into more than 80 different countries and provide employment for more than 9,000 people.

An International Division

From an organizational and operational standpoint, one of the major milestones in the development of RCA's overseas activities came in 1945 with the establishment of the RCA International Division.

Prior to the establishment of this division, the export and foreign licensing activities of our company and the supervision of its overseas subsidiary program had been parceled out on a functional basis among various domestic divisions of the company, which were, of course, primarily concerned with their respective activities in the United States.

The establishment of the international division has centralized responsibility and authority for export, foreign licensing, and foreign subsidiary projects. The division vice president reports to an executive vice president of RCA who is in charge of sales and service functions. In turn, he reports to the president. The president of our company is a traveling executive, and he knows as much about the international business as any of us—if not more—so we have no difficulty in gaining corporate status or recognition.

The relationship between the international division and our product departments is very similar to that of a distributor. Our problem is to plan our sales requirements sufficiently in advance so that we can place firm orders in the factories for the products. Our orders are then treated in the same way as those from domestic distributors. Moreover, our organizational format guarantees that the foreign side of our company is not subservient to the domestic. It also insures that export systems will not be developed at the expense of licensing or foreign subsidiary programs—and vice versa.

How to Market

With this brief summary of our history as background, I would now like to look at some of the major problems confronting most United States companies in their overseas activities. The key question is, of course, whether the potential of a given foreign market is best cultivated by exporting product and service from the United States, by entering into licensing and technical aid agreements with existing local manufacturers, or by the establishment of one's own manufacturing and distribution facilities.

Of course, there is no reason why a company should not engage in all three activities—export, licensing, and manufacturing—in the same market at the same time. We do that in many places. But a firm should make sure that it is using the best balanced and the most remunerative combination of each of these three basic approaches in tapping the potential of each particular market.

Most United States companies started their foreign operations with an export activity. They began selling a product or a service in the United States and soon received a few unsolicited orders from foreign sources. Usually the next step was to set up an export division as part of the domestic sales department and to inaugurate a search for overseas orders. A United States-based export firm is hired, independent distributors or manufacturers' representatives abroad are signed up, or company-controlled sales branches are established in principal foreign markets.

Ordinarily, when a foreign market becomes big enough and the profit potentialities appear sufficiently bright, or when currency or tariff restrictions start impeding exports from the United States, firms begin to think about building local production facilities. In some of the more highly developed countries of the world, serious economic and political obstacles to both importation of products from the United States and to local manufacture by United States controlled subsidiaries may arise. In such situations, the United States company often finds that its best approach is to sell know-how to the established foreign manufacturers and license them to use its patents, copyrights, or processes.

In foreign activities as in domestic business, the biggest profits accrue to those who base their decisions and actions on realistic, integrated, and well-conceived plans. There is no standardized and unchanging formula that can be set forth, since marketing strategy and tactics depend upon what the individual company has to offer the foreign consumer at a particular moment and on the conditions in the foreign market at the time the offer or consideration is given.

Where to Market

Obviously the first step in the intelligent planning of overseas operations is to work out a running inventory of what a concern has to offer and what is available for productive employment abroad. These "assets" are not limited merely to those on a balance sheet. The following items might be listed in such an inventory:

Certain products or services which have been developed in the United States.

A well-known trade-mark and a market acceptance which already extends beyond the boundaries of our country. This is particularly true in our case, with our monogram and dog-and-horn emblem.

An experienced organization with a fund of knowledge about how to make and merchandise a product or service. Our biggest problem is in this area, incidentally. We have an able and experienced organization to be sure, but a shortage of trained manpower willing to work overseas continues to plague us.*

Valuable patent rights or industry leadership in certain technical processes.

A certain amount of cash or equipment to be invested overseas, or a credit standing which permits the marshaling of additional resources for this purpose.

* For a further discussion of this problem, see the chapter on personnel management, p. 116.

With a list of assets prepared, the next step is to take a look at the prospective markets abroad. The list from Aden to Zanzibar should be covered, and a country-by-country and product-by-product study should be made.

Of course, this is a gigantic task. The markets need to be studied intimately. For our part, we ask ourselves such questions as these:

> Are products or services similar to ours already being sold in the market? Of what quality and at what price?
>
> What are our chances of competing with the established brands? Is there competition from local sources of production? From other exporting countries? From other United States producers?
>
> If no local market exists at present, can one be developed? What are the economic conditions and prospects for the country? Does it have dollars to spend on our product?
>
> Would it pay to modify our product to meet local demands?
>
> What distribution and service facilities are available in the market? What advertising media are available for building up a demand?

Special Problems

The foregoing, of course, are only a few of the questions to ask in deciding what potentialities exist abroad. A whole series of problems arises from the nature of the particular operation in which a firm is engaged. At RCA, for example, we have a collection of issues revolving around the procurement of licenses:

> We export a good many millions of dollars worth of products each year. These products generally fall into two categories: consumer goods products—radio, TV, white goods, records, high fidelity equipment—which require no licenses; and technical products, which may be restricted in one way or another. They may include anything from a multimillion dollar communications system down through various types of aviation equipment and certain military items to radio tubes.
>
> In some cases where RCA has produced products for United

States military forces we have had to check to make sure they have been declassified before we can send them to a foreign government. In addition, we may need an export license. Furthermore, we supply our factories overseas with certain raw materials which they cannot procure from any other source. An example is raw nickel, used in connection with the manufacture of phonograph records. Nickel is a strategic material, and consequently is controlled as part of our national stockpiling program. We have to get an export license to ship such products.

Once the nature and size of the potential in a particular market has been determined, a company must decide whether or not it is worth exploiting and, if so, in what manner. Some businesses find, for example, that it is difficult to compete with European-made products in a certain market because of lower labor costs or customer preference for certain European-style features. In such a case arrangements might be made to have a particular product built in Europe by a company in which the parent firm has a financial interest, or by an independent manufacturer. Similarly, difficulty in securing payment in dollars in sterling bloc markets may be an obstacle. It may then be necessary to locate the product supply in a soft currency country or engage in "switch transactions" so that profits can eventually be brought back to the United States in the form of dollars by trading in foreign currencies.

Many United States companies have been able to build up a sizable volume of business in the sale of component parts to their foreign licensees. This is a sales opportunity which we believe should be seriously considered.

The opportunities to build sales volume and profits from overseas activities are very attractive today and should grow substantially in the years ahead. However, competition from European and Japanese industry is becoming increasingly keen and must be taken into account. Many of these countries must export to live. England and Germany, for instance, have lost important markets back of the Iron Curtain and elsewhere in the world which they held before the war, so they are making a determined effort to move into Latin America and Asia. In addition, the communist bloc is making a strong bid to supply both capital goods and consumer goods in Europe, Asia, Africa, and Latin America. In the face of this competition, United States industry must exercise the same diligence and apply the same critical analysis to the foreign market that have been characteristic of its domestic operations.

GROWTH OF AN EXPORT BUSINESS*

Quaker Oats Company started its foreign activities many years ago, thanks to a few vigorous executives who could see the trend of the times. In those early days we did not have much to sell, but we did have a few clear-cut advantages over our competition:

> U. S. grain costs were low compared with European costs.
>
> We had an improved technique: our rolled oats cooked faster than the old Scotch oatmeal.
>
> We had a marketing approach which was revolutionary at the time: we marketed Quaker Oats in a branded package. All oatmeal used to be sold in barrels until Quaker Oats developed the branded package as a replacement for the bulk item.

But we have changed vastly since then. Although Quaker Oats was our original product, it no longer constitutes the bulk of the business. We now mill wheat flour; make animal foods; produce Aunt Jemima Pancake Flour, corn meal, and cereals like Puffed Wheat and Puffed Rice. Recently we have even gone outside of the grain family, and started to manufacture Ken-L-Ration Dog Food and Puss'n Boots Cat Food. Finally, we have a foot in the chemical field with a product called Furfural.

Oats Abroad

Taking a closer look at our history, we find that Quaker Oats sent its first man abroad to be resident executive in Europe in 1898. In

* By Mr. Hart.

1899 we formed our own sales company in the United Kingdom, called Quaker Oats, Ltd. We started manufacturing in Germany in 1908 and in Canada in 1900.

The period after World War I was again one of expansion. Our Canadian export to England was shut off, so we had to increase the size of our mills in the United Kingdom. We also started manufacturing in Holland and Denmark and expanded facilities in Germany.

We went to India, Africa, Asia, and South America during these years in order to intensify work that had been started before the war. In the 1920's we had our own resident man in India, South Africa, China, and South America. We were among the early brand merchandisers in many of the distant world markets. In this same period we started licensing manufacturers in Mexico and Argentina.

Postwar Developments

There have been two major developments in our export marketing operations during the postwar period.

In the first place, we were forced to supply from sterling and other soft currency areas to maintain our markets. Our company had long been aware that exchange rates and duties affected our export profits. Indeed, in the past, stimulated by these factors, we had begun to manufacture our product locally on a small scale. But large areas of the world became closed off to export because of exchange restrictions during the postwar period. It was to by-pass these currency restrictions that we established export production in the sterling and soft currency areas.

During and since the postwar period we have increased our rate of expansion—particularly in South America—by enlarging our export operation and adding new local manufacturing. This second major development was partially the result of the exchange problem. Brazil, for instance, closed the door in 1947. After hanging on for a little while, we started manufacturing locally to compensate for the lost export market. In Colombia we established a wholly owned manufacturing operation from scratch in 1950 because duties had been increased and exchange became difficult. Two years ago we bought out our Argentine licensee, and we are presently expanding there.

The Company Today

The latest consolidated statement of our United States and Canadian companies shows sales of $276 million and a net income of just over $10 million.

In the foreword of a recent annual report, we stated that net earnings of the nonconsolidated overseas subsidiaries for the past year were approximately $1.5 million, a figure which does not include either our Canadian subsidiary or the American export business. We do not publish the figures of our total overseas sales, but I can assure you that they represent a sizable portion of our business. Thus, in spite of the increased business and phenomenal growth of the United States markets, our foreign business constitutes a substantial part of our over-all operation.

QUESTIONS AND ANSWERS*

From the floor: Do you find that the different customs and economic conditions of other countries make product adjustment necessary?

Mr. Hart: We started by taking a product we made here—like Quaker Oats—and trying to convince people overseas to use that item the way we did. Two things happened: they wouldn't use the product at all, or they wouldn't use it in the same way. In the second case, we were at least partially successful; in the first, we had to change the item altogether.

But gradually we came to realize that we were not really in the oatmeal field at all—we were in the food business. What do you do

* Businessmen present at the panel session on which this chapter is based raised certain questions which brought about the discussion reported more or less verbatim on these pages.

when you are in the food business? You make things people want to eat. So we have designed products to fit the particular markets where we operate. Some of the items we have developed are not made in the United States at all, and wouldn't be suited to the tastes of our customers here.

Mr. Burnstan: We had a similar experience with automatic transmissions and overdrives. Overdrives are fast disappearing in the United States, but everybody wants an automatic transmission. This isn't true in Europe, where the only item you place on a car that pays for itself is an overdrive. In an area where gas costs 90 cents a gallon, an overdrive becomes a very important unit.

Mr. Watters: Among other products, we distribute a line of electric toasters overseas. We had a difficult time with them in some South American markets, and couldn't understand why. Finally we went down and discovered that people just don't like toast in South America!

Radios are another example. It is impossible to sell our line in some parts of Latin America and the Middle East for two principal reasons:

> In the first place, our domestic radios do not have short-wave except in a special model, and foreign consumers insist on sets which can receive that frequency. Secondly, people in many parts of the world prefer the German-type styling with big cabinets and dark wood, because they feel it brings them prestige. When a Middle Eastern or South American family makes an investment in a radio, they are buying a major piece of furniture, and they want something sizable to show for their money.
>
> Consequently, we went to Germany and made a deal with a manufacturer to produce a line of RCA radios. Internally, the radio is designed to American standards. The circuitry is ours, and the tubes used are RCA tubes because we are interested in the renewal market. But some of the sets have seven bands, and they are great big pieces of furniture.

Mr. Hart: We have found that language is at its colloquial worst when used to describe likes and dislikes in foods. It is virtually impossible to understand a consumer survey on food without a real knowledge of the language. So we have our overseas executives go to cooking school and learn how to produce every type of product which interests us. Our managers, skilled as they may be in administration, don't like to get their noses into the kitchen pots, but we require them to do it all the same, and we've eliminated expensive multithousand-dollar consumer surveys by doing so.

From the floor: How good are local sources of market information? Do you have to utilize United States firms, or can you use French, English, or German companies?

Mr. Hart: In the United Kingdom, research organizations are fully comparable to those we have here. On the Continent, too, they are pretty far advanced. When you get to the Belgian Congo, Malaya, or Portuguese Africa, however, you have a different problem.

Mr. Burnstan: Our experience has been different. We had an elaborate survey made on the Continent, but had to go back and do it all over again. The people who were doing it were keen enough, but they couldn't understand what we, as Americans, needed to know to market our product to the German people.

From the floor: Is it difficult for the international operation to get as large a share of company money as it would like?

Mr. Watters: In our company we have no difficulty in getting money for projects which are valid and for which we can show a proper profit return. We are affected by the availability of money in RCA, which, of course, is determined to a great extent by domestic production. On the other hand, our percentage of profit on net sales of exported goods—including dividends remitted by our overseas companies—is significantly higher than that of any of our domestic activities. Because of this, we are quite respected citizens in the corporate scheme of things.

GOVERNMENT POLICY AND BUSINESS ABROAD

Dan T. Smith, Samuel C. Waugh, Leslie Mills, and Roy Blough

GOVERNMENT AND EXTERNAL COMMERCE *

IN 1803, PRESIDENT THOMAS JEFFERSON bought the entire middle section of the United States for $15 million, or about 4 cents an acre. At that time the area was known as the Great American Desert. It is now referred to as the "breadbasket of the country" and provides a substantial portion of our food requirement each year.

Three months prior to this purchase Jefferson sent a secret message

Note: Mr. Smith, who acted as moderator for the panel on which this chapter is based, is Professor of Finance, Harvard Business School; Mr. Waugh is President and Chairman of the Board, Export-Import Bank; Mr. Mills is a Partner, Price Waterhouse & Co.; and Mr. Blough is Professor of International Business, Columbia University.
* By Mr. Waugh.

to Congress asking for an appropriation to explore the possibilities of trade with the Indians along the Missouri River. Congress responded to that request with an appropriation of $2,500 to develop "the external commerce of the United States." The money was used to finance the Lewis and Clark Expedition.

That figure of $2,500 to develop "external commerce" takes on real significance when it is set against the $25 billion which represents our two-way external trade this year.

A Long Way to Go

We have come a long way in the last 150 years! But we still have a great distance to go. As a matter of fact, I would say that full expansion of "external commerce" still lies ahead of us.

One of my first assignments in Washington, in 1953, was to represent Secretary John Foster Dulles at a meeting of businessmen who were concerned with the problems of foreign investment. They met to discuss what steps could be taken to encourage the investment of private capital overseas.

Since that time, the subject has become one of the most discussed topics in the government and among private businessmen. Unfortunately, however, we spend 75% of our time discussing what American business can do abroad and only 25% actually trying to create an investment climate abroad which will attract available capital.

Our efforts in this direction are not being made in a vacuum. In the years since that first meeting, I have attended countless discussions all over the world—all dealing with the same subject. From these meetings, formal and informal, I have discovered that there are three basic facts of international and economic life which must be considered as we fashion policies designed to encourage overseas investment.

The Three Facts of Life

In the first place, all the countries in the world are more or less dependent upon United States markets. Our industrial economy now produces a $400 billion gross national product each year. We are the largest sellers and the largest buyers on the globe. As a result, economic conditions here have a powerful impact on conditions abroad. To illustrate:

> In 1949, for instance, our gross national product fell about 4%. Nobody paid much attention to the decline at home, but our imports from Europe dropped 22% during that period; our imports from Chile fell 36%; and our imports from Egypt were cut by nearly 50%. Thus a proportionally small drop in our GNP caused a large decrease in United States buying power abroad.

Secondly, any military or political pact is built on sand unless both parties to it have strong economic structures.

Finally, the foundation of many of our bonds with the countries of the Free World in the postwar years has been fear. This fear must now be replaced by the ties of trade, for the Soviets are seeking to relax international tensions and thus destroy the underpinnings of our alliances. I do not mean to minimize the force that a similarity of ideals exerts in holding countries together. But the strongest cement I can think of is trade.

These facts force us to the conclusion that we must have an atmosphere conducive to trade and investment if we are to hold the free nations of the world together. Given this situation, it is self-evident that our government has an obligation to help create and maintain a world climate that encourages international economic activity. The Congress of President Jefferson recognized this governmental responsibility when it appropriated $2,500 for the development of "external commerce." Our present-day government should recognize it also.

In order to be consistent with our American heritage, however, the obligation may be met indirectly rather than directly. There are many examples of such indirect action—one of the most successful is the Export-Import Bank. Because of my connection with the Bank, I want to summarize its achievements as an illustration of the importance and effectiveness of indirect governmental assistance in this field.

Export-Import Bank*

If all countries had stable economies, freely convertible currencies, no exchange problems, and sufficient dollars to buy United States goods and services—and if the commercial banks of the country were in a position to make immediate and long-term loans—there would be no need for an Export-Import Bank. But these conditions do not exist. American business must compete in foreign markets as they are today, and an element of that competition is the matter of financing. It is the responsibility of our government to aid those firms that wish to enter the foreign field; the Export-Import Bank helps implement that responsibility.

The Bank, unfortunately, is not very well known in this country, although it has existed for 22 years. During its lifetime, it has authorized something over $7 billion worth of loans, and has paid out more than $5 billion. We have some $2.6 billion outstanding today and between $600 million and $700 million worth of authorized loans that have not as yet been taken up. Our capital is $1 billion, and the loaning power is an additional $4 billion.

The Export-Import Bank has always paid its own way, paying interest to the United States Treasury on every dime that it borrows from the government. Its annual earnings have now reached the $60 million mark. The Bank does not compete with private capital, but endeavors instead to work with and through private banks, both here and abroad. Its charge-offs have been less than $500,000 or one one-hundredth of 1%.

What is the task of the Bank today? In large part the answer hinges on current world economic conditions. During the last few years we have seen a transition from a sellers' to a buyers' market. The competition we are meeting from abroad is increasing, as countries recover from the damage that World War II inflicted on their economies. In addition, we face growing competition from the U.S.S.R.,

* For a further discussion of the Export-Import Bank, see statement by Sidney E. Sherwood on p. 294.

which has become a powerful world economic power. Finally, the governments of some 11 countries are helping their manufacturers and exporters to develop foreign trade. In view of these four conditions, the role of the Export-Import Bank is vital in bolstering the strength of our world economic position.

Given the need for governmental participation in the international economic picture, the pattern of indirect assistance which the Bank has followed holds out the most promise. In the new policies which we develop to encourage businessmen to invest overseas, we would do well to duplicate the general approach of the Bank and follow its example of indirect aid rather than adopt programs of outright subsidy.

TAXES AND FOREIGN INVESTMENT*

It is a truism that United States tax policy has a marked effect both on firms doing business abroad and on the rate of new overseas investment. Consequently, I believe that some changes could be made in our current tax structure which would stimulate businessmen to operate abroad.

But the simple statement that domestic taxes are related to overseas investment is not enough. The question is *how* they are related—and *how much*. Some surveys appear to suggest that domestic taxes have a limited—or even negligible—effect on businessmen who are deciding whether to invest abroad. In a sense, those surveys may be accurate, since no business is going to abandon profitable opportunities overseas merely because the tax picture is difficult. Nevertheless, business is now so tax-conscious, and our burden is so great, that domestic rates must be considered a significant element in any analysis of foreign investment. When they are so considered, their influence falls on the negative side.

Fundamental changes in our laws could well stimulate the flow of private United States capital into foreign investment. Let me make clear before I go on, however, that I am not concerned with the gim-

* By Mr. Mills.

micks and gadgetry of loopholes. Rather, I am interested in our basic tax policy which now tends to discourage the export of capital on a long-range, broad basis. The real problem lies in the philosophy of our tax pattern, which imposes a heavy burden on business income derived from foreign sources.

The Citizenship Theory

Despite the dangers of oversimplification, it is fair to say that the fundamental difficulty springs from the so-called citizenship theory which we apply in taxing foreign income. Our system is based on the concept that individuals and corporations should be taxed as United States citizens, regardless of where they make their money. This attitude stands in strong contrast to the thinking of the British Commonwealth countries, for instance, who believe that income should be subjected to tax only in the country where it is earned. Our system, then, rests on the essentially sound but sometimes detrimental, idea that citizenship automatically carries with it the obligation and privilege of paying United States taxes.

In practice our theory means that a firm's total tax burden is always set at least at the United States rate; on the other hand, if the foreign rate is higher, taxes are assessed at that level. Since our corporate income tax is one of the highest in the world, a United States firm now doing business overseas is obviously paying a very high percentage. Furthermore, if a foreign country receives a large part of its revenue from other tax sources, the American enterprise will be paying a share of those duties as well.

This policy has many effects, not the least of which is the incentive it provides for the foreign country to increase taxes on United States businesses. Superficially, it looks as if these funds actually come out of the United States Treasury, rather than from the company itself. Thus, if a country wishes to stimulate investment it is unlikely to offer tax reductions, because the United States firm will not receive any benefit from them. It will still be paying a high United States tax rate. In the last analysis, the fundamental decision we made when we first set up our tax structure in 1921 ought now to be re-examined.

Credits and Confusion

Another difficulty arises when a company tries to figure out which foreign assessments it can subtract from its income for United States tax purposes. American business is necessarily complicated, and foreign business even more so. Consequently, when you try to coordinate the system of the United States, which is based on our economic pattern and way of doing business, with the tax and economic systems of other countries, major difficulties are bound to develop. These problems are constantly before the courts, the Treasury Department, and the tax administration.

Furthermore, tax credit provisions do not provide any real incentive or tax relief for businessmen. All they accomplish is the removal or reduction of double taxation—which everyone feels is inequitable.

Since the 1940's we have seen one major deviation from the citizenship theory of taxes. An example of true incentive, it allows a rate reduction for the so-called Western Hemisphere Corporation. Basically, it is a device for tax reduction on corporations conducting business in accordance with certain very restrictive qualifications. In practice the plan applies only to domestic corporations, and the restrictions are very complicated and legalistic. But at least the theory behind it is sound.

All these variations and possibilities can confound even the most sophisticated businessman.

I am reminded of the story about the executive who asked his tax adviser if a one-armed man could be sent to help him with his return. The consultant was naturally rather mystified, and replied, "Well, I don't think we have any. Why do you want a one-armed man?" "All these experts you have sent me in the past," said the businessman, "answered my questions about what I should do by saying that on the one hand you can do this, and on the other hand you can do that."

This whole area was discussed in the Supplement Report of the Mills Subcommittee on Federal Tax Policy for Economic Growth

and Development. This report puts its finger on the problem in the
following quotation from a paper read before the committee:

> "United States taxation of foreign source income is cumbersome,
> formalistic, and frequently inequitable. It is inequitable in that it
> imposes different tax burdens on similarly situated taxpayers, and
> does not consider the activity in the foreign country. The differ-
> ence in tax burden arises solely from variation in the legal form
> in which business activity is conducted."

Fortunately, the administration began to move in the right direction when it presented a bill to the Congress in 1956 which was designed to stimulate investment abroad (HR 7725). Secretary Humphrey's letter of transmittal when he sent the act to the Ways and
Means Committee included this statement:

> "The purpose of this recommended legislation is to facilitate in-
> vestment abroad of capital from this country. At the present time
> our business firms are at a disadvantage in countries with lower
> taxes than our own when they have to compete with lower capital."

But this particular bill was severely criticized by the tax fraternity.
They claimed it was complicated, excessively restrictive, and would
not achieve its purpose. Basically, I think their comments in this
case were well-founded because the bill is merely an extension of
the Western Hemisphere Corporation concept, embodying the same
complications to which I have referred. Again, however, it was a
step forward in theory, if not in practice. Unfortunately, the bill was
not even considered by the Ways and Means Committee and therefore died until the 84th Congress.

The Triumvirate

Why are we failing to do something really constructive? The fault
lies with the tax administrators, the courts, and the Congress. It is
not a situation that can be blamed on any one administration—and
surely not on this one—but rather on those in Washington who have
administered the laws over the years. As a group, tax administrators

still feel that it is fine for United States enterprise to go abroad. On the other hand, they are convinced that an ever-present reason for entering the foreign field is to escape payment of a fair share of taxes in this country. A firm must prove its case to the contrary with a clear preponderance of the evidence. Thus the Internal Revenue Service interprets congressional statutes in the most restrictive way possible. No one can question the administration's responsibility for the protection of revenue, but IRS might do well to read sympathetically statements like that of Secretary Humphrey which I have just quoted.

The courts are equally restrictive. Whenever questions come up for adjudication, the courts create great complications by hair-splitting on the fundamentals involved. Furthermore, the attitude of many judges is one of: "By God, if you are going to get a reduced tax bill by doing business abroad, you have got to prove, and really prove, that you are entitled to it."

The third party in this triumvirate—the Congress—has shown the same attitude. In 1954, Congress almost passed liberalizing provisions for those doing business abroad. They failed to do so because they needed "more time to study it"; but they promised to give their approval at the first opportunity. Yet that same Congress, in that same year, re-enacted a provision which decrees that anybody who gives any advice on forming a business abroad must file a report within 30 days describing the matter fully whether or not the advice was acted on. Because of this provision, if a company calls on me for professional advice, I have to say, "You may not think it wise to talk with me; I am obliged to file a report about it." Needless to say, this is a highly restrictive measure in itself. But beyond that, such a proviso looks to businessmen like a device to ferret out wrongdoing. There are, I am sure, situations where information on the formation of foreign corporations would help the Treasury in its policing job. But I wonder if the benefits gained from such information outweigh the damage that is done by the creation of a climate of suspicion, which implies that there is something wrong with doing business abroad. In addition, such restrictions convey the impression to businessmen that Congress is fundamentally unfriendly to overseas enterprise.

Search for a Solution

Many solutions to the problem have been suggested. Some of them are technical and complicated and subject to vigorous criticism; others are worthy of consideration. One which was recently proposed, for example, would attempt to stimulate investment abroad by applying the amortization theory. A five-year period of amortization for tax purposes would be offered to anyone investing money abroad.

Though such a measure would indeed act as a stimulant, we ought rather to consider the simple solution of exempting all income earned abroad from taxation until it comes back to the United States. Then it should be treated as a capital gain.

My education in politics goes only far enough to assure me that a proposal like this would create problems upon problems. All our states do not have seaports, for one thing! Nevertheless, I believe such a statute should be enacted.

If there is any merit to this exemption plan, it might be worked out in the form of a treaty. We now have trade agreements with a great many countries. If we could make a give-and-take deal with a foreign country, by which we would get concessions from them on taxes, and simultaneously give United States tax advantages to our people who are operating there, we would have gone a long way toward establishing a good climate for investment and stimulating the flow of private United States capital into overseas areas.

FOREIGN POLICY AND INVESTMENT ABROAD*

As the "academic" contributor to this chapter, I shall discuss some of the more general aspects of the relation between United States Government policy and United States business abroad. In view of the great breadth of the topic, some limitation of the discussion is neces-

* By Mr. Blough.

sary; accordingly I shall center my comments on policies relating to investment abroad, although many of these also have a bearing on other types of business activity overseas.

There are two points which we should keep in mind when examining the bearing of government policy on foreign investment.

In the first place, United States Government policy is by no means the only force that is affecting the volume of our investment abroad. I would suggest, moreover, that such policy is neither the chief factor promoting that investment nor the primary obstacle to its more rapid increase. However attractive the government might make its policies, it could not stimulate a great flood of investment to other countries— at least not until various other obstacles had been removed. While under present circumstances the efforts of the United States Government may add up to a relatively minor total, it is by no means a negligible one, as will appear.

Secondly, we should be clear about what results we wish governmental policy to achieve. Are we really seeking to promote the broad national interest or only some particular type of business operation? Presumably it is the former, but many proposals in this field which are put forth as promoting the national interest would actually benefit only a very limited group. Such policies—for example, total or partial tax exemption—would indeed stimulate the activities of the group requesting them but at the expense of other businesses and the taxpayers as a whole. It is not difficult to stimulate particular activities through governmental policy; it is much more difficult to promote the national interest. Yet we tend constantly to generalize narrow group interests into an alleged broad national interest.

Again, when we speak of "the national interest" of the United States, are we referring to economic interest in the sense of enlarging the gross national product of the country in the present and relatively near future? Or do we have in mind "the national interest" as defined by the enhancement of our moral leadership, world political stability, military security, avoidance of war, and the resulting longer-run economic benefits? These goals might be achieved by strengthening our friends economically through overseas investment, as a part of the effort to promote the broad objectives of our foreign policy.

The Key Is Foreign Policy

In my opinion, it is this last consideration—foreign policy—which is the most persuasive argument for governmental action to encourage investment abroad. It is also the chief motivation for today's governmental policy in this field. Unless we are successful in our efforts to build and maintain a free and peaceful world, there will not be much left of our economy—or that of anyone else. It is the task of the foreign policy of this country, in concert with other nations, to maintain peace. Our policy on investment abroad should be directed to helping accomplish this task.

Within this framework of objectives, there are two general groups of policies that can be undertaken by the government to promote investment overseas:

(1) Short-term policies, relating specifically to the investment itself, or having a direct bearing on it. Tax policy is an example, for taxes clearly have an impact on the attractiveness of business operations. Also in this group are investment guarantees in the form of insurance protection against the risks of expropriation, adverse foreign exchange developments, or devaluation; these risks have a specific and important bearing on our willingness to invest abroad.

(2) Longer-range policies, which are no less significant in their effects on investment, but much less direct in their impact.

Long-Range Policy

The remainder of my comments will concentrate on these longer-range policies, which can be brought together under a number of subheadings.

The first group is made up of those policies which affect the supply of dollar exchange in the hands of businesses and governments abroad.

American businessmen who have listed the principal obstacles to their investing abroad have commonly given first priority to their fear that foreign exchange restrictions imposed by the host countries would interfere with the transfer home of earnings and the repatriation of capital. There are various causes of such restrictions; one which our policies might help remove or reduce is the so-called "dollar shortage" or "dollar gap." In the period since the war the total volume of our exports has depended on the number of dollars available to potential purchasers. During much of this period, purchasers in other countries who have sought to buy more from us were restrained by their inability to secure dollar exchange. This unsupplied demand for dollar exchange has been a substantial, and often the major, factor necessitating foreign exchange restrictions. Policies which helped remove or reduce the dollar gap would thus stimulate both United States exports and United States investment abroad.

One might think that the export of United States products is an alternative to investing abroad, and in some situations this undoubtedly is the case. In the main, however, exports have proved to be a first step toward overseas investment. Most businesses currently investing abroad started their international operations by exporting their products, and later shifted in whole or in part to investment for reasons which are explored elsewhere in this book.

Among the specific policies which affect the dollar gap are our tariff system and our customs procedures. These brakes on imports restrict the volume of dollars that businesses can earn by exporting to us. Such restrictions operate to limit United States investment abroad not only because of their immediate effects but also because of their implications for the future repatriation of earnings and capital—transfers which require that dollar exchange be in the hands of foreign businesses and governments. The larger the flow of private investment overseas, the larger the future volume of earnings to be received and capital that our investors may wish to repatriate—and accordingly the larger the volume of dollar exchange that will be required. The expectation that tariffs, complex customs regulations, and even import quotas will continue to limit the number of dollars that other countries can earn may well give pause to prospective overseas investors.

Another group of policies relates to the movement of trade throughout the world. Discriminatory or burdensome restrictions impede overseas investment by limiting the size of prospective markets, giving cause for fear of new and arbitrary restrictions in the future and discouraging exports, which, as previously mentioned, are the leading edge of overseas investment.

Restrictions on the free movement of goods in international trade are imposed both by governments and private business agreements. On the governmental side, foreign exchange restrictions, import quotas, "barter" and other bilateral agreements, tariff preference systems, and other devices, discriminate against the goods of certain countries, reduce the flow of world trade, and limit the market size.

On the private side, cartel agreements and other arrangements among the businessmen in different countries restrict production and international trade and are inconsistent with our basic beliefs in the value of competition.

After the war, when the situation with regard to trade restrictions was exceedingly bad, the United States took a leading role in promoting freer and nondiscriminatory trade. In recent years, I am sorry to say, the government seems to have lost some of its enthusiasm and has withdrawn from a position of leadership. One example of this shift is the failure of Congress to pass the bill authorizing our participation in the proposed Organization for Trade Cooperation. Another is the changed and now negative stand of the Administration toward proposed international measures for investigating, publicizing, and otherwise discouraging private international restrictive business practices.

World Economic Stability

In the third set of long-range policies are those which have consequences for world economic stability. Some people have argued that the high profit level prevailing at home is one reason that United

States capital does not go abroad. Therefore, they say, a depression here would increase the attractiveness of overseas investment by reducing profits on domestic investment. This proposition seems fallacious to me: a recession or depression here would so upset business abroad that the appeal of foreign investment would diminish if it did not disappear entirely. The strength of our domestic economy is an integral part of global stability.

In our efforts to maintain vigor in our own economy, however, we need to be careful not to follow policies which would be detrimental to world economic stability. For example, consider one aspect of our import policy: When business is bad, the pressure to restrict imports by raising tariff rates and imposing quotas greatly increases as compared to times when business is good. But reducing unemployment by restricting imports does not get rid of the unemployment; it merely exports it to our trading partners abroad. This is shortsighted indeed; it militates against world economic stability, and discourages our investment abroad.

One segment of the world economy that is especially prone to violent fluctuations is the market for raw materials or primary products. Fluctuations in the demand for and prices of these products cause great economic instability and damage in the primary-producing countries, are an important factor tending to weaken their political stability, and give rise to strong pressures for quick industrialization at any cost, even along uneconomic lines. If these fluctuations could be eliminated or substantially reduced, the countries involved would be far more attractive to prospective United States investors. I recognize the difficulties inherent in stabilizing the markets for these products, but I regret that the United States Government has thus far shown little inclination to join with others in cooperative efforts toward developing a practical stabilization plan.

Promoting an Economic and Social Base

The last series of policies I shall mention includes those designed to help build up the economic and social base in the less developed countries. Such a base is necessary if much United States investment is to be attracted to those countries. The establishment of a succccess-ful manufacturing industry, for example, requires adequate power, transportation facilities, sewerage and other public health facilities, and workers with some degree of skill and education. These founda-tions, on which industry rests, simply do not exist or are grossly inade-quate in vast areas of the world. Until these foundations are laid, there is not likely to be much foreign investment, especially by smaller enterprises which are not in position to set up their own facilities.

Many countries are not in position to build up an economic and social base, except very slowly, unless they have outside help. Several programs of the United States Government are designed to help such countries build up this necessary foundation. Our technical aid program, our participation in the Technical Assistance Program of the United Nations, our economic aid program, and our policy of lending funds derived from the sale of surplus agricultural com-modities abroad have been of this character to a considerable extent. Construction of power and transportation facilities has been aided through loans by the Export-Import Bank and the International Bank for Reconstruction and Development, of which the United States is a leading member.

One proposed program for helping finance the parts of the eco-nomic and social base that do not lend themselves to self-liquidating loans is SUNFED—the Special United Nations Fund for Economic Development. The United States has consistently opposed this pro-posed agency, ostensibly on grounds that we could not afford the cost, but perhaps chiefly for reasons having to do with the enlarge-ment of the role of the United Nations and the loss of control over the use of funds appropriated by the United States Congress.

This is not the place to examine the desirability of any specific proposal, such as the SUNFED, but I would like to stress the point that private investment will not be substituted for public investment in the construction of the economic and social base. We shall need more public investment for this purpose, if we are to speed the flow of private investment.

In summary, then, there are many indirect ways in which policies of the United States Government can stimulate private investment overseas in the interests of promoting our broad foreign policy objectives. It behooves us to contribute our ideas to the creation of these programs and our support to their implementation.

QUESTIONS AND ANSWERS*

From the floor: Mr. Mills' proposition that we exempt certain foreign income from taxation is a good one. Perhaps we might go a step further and suggest that the money made by domestic concerns on the goods that they export be exempt as well. In this way we can strengthen our firms against overseas competition.

Mr. Mills: That is a good thought. It is obvious that no investor is going to invest abroad, considering the risks involved, unless he receives a higher yield than he can realize now. Investors will supply capital anywhere if the yield is high enough.

I don't believe we should subsidize anybody, but I do think that we ought to create a situation which will make the yield high, and the cheapest way to do that is to reduce taxes. I don't consider this a bonus or a subsidy.

Mr. Blough: I don't agree entirely with Mr. Mills, but I am even more concerned by the comment from the floor. What is the purpose of tax exemption anyway? I presumed it was to stimulate investment abroad. If so, how would the proposed exemption on profits from exports accomplish this? We want to encourage investment overseas, not simply sales abroad; and no one will set up facilities in other countries if he can make as much or more money by exporting goods made in the United States. As has been pointed out, the failure to make profits on exports is one factor which encourages overseas investment.

From the floor: Theoretically, it is true that if there are two or more

* Businessmen present at the panel session on which this chapter is based raised certain questions which brought about the interplay of ideas reported more or less verbatim in this section.

systems of taxation involved, a company should pay only the highest tax. In most cases, of course, this is the United States tax of 52%. But this principle is, in fact, so hedged with conditions that it does not work. It is generally true that a good, profitable opportunity will not be passed up because it is highly taxed, but I know of a number of cases where the proposition simply became impossible because the rates went up to 85% and 90%. If United States authorities would implement the 52% principle, we would see real progress. It might not stimulate investment by making foreign operations more profitable than those in the United States, but at least they would be on a par with domestic operations.

Another problem is foreign control. One of the great impediments to increased foreign investment is the insistence of foreign governments that control must rest in the hands of foreign individuals or governments regardless of the relative value of the assets in the country and the money which is to be brought in for development. This principle ought to be eliminated, possibly by treaty.

Concluding Note *

As one who has been concerned with tax policies in the Treasury during the past few years, I want to comment on some of the observations that have been made in this chapter.

The number of worthy causes that can be furthered by differential tax treatment is overwhelming. A vast number of domestic exemptions or rate reductions are urged to stimulate industrialization in one area or keep industry from moving from another section, to promote decentralization, to aid civil defense, and to encourage particular professions or investments. Special tax treatment or tax exemption is the first and most obvious device that occurs to people when they want to foster some program. If one starts consenting to, or encouraging, differential tax treatment, the tax base withers away to the point where rates on the remaining taxable income would have to be considerably higher than the present exorbitant levels.

* By Mr. Smith.

Furthermore, in the area which the authors of this chapter have analyzed, we run into a special difficulty. We have to define "foreign income." The number of man-weeks that have gone into trying to work out this little "technical problem" is considerable. Every group having anything to do with foreign business seems to want to be included in a definition which will qualify for this advantage. Because of this "technical problem," legislation which was well advanced in 1954 died aborning. The definition of "foreign income" is a chronic problem that is going to make the adoption of differential tax treatment very difficult indeed.

As regards the proposal for tax exemption for income from exports, American businessmen are active in Washington, calling the attention of the government to instances where foreign countries are subsidizing their exports in various ways. They want us to protest, and we do. As a matter of fact and of principle, this Administration is opposed to the subsidization of exports by us as well as by others.

One other matter further complicates this question. Obviously, any tax concessions would have to apply to existing companies as well as to those considering overseas investment. But, by definition, established investments do not need any encouragement—they have been made under the present law. How, then, do we balance the inequities of such unnecessary windfall benefits against the need for encouraging new industries?

In closing let me say that I am not very hopeful about any substantial tax reductions in this area in the near future. An attempt was made in 1954 as part of a general tax revision. The chances of special tax reductions for this one kind of income without general reductions do not seem good. I greatly hope that the time will come when the tax level as a whole can be lowered, but that time is still uncertain.

RETURNS AND RISKS ON INVESTMENT ABROAD

Lawrence E. Thompson, Robert H. Strange,
Maurits E. Edersheim, and N. A. Bogdan

THE TWO WORDS which dominate the title of this chapter—returns and risks—neatly summarize the whole problem under discussion. Obviously, return has to be commensurate with risk in an investment situation. Risks are always involved, but no one is willing to take them unless the returns are adequate to protect him against possible losses and attractive enough to indicate that a profit is to be made. Generally, investors choose between foreign and domestic investments on this same basis. But there are particular problems in foreign investment which affect returns and risks, and the authors of this

Note: Mr. Thompson, who acted as moderator for the panel on which this chapter is based, is Associate Professor of Business Administration, Harvard Business School; Mr. Strange is a Director, Scudder Fund of Canada, Ltd.; Mr. Edersheim is General Partner in charge of foreign operations, Burnham and Company, and Mr. Bogdan is President of American Overseas Finance Corporation.

chapter have outlined them in a way that should be helpful to the reader.

There is one special aspect to the foreign investment problem which businessmen should understand: the need for education. The general public is almost completely uninformed in this field; few know the true story of foreign investment or the facts of past performance. The efforts that have been made to date to fill this gap are sound, but they mark only a beginning. Those of us who are concerned with private investment bear the responsibility for pushing ahead on this front.

Given this situation, it is significant—and somewhat surprising —to note that public interest is increasing. While we have not had a great deal of indirect or portfolio investment in the past, the growing amount of direct investment through investment firms and indirect investment through the formation of trusts and banking organizations designed to supply medium-term loans constitute a series of developments which promise to provide an increasing flow of money abroad.

Obviously such a program calls for different types of management and research, more publication of results, and wider coverage of progress. Though this work lies ahead I think those who are in this field can be very pleased—although not complacent—with the progress made thus far.

INVESTORS IN SEARCH OF INVESTMENT*

I would like to cover two general areas of the very broad subject which has been raised in this chapter. In the first instance, I want to raise the question of why large numbers of Americans have a growing interest in investing some portion of their capital in foreign businesses. Secondly, I am concerned with how the individual and the institution can find and supervise good investments overseas.

The answer to the first of these questions seems to me very sim-

* By Mr. Strange.

ple, and at the heart of all forms of American investment abroad, be it the purchase of a share of Standard Oil of New Jersey, the decision of an American business firm to extend its operations to other countries, an individual's plan to buy agricultural land in Argentina, or the investment in or the lending of money to foreign enterprises. The clear answer is that the investor feels he can invest his money at least as profitably abroad as he can at home.

The oil industry provides one good example of why the investor is tending to look abroad for opportunity. The growth in consumption of petroleum products since the end of the war in this country has been remarkable, but in some other nations it has been even stronger and more consistent. Similarly, in a number of lands the rate of growth in electric power consumption has been more rapid than ours. Neither of these events has gone unnoticed by United States businessmen or investors. The extension of our oil and electrical interests abroad and the growing number of United States shareholders in such companies as Royal Dutch Company, British Petroleum and Phillips Lamp bear out this observation.

This faster rate of growth is not, of course, the only reason capital investment abroad is expected to produce relatively attractive returns. It is not necessary that a foreign economy grow *in toto* to an equal or greater degree than ours in order to attract interest. Technological developments overseas, like the discovery of polyethylene, the development of transistors or the earlier use of jet aircraft can provide a stimulus to capital participation. Moving to seemingly more mundane fields, it is even possible that selective industries and companies in relatively static economies may provide investment opportunities that are attractive. Such an enterprise as packaging seems to have a most promising future in some mature countries.

Before leaving the subject, I would like to touch lightly upon that all important divisor, *price*. With the benefit of hindsight, we can see that the price of many foreign investments in recent years was low relative to their underlying or subsequently developed values. This was particularly true in the case of German and Japanese investments. Such large disparities between price and real or future value probably no longer exists, but it is possible that the more adventuresome investor may yet find some.

In dealing with the second general question—how can individual and institutional investors find and supervise good choices in the foreign field—I would like to borrow an instrument developed and popularized by the Harvard Business School and set down a brief case history of the techniques with which the Fund, Inc., Scudder, Stevens and Clark meets the problem.

A Case History

Although the field of overseas investment was not completely alien to us in the regular conduct of our business, we developed a strong feeling after the war that better methods for finding and supervising our clients' international interests could be worked out. Accordingly, in the fall of 1952 we approached the SEC and various other American and Canadian government departments with the idea that a publicly distributed and nonresident owned Canadian corporation might be established for this purpose. For many years there had been a substantial number of such privately owned companies, but there were no publicly-distributed, SEC-approved NRO Canadian firms.

To qualify as a non-resident owned Canadian corporation, at least 95% of a company's shares must be owned by holders who are not residents of Canada. In our case, the corporation's investments are confined to securities of companies deriving the bulk of their income from sources outside the United States. Since two-thirds of our investments must be made in Canadian corporations, we felt it most important to go into partnership with Canadians who were well qualified in their own and other investment fields. Accordingly, in conjunction with a group of Canadians who had many years experience in the operation of Canadian and Scottish Trusts, an office was established in Toronto. We invited a group of outstanding Canadian and American businessmen with wide experience in the operation of foreign companies to serve on the board with our own directors. These men have played an active and invaluable part in the daily conduct of the trust, in the operation of the executive committee and on the board of directors. In addition, the firm of Scudder, Stevens, and Clark, with its research department of over forty trained experts, serves as investment advisor to the trust. We decided to make the shares available not only to our investment counsel clients but to everyone who wanted to pay $32 apiece for them. Consequently, Lehman Brothers, in association with a large group of investment firms, underwrote and publicly distributed $30 million of stock in the trust in 1954. With the underwriting of an additional $10 million in August of 1955, the trust has now grown to approximately $55 million. The asset value of the original shares rose from $30 to $45 in the first two years.

In addition, we now hold securities in two South African companies, two jointly based in the Netherlands and the United Kingdom, two British, one Peruvian, one Rhodesian, one Belgian Congo, and one Dutch firm. These holdings have an aggregate market value of almost $8 million.

Obtaining Information

The primary problem in the selection and supervision of foreign investments is the acquisition of adequate current information. A great deal has been accomplished along these lines in the past ten years, though there is still plenty of room for improvement. Basic industry and economic reports of foreign governments are often models that we could well imitate. Our own Department of Commerce has done an excellent job in issuing current statements of basic tax and economic data. Some investment houses print reports on individual foreign companies and conditions abroad. Moody's, Investment Service in London is an excellent equivalent of Standard & Poor's Corporation. Company and directors' reports abroad have often improved as much as those in this country.

In conclusion, I feel that there are a large number of favorable opportunities abroad for investors with the necessary determination and intelligence, given the right kind of information and an effective vehicle for putting that information to work.

PRIVATE INVESTMENT *

Individuals and diversified funds have only just begun to invest fairly large sums of money in foreign countries other than Canada. Up to the first World War, we were a capital importing nation. In the 1920's, however, we attempted capital exporting at a fairly good rate, primarily through high yielding government and corporate bonds. But the depression of 1929 and later the threat of World War II killed the trend.

During the first few years after World War II, international conditions discouraged real interest in global investment of private capital. But as the years passed, the situation changed radically. After 1950, world recovery—especially in Western Europe—proceeded much faster than anyone had expected, while equity values rose in this country, making many foreign situations look attractive in comparison. Foreign investment was on the increase.

Despite the publicity about specific foreign issues, however, few people realize the extent to which private investors are purchasing overseas securities today. I do not know of any official statistics on the subject, but I would estimate the amount at a minimum of $2 billion. In Royal Dutch alone—by far our most widely held foreign issue—we have invested $500 million.

Until now, most of our investment abroad has been done with companies domiciled in Western Europe or South Africa. We invest with them because only the Western European centers—where South African shares are also actively traded—are sufficiently developed to create a good public market for buying and selling. South America, for instance, has been suffering from a lack of sufficiently important capital markets, while other parts of the world have been too near areas of conflict for investment purposes.

Incidentally, investors should understand that stock purchases in

* By Mr. Edersheim.

foreign companies will not generally lead to ownership. Though this has occasionally happened, most firms have regulations which make it impossible. An American could own millions of shares in Royal Dutch, for instance, but could never have more than six votes.

Increased private investment raises several questions:

- What are the risks involved?
- What return can be obtained?
- What is the significance of this investment for our foreign policy?
- What can the government do to promote this type of investment?

Let us take a look at each of these issues in turn.

Investment Risks and Returns

There is no doubt that investing abroad entails more risk than does investing in this country. Foreign companies do not publish as many details of their operations for the benefit of their stockholders as does United States business. Furthermore, it is obviously more difficult to follow a situation from a distance. There are no regular newspaper reports to read, for example, so the investor must depend to a great extent for his information on the person who studied and recommended the venture originally. Therefore there is less opportunity for him to exercise individual judgment. Also, the company sometimes operates under different laws, which are often designed more for the benefit of the national stockholders than for ones in other lands.

> For instance, stock dividends are tax free in this country until sold, when they become taxable at the capital gains rate; in other countries, they are taxable as ordinary income. On the other hand, different kinds of distributions are taxable here and tax free abroad. Most foreign companies will act in a way most favorable to the local holders because of their unfamiliarity with tax laws in other countries.

There are other problems involved too: in many countries, the local political situation has a much larger bearing on operating a company than it does here. The limited capital markets in many countries make the shares of a foreign company more risky; for example, while shares can be bought abroad, resale is much more difficult. In addition, foreign exchange restrictions are a constant threat.

Consequently, even more care should be exercised in selecting foreign investments than in investing locally. Amazing as it may seem, United States investors have not always observed this warning. While most foreign stocks have been bought after a thorough study and for well-thought-out reasons, some—especially during the height of the foreign securities boom in the spring of 1955—have been bought essentially on "romance"—Virginia, Orange Free State, and E.M.I., to mention a few. In this connection, it is wise to take the argument that some foreign issues are statistically cheaper than their domestic counterparts with a grain of salt. They may be less expensive —but other factors should be considered in making a purchase.

Basically, capital is short, especially in many underdeveloped countries and even in a number of Western European nations. Consequently, there is not so much competition for an attractive investment objective, and the price does not go up as much. The lack of a large stock buying and selling public has often restricted the floating supply of money. It is true that the price will often rise when United States investors start to buy, especially since the capitalization of most foreign companies is small as measured by our standards. However, we have often seen that United States buying brings a stock up too high, so that it drops sharply when our purchases cease. I would like to cite two typical examples:

> When Unilever declared a stock dividend, the price of the stock went down instead of up—even though it still looked very cheap on the basis of earnings. Amsterdam cabled our firm, and simultaneously we cabled them saying, "Market action Unilever disappointing." Why did this happen? Because everybody in Holland has had Unilever for years, and Hollanders are not going to buy it after a big rise. To add to this, the comparatively small segment of the United States public which is interested in such an issue already owned it. There simply is not a large reservoir of additional buying power abroad for top-grade stocks.
>
> We heard that Potgietersrust, part-owner of the world's largest

platinum mine, was going to raise its dividend. We considered trying to place the stock, which was then yielding 8%, in this country. It was selling at $1.50. We asked our South African correspondent what he expected the dividend to be and where the price of the stock could go. He prophesied that the company would raise the dividend to a level yielding at least 12% on the present price and declared that the shares might go to $2. We pointed out that it would not be worthwhile for the United States investor to take a geographical risk and pay high expenses, and asked why such a conservative stock could not double and yield 6%. In reply, he claimed that such a development would be impossible unless Americans bought it, because he had plenty of situations which were just as attractive and yielded 10% plus.

Consequently, the investor is well advised to look for other positive factors in a company besides the immediately obvious yields and price-earnings ratios.

Notwithstanding the risks, the various trends abroad offer promise of growth in volume, and earnings greater than the growth potential of equivalent United States companies. In the first place, it is reasonable to assume that the general living standard overseas will rise faster than it will here because it is starting out at a much lower level. For instance, the number of cars outside the United States, the consumption of gasoline, the number of radio sets in use, the telephones, and the miles of new railroads being built have increased much more rapidly in foreign countries. Many firms have expanded at a greater rate the last few years than have their counterparts here —and they probably will continue to do so.

Secondly, in many nations, the economy is still freer from government controls than is ours. There are no antitrust laws, no fair trade laws, and consequently individual enterprises can develop the way they want to.

Finally, there are natural resources. A diversified portfolio should represent *all* natural resources, but sometimes the best—or even the only—companies controlling resources which we do not have in America are foreign firms.

I should point out here that the investor ought not to apply the same standards to overseas opportunities that he uses in this country. Furthermore, the economic and political picture of the nation involved should be studied carefully.

Needless to say, the return abroad depends on the degree of risk one is willing to take, just as it does in the United States. Companies domiciled in Western Europe, by and large, do not pay much higher dividends than similar firms here. They prefer to finance their expansion internally in view of their limited capital market, and their profit margins are sometimes set higher than ours. The return on investments in underdeveloped countries is much higher —but so is the risk. South African securities, for instance, yield 10% to 12%, and many South American situations offer very substantial returns.

But there are advantages to Western European investment despite lower rates of return. A good company sells at seven times its earnings. In this country a similar quality company might sell at fourteen times its earnings. The practice of internal financing means that the equity value is building up all the time. These firms are making money, so their earnings and intrinsic value are rising.

As an illustration, look at the case of Royal Dutch. They reinvest 82% of their earnings. The company has been very successful, so the stock which just recently was earning $8 per share is now earning near $13 per share. Consequently it becomes very cheap, even to the Dutch. They are willing to pay seven times $13 because the chance for further advancement is excellent.

In summary, the fact that Western European countries have so much internal financing makes them very strong and assures a continuous rise in profits.

Adjunct to Foreign Policy

There is one aspect of the private investment picture that has been overlooked: its importance as an adjunct to our foreign policy. Though the government is trying to promote direct foreign investment by the large companies with guarantees and tax concessions and is seeking to stimulate foreign trade, it has done nothing to encourage overseas investment by individuals. On the contrary, the Securities Exchange Commission and the New York Stock Exchange have made it harder to invest abroad in some cases. Presumably, existing laws force them to do so. But wherever the blame may be, the effect is damaging.

Only in the last few years have some steps been taken to promote foreign securities and make them more attractive to the American public:

Several important companies like Royal Dutch have listed their shares on the New York Stock Exchange or on the American Stock Exchange.

Other companies have not gone as far as listing, but have created American Depository Receipts—shares issued by an American bank against the deposit of shares of the same company abroad. These receipts have made it much simpler to trade issues, since the shares need not be sent abroad for transfer whenever ownership changes. Furthermore, the dividends are sent in dollars to the registered holder by the American bank.

A number of firms, all members of the National Association of Security Dealers, have improved their means of acquainting clients with foreign issues and have facilitated trading by creating better markets in this country for the various issues.

Possible Changes in Law

But more needs to be done. For instance, the present law prevents members of the National Association of Security Dealers from participating in the distribution of any new issue which is not fully registered with the Securities Exchange Commission. This provision should be altered. Because of it, United States stockholders in Royal Dutch suffered a considerable loss in 1947 (the company is now registered) and, more recently, investors in Phillips Lamps had a similar experience.

The SEC requires registration (in reality, full disclosure) of every new issue in this country, thereby keeping a control over such issues. But registration for a foreign company is often a very expensive, complicated, and time-consuming operation because of its different bookkeeping system and the particular legal requirements under which it operates.

Recently I was asked by the managers of a well-known foreign company listed here whether or not they should register a new issue. In view of the time element involved in registration and the limited interest in their stock, I honestly could not recommend it. Domestic companies have to accept this delay, of course, but they can plan for it. Furthermore, they have to prepare fewer new figures and, in many cases, have a better capital market to work with.

Perhaps a middle way could be found—for instance, a special clearance could be devised so the SEC could exercise some degree of control. But at the same time it could state clearly that the issue has not complied with all requirements and is, therefore, a more risky proposition for the investor. The New York Stock Exchange might work out a special type of listing and develop a uniform system of deliveries and mutual recognition of arbitrage positions with the other recognized world stock exchanges. Possibly Congress could declare foreign companies officially free of our antitrust laws insofar as these laws pertain to their operations outside the United States. Most foreign companies probably cannot actually be indicted under the strict interpretation of the law—especially not for operations conducted abroad. In the case of Royal Dutch a few years ago, for instance, the indictments did not stand up. But many foreign companies fear these laws all the same, and have not promoted their shares in this country or created American Depository Receipts or listed themselves because of the regulations. Finally, the government might give private investors abroad the same tax exemptions granted to American corporations on at least part of their foreign income.

The concessions should not be one-sided, however; other governments and companies should realize that it is a great advantage to have private American capital invested in their large enterprises because it gives them access to a more sizable capital market. There is much that can be done in foreign companies to increase stock desirability to Americans. They could cooperate by improving stockholder relations, annual reports, and by issuing American Depository Receipts.

If only some of these conditions can be fulfilled and if the world situation remains comparatively calm, we may witness a period of much larger and more widespread private investment abroad than ever before. It would, of course, be best for the world economy if this investment stream could be guided to the underdeveloped countries. However, more stable conditions will have to be established in many of these areas and improved financial market centers must be set up. For the moment it is better to invest in those countries indirectly through the various diversified investment trusts which just recently have begun operating.

In conclusion, let me point out that the various kinds of private foreign investments provide an ideal way to aid the Free World. There is no cost to the government. Since no effort is made to obtain control, there can be no fear of "dollar diplomacy." Private investment gives us the opportunity to provide financial support and to demonstrate confidence in the political stability and the financial skill of our allies and friends. Finally, it makes it possible for us to demonstrate the advantages of a free enterprise, capitalistic system in effective and convincing fashion.

THE FUNCTION OF LENDING*

For some reason, foreign lending usually gets lost in the shuffle in any discussion of foreign investment, and very few references are made to it. Nevertheless, lending involves about the same basic risk as does any other form of investment, though perhaps the emphasis and the degree of risk are different.

> For instance, though a loan is usually extended in dollars, it is still subject to difficulty in case of devaluation of the obligor's currency. In a devaluation situation, more local currency is needed to

* By Mr. Bogdan.

buy the dollars owed. If the debtor does not have enough local currency, the lender is caught in the same position as the investor.

By the same token, a loan is subject to the usual risks of inconvertibility and transfer delays. If a country that owes money abroad runs into exchange difficulties and has to resort to exchange control, it is just as difficult for it to transfer the interest on a loan as it is to transfer dividends on an investment. Thus, by and large, one can say that loans are serviced on the basis of the same policies and restrictions as any other form of investment.

Apart from the transfer risk, however, loans are usually subject to *less* governmental interference in the obligor country since they do not carry ownership with them. Foreign governments are somewhat less prone to interfere with the servicing of a loan than with the exercise of ownership rights, and have so demonstrated over the course of many years. On the other hand, a loan depends much more on the basic will of a debtor to pay than does an investment in equity. It is easier for a foreign company to pass a dividend due a foreign stockholder than it is to default on an obligation to pay interest. All it has to do is to say that it did not make enough money, or that it wants to reinvest the funds in the business for a future expansion program.

But interest stares them in the face. They have to meet maturities and amortization payments. Any failure to meet such payments is considered a default, and one act of default has very serious repercussions on the credit standing of the particular debtor, and even on the standing of the entire debtor country.

Three Types of Loans

The past record of lending is mixed. Short-term lending—the normal commercial bank operation—has worked out fairly well. Very few banks have lost money in their short-term loans abroad, over a period of time. They may have been hung up or frozen for temporary periods in one country or another, but in the long run, they have been paid back.

Long-term lending, on the other hand, has a poor record, and its lack of success between the wars has scared off lenders for many years. There is a reason for its failure, of course. Before the first World War, and then between the two wars, most of the so-called long-term lending was done through public bond issues. These issues were negotiated at the governmental level on the borrowers' side. The bond purchaser had no voice in the negotiation of the deal. He was never given any chance to control, investigate, or analyze the use that was going to be made of the proceeds of the loan. Whenever things became difficult, the debtor in the foreign country found it all too easy to say "Well, here we got this money, but we don't know who lent it to us. It is from an anonymous and impersonal group of bondholders somewhere in some foreign market. We have no direct contact with them. They have never been to see us and, therefore, they can perfectly well wait for their money"!

The record of the so-called medium-term or direct type of loan—with which I intend to deal in more detail—is as yet undetermined. Relatively little medium-term lending has been attempted in the past. Today, however, it serves an extremely useful purpose, and one that is similar to any other type of investment. It is particularly worthwhile if it is set up on the basis of direct negotiation between lender and borrower, serves a well-defined need, and is carefully selected with an eye to its effect on the country involved and the governmental policies being followed.

Many people feel that the difference between investing in equities and lending is simply that equity investment stays in the country more or less permanently. A man who buys shares, for instance, or a direct investor who establishes a manufacturing operation puts foreign exchange into the foreign nation, and there it stays making a contribution to the recipient country's balance of payments. But in fact even short-term lending fulfills the same permanent function since it provides revolving working capital to finance exports and imports. No country can exist for very long without such working capital. Therefore, to the extent that it remains available to a foreign nation—and there is no reason why it would not remain available under normal circumstances—it represents an addition to that country's balance of payments position, and plays a direct part in facilitating foreign trade.

By the same token, a medium-term loan, even though it has to be repaid at maturity, has an important impact on the economy of the borrowing country. Such a loan serves a specific and productive purpose. When it is used to finance the purchase of equipment, of machinery or other types of capital goods, it makes exactly the same contribution to the borrowing country's economy as does any investment in equity.

A concrete step toward developing this type of lending in this country was taken a little over a year ago. Encouraged by the government, five of the leading banks decided it was time to go beyond the narrow bounds of commercial banking and create a vehicle for the extension of medium- and longer-term loans which would serve basic economic purposes. With this thought in mind, the American Overseas Finance Corporation, to which Mr. McCloy referred in his chapter, was formed as a pilot operation to see what could be accomplished in that direction.

The AOFC is organized under special laws and Federal Reserve regulations which do not permit it to accept deposits. Rather, it is authorized to issue its own securities, proceeds of which provide the funds needed by the corporation for its operations. Naturally, the potential purchasers of AOFC's securities demand a reassuring picture, so it was felt from the start that it might be useful to have the United States Government participate in the operation by granting certain guarantee facilities, particularly against political risks.

AOFC's first step, therefore, was to work out an agreement with the Export-Import Bank under which the latter would extend certain guarantee privileges up to one-third of AOFC's loans, provided certain standards and conditions were observed. Unfortunately, these arrangements have not worked out too satisfactorily. Instead of encouraging and supplementing private capital, as the law and Congressional policy say it should, the Export-Import Bank seems to be in competition with AOFC. This is a rather unexpected example of a government agency offering outright competition instead of encouraging private initiative. However, AOFC is only just beginning and recent discussions in Washington have indicated that ways and means can perhaps be found to increase cooperation.

I hope that insurance companies will provide another source of loan capital to first-class foreign obligors in years to come. They have been extremely reluctant to go into the foreign field in the past, and have confined their foreign investments almost entirely to Canada. Of course, they are subject to certain restrictions. But if they took advantage of the exemptions now available to them, the amount of money released for investment abroad would be quite substantial. The New York life companies were recently granted a little additional relief, and it remains to be seen whether or not they will take advantage of it. I suspect it is going to be a very slow process. It is to be expected that insurance companies, once they decide to take a fresh look at the foreign field, will start out by being more interested in loans than equity investments. However, I believe that all these sources—AOFC, insurance companies, and possibly the International Finance Corporation—will eventually find that lending and investment in equities can be combined very profitably and constructively.

In summary, a beginning has been made in foreign lending, just as it has in portfolio investment. If we are prudent and patient, I think we will see important developments in the years ahead.

QUESTIONS AND ANSWERS*

From the floor: One very important phase of overseas investment has been omitted in this chapter. Many years ago a Scotsman made the observation, "The basis of credit is in the person." But we tend to talk about foreign investments in the abstract without distinguishing the psychological or moral background of the individual in-

---

* Businessmen present at the panel session on which this chapter is based raised certain questions which brought about the interplay of ideas reported more or less verbatim in this section.

volved. All the stamps of lawyers and votes of commissioners from Honduras, Guatemala, Paraguay—or what have you—are worth about as much as a snap of the finger. We need to be clear about all the details of a loan—with whom it is made, its historical and ethical background, and the reliability of the borrower.

From the floor: The matter of tact enters into this question, of course, and also the changing climate of the times. Some countries that have shown bad faith in the past may be better in the future. But I agree that it is unfortunate to skirt around those factors; we are probably too polite about them in public discussions. We talk about risks and make general statements, but there are a lot of places where no sane man would ever invest.

Mr. Bogdan: When I referred to the need for telling the full story, and particularly the past record, I had that precise question in mind. I firmly believe, however, that if the whole record were placed before the public, people would be very much surprised to find how few countries have shown bad faith in the past and how remarkably good the over-all story really is.

From the floor: You may be right in the aggregate—but look at Latin America for instance. All you have to do is go back to 1870 to show constant devaluation and constant defaults.

Mr. Bogdan: I don't necessarily call that an act of bad faith—and this is not a question of "the aggregate." In detail, the record is excellent.

From the floor: There is room for improvement in the United States tax structure with reference to the treatment of income from foreign investments. Personally, I don't favor any substantial changes in the United States tax patterns to accommodate the needs of American investors abroad, but there are two aspects of the present law that deserve attention:

   • Section 902A of the Internal Revenue Code provides that an American corporation which owns 10% or more of the stock of a foreign corporation will receive a credit not only for the taxes it has paid on dividends but also for any other taxes paid by the foreign corporation. I feel that the potential for American investment abroad would be improved if the 10% restriction were removed.

• Section 902A extends only to corporations: a company investing abroad can receive a very substantial tax credit, but an individual cannot. In the more sophisticated systems, particularly the United Kingdom, full credit is allowed the individual investor for taxes paid on dividends declared by foreign companies. Possibly we could pattern our law on theirs in this regard, with a reduction of the 10% figure in the case of individuals.

From the floor: If somebody makes an investment in foreign land or stock, are the titles pretty well assured by a public agency?

Mr. Bogdan: That varies tremendously from country to country.

Mr. Edersheim: If you buy a listed security, it is just as well protected as United States Steel. It is true that after the war many securities were lost. They were not always recognized by the country involved, but I think that this situation has been changed since 1949. Listed securities abroad now have the same kind of title as in this country.

From the floor: If a company should lend some money on a mortgage on a secured basis, is there a public record of it comparable to the one in this country?

Mr. Bogdan: There again, it differs a good deal depending on the country. In Mexico, for instance, protection is not quite adequate; in other Latin American countries it is. Western Europe, by and large, maintains good records. But there may be trouble when it comes to enforcement, quite apart from the element of registration and record.

From the floor: Isn't it true that it is becoming more difficult to invest money profitably in Canada? I understand Canadians now rather resent us coming up there with our money.

Mr. Strange: I think it is quite true that the Canadian newspapers have emphasized the question of the entry of United States capital, though not as much in portfolio investment as in record investment. There are a number of reasons for this, in some cases hinging on specific problems. You would have a difficult time buying a chemical plant or company in Canada, for example. But generally speaking, I don't think that this is as serious as some newspapers intimate.

From the floor: Aren't some other funds having difficulty placing their money?

Mr. Strange: I think this is a misapprehension. When we raised $30 million at the start, many people were worried about other funds. They thought we would force up the price of securities in Canada. As a matter of practical fact, I can think of only one instance in which we had any percentage effect on the price of the security. In more instances than not, we purchased securities at somewhat less than prevailing prices. I am investing money there every day now, and I don't find the situation changed.

From the floor: I think the trouble is the scarcity of good Canadian companies. Everybody naturally is seeking them, and this makes them even scarcer. Also, I think that this talk of resentment against United States capital is overemphasized. I think Canadians—and investors in most countries—feel a little nervous about the effect of American investment, and we must watch it. But it does not seem too serious to me.

Part Three

OVERSEAS VIEWS OF UNITED STATES BUSINESS

INDIA'S EXPANDING ECONOMY—
RETROSPECT AND PROSPECT

Gaganvihari Lallubhai Mehta

A DIPLOMAT, according to the old saw, is a man who thinks twice before saying nothing. This caution, so characteristic of those in my profession, seems even more appropriate for me in this particular discussion. For commercial and economic subjects are so complex that it is even possible for two experts in a single field to take two totally different approaches with equal confidence.

Nevertheless, I want to describe the economic development of India, and in so doing try to provide a picture of the attitudes and problems of one of the world's new nations.

Our economy today is in a crucial state. The First Five-Year Plan, formulated in 1951, ran its course with a fair measure of success and the Second Plan is being put into effect. The experience gained in implementing the First Plan gave us an idea of the methods and

Note: Mr. Mehta is Ambassador of India to the United States and Mexico.

limitations of economic planning and a more precise assessment of the problems which would have to be faced during the next five years. This is, therefore, an appropriate moment to review what has been achieved so far and to outline the prospects for the years ahead.

A STORMY CLIMATE

As a member of the Planning Commission which drafted the outline of the First Five-Year Plan, I recall vividly the atmosphere in which we began our work. The task was a formidable one. We confronted an economy lopsided in its growth and seriously affected by an acute postwar inflation coupled with shortages of essential commodities and raw materials. In a sense, this imbalance was a concomitant of our retarded development under foreign rule. Although India had begun to develop industrially during the previous thirty years, the national economy was still basically stagnant. Standards of living in the country were woefully low; production and consumption of food, clothing, and elementary necessities were far under a decent minimum; and per capita income was among the lowest in the world. India thus presented a gloomy picture of a country with subsistence agriculture and only incipient industrialization, inadequately developed resources, and rural areas that were largely neglected. We were, indeed, more planned against than planning.

The last World War further complicated this already backward, unbalanced economy. It left inflation and economic shortages in its wake, and severely distorted the normal patterns of production, investment, and trade. The transfer of power from British to Indian hands coincided with the always difficult transition from a wartime to a peacetime economy. To complicate the situation still further, the achievement of independence brought about a "revolution in expectation." Popular demands for economic relief and advancement necessitated positive steps on the part of the national government.

Thus the First Five-Year Plan was formulated with a legacy of economic backwardness and neglect, in an environment of inflation and scarcities brought about by the war and the partition of the country, on the one hand, and an atmosphere of hope and expectation, on the other. Only active measures in accordance with a well-conceived and coordinated development program could meet our needs.

A REALISTIC PLAN

Though we vitally needed more rapid industrialization in order to diversify the economy, improve standards of living, and provide opportunities for employment, circumstances required that the First Plan give high priority to other programs. We had to work out schemes that would overcome shortages of food and essential raw materials, expand the supply of consumer goods by fully utilizing the capacity of various industries, and rehabilitate the railway transport services which had been overstrained during the war. It was for this reason that the Plan attached importance to the development of agriculture and irrigation, and sought to revitalize the villages and rural areas through community development projects and extension services.

After taking stock of all the resources that we could mobilize—financial, technical, and human—and assessing the probable availability of resources from outside the country, we formulated the Plan on a fairly realistic basis. At the end of its first year, the Korean boom intervened. We made good use of the resulting improvement in our trade position by taxing away the windfall of surplus earnings from our exports and utilizing the funds for development. To some extent, this helped reduce our reliance on external resources.

During the five-year period both federal and state taxation were increased substantially, and large amounts were mobilized through public borrowing and some savings. We were also fortunate in obtaining over $500 million in external aid in the form of loans and grants, mainly from the United States. In addition we were able to use sterling balances to our credit in London. The actual aid (that is, grants as such) constituted about one unit out of every twenty of the total investment in the public sector. Thus it is clear that we have tried to raise ourselves by our own bootstraps in planning our programs. We have not only endeavored to mobilize our existing resources; we have augmented them by demanding whatever sacrifices we reasonably could from our own people. While we are deeply grateful for the assistance we have received from abroad, we can legitimately pride ourselves on evolving a program of self-reliance.

Let me pause here to emphasize that all this has been done by democratic process. If I may borrow an historic phrase from one of the greatest Americans, we believe in planning of the people, by the people, and for the people. We believe that the economic development of India should be based on the needs and demands of the people in the villages rather than on *a priori* doctrines and rigid theories. Economic planning in India is fundamentally democratic in character—in its conception, formulation, and execution. Public debate, both inside and outside of Parliament, preceded the adoption of the Plan, and the program has been operating ever since through persuasion and agreement rather than through compulsion, coercion, and violence.

Undoubtedly, this is an unusual experiment. In these days of regimented economies, when economic planning has been regarded as tainted by totalitarianism, India is seeking to show that a new way of life for its masses can be consciously and purposefully brought about by the state through democratic means. For we believe that the plan is for the man, not the man for the plan.

HOW DID IT WORK?

What was the result of this planned effort during the five years after 1951? The national income registered an increase of about 18% by the end of the First Plan period, as against the 11% that had been envisaged. The output of food in 1954–1955 was 65.8 million tons, exceeding the goal by about 4 million tons. The index of agricultural production rose by 13% and industrial production went up by about 11%. A year before the termination of the Plan period, the production of cloth exceeded the target by 387 million yards. Equally good performances were registered in jute, cement, paper, chemical, and light engineering industries. During this period of development, price levels remained stable and the cost of living registered a small decline. Our payments position externally held stable at a much higher level of exports and imports than before, and we were able to repay an amount of almost $100 million which we had borrowed from the International Monetary Fund as short-term accommodation during a period of food crisis in 1949.

But the measure of the Plan's success should be determined by more than the achievement of physical targets, important though that is. A new spirit was developed among the people—a spirit of enthusiasm and confidence. Everywhere about the country, people in the villages were demanding schools and medical dispensaries, roads, bridges, railway connections, and, above all else, more water through irrigation works, large and small. The "apathetic" masses were awakening and cultivating a healthy discontent with their living conditions and the lot which they had inherited through generations. The spell of stagnation had been broken.

The progress of community development projects is one of the most hopeful signs of this resurgence. A useful yardstick of the success of such projects, and of the national extension service, is the size of the voluntary contributions made by the people under various schemes. The estimated total of these contributions—made in cash, materials, and labor—reached a figure that was nearly half of the expenditure incurred by the government during that period.

With these achievements of the First Plan behind it, the government formulated the Second Five-Year Plan and placed it before the public. Before I come to the salient points in this Plan, however, I should like to refer briefly to some of the basic ideas on which it is constructed.

A SOCIALIST PATTERN OF SOCIETY

To begin with, our broad objective is to build a socialist pattern of society—an objective which has been widely accepted in our country. With the gross poverty of the people, a majority of whom still live on a subsistence level, with squalor and ill health, with chronic unemployment and underemployment, and with wide disparities in income and wealth, it is inevitable that there should be an insistent demand for economic betterment and equality. Lacking large capital resources and confronted by serious economic ills and social evils, there is little hope that the requisite degree of amelioration will be achieved solely through private action and enterprise. We are trying to do in decades what has been achieved elsewhere in over a century.

We need not be afraid of words—whether socialism or any other "ism." As a matter of fact, in Washington they are saying that most *"isms"* have become *"wasms"*! Today, all civilized governments seek to establish for their people some kind of welfare state or society which can make concerted efforts to improve standards of living, provide the widest possible social and educational opportunities, ensure an increasing degree of economic security, adopt measures to prevent inflation and offset depression, and enlarge the scope of essential social services for the satisfaction of basic human needs. In this sense, as Sir William Harcourt, a former British Chancellor of the Exchequer, observed in introducing the Death Duty Bill in Parliament, "we are all socialists now." No sensible person could support unfettered exploitation of economic resources for private gain. No healthy adult citizen has the right to enjoy fruits of other people's labor without contributing a fair quota of his own.

Economic development anywhere today involves a certain measure of control and regulation in the wider interests of the community. Surely we cannot agree with the multimillionaire oil magnate who recently remarked that "Communism began in the United States when the Government took over the distribution of mail." Even in free economies, the state does intervene to guarantee prices, subsidize and protect domestic industries and transport services, and assist national investments abroad.

In the last analysis, the functions performed by the state in a national economy depend on the conditions in the country. In a nation like the United States, for example, where there has been a balance between population and resources, it has been possible for private enterprise to achieve economic development together with increasing social equality and security.

But our problem is a different one. We have too many people forced to work with too few available resources. If economic growth were left entirely to private interests, our progress would be slower and more uncertain and the priorities established might well be out of harmony with the basic economic needs of the country. The limited resources available might be utilized for purposes which are not socially desirable and needs which are not urgent. It is this relation between people and resources, and not any doctrinaire considerations, that has actuated us to organize our development according to a pattern of over-all guidance by a democratic state, in conformity with a system of planned priorities which are adjudged necessary for the achievement of social and economic stability.

I should also point out that the scale, structure, and pace of our industrial development has to be adapted to an economy with large resources of manpower but inadequate capital. We have to maintain a balance between human labor and machinery and cannot indiscriminately adopt the labor-saving devices which are suited to conditions elsewhere. Our emphasis has to be on small-scale and rural industries and on what we might call "labor intensive" industries. We are not unaware that such an economy cannot provide the same standards of living as employment based on an intensive use of capital. But we have to build on our own foundations and in our own environment. We can and should be able to do without a number of products, facilities, and services which are regarded as essential in more developed countries—at least during the time we are trying to provide the necessities of life to the mass of the people.

The Second Five-Year Plan called for a substantial increase in investment—its total magnitude being over $10 billion. Although not all the resources were in sight when the Plan was formulated, we had fairly clear programs for the further intensification of efforts in mobilizing domestic resources. Our schemes, when they mature, should extend the areas under irrigation and augment industrial production. This, in turn, will provide some necessary additional resources. We also expect that friendly countries will continue to give such aid as is possible during these crucial stages of our economic growth. If there is a gap left after all these sources have been tapped, we will not be distressed. It will serve as an incentive for the people to strive even harder to attain the social and economic objectives set forth in the Plan.

For a plan is not a mere inventory of schemes; it must stimulate effort, inculcate initiative, and strengthen creative forces. In all such projects and endeavors, there is always embodied an element of hope. A sound and progressive economy should be able to generate its own momentum and derive strength from the people. Browning said that it was better to strive for a million and miss it than reach out for a hundred and get it. If you feel that this is poetic license, not wholly relevant where hard economic facts are concerned, let me quote what a distinguished Harvard University economist, Professor J. K. Galbraith, said recently about the magnitude of our Plan:

> "A large plan has the obvious advantage of being a direct inducement to a large effort.... Moreover, it would seem important that people feel that the government is making a maximum effort on their behalf. Against the dangers of a big programme must be set even greater dangers of frustration of the democratic spirit which would follow from one that seemed reluctant, inadequate or even insufficiently bold." *

In drawing up our Plan we had to consider, against the risks of inflation, the prevalence of chronic unemployment and underemployment with its maladjustment, waste, and social discontent. We did not have a totalitarian conception which laid down the quantum of everyone's contribution in short and precise terms and measured it by bureaucratic yardsticks. We proceeded by the method of trial and error and tried to maintain a degree of flexibility while keeping our objectives steadily in view. Above all, we continuously reminded

---

* John Kenneth Galbraith, *Economic Planning in India: Five Comments,* Studies Relating to Planning for National Development (Calcutta, Indian Statistical Institute, March, 1956), p. 2.

ourselves that the human being on the farm and in the factory is at the center of all our national effort.

THE PLAN IN DETAIL

Although the absolute expenditure on agriculture is set higher than during the period of the First Plan, the Second Plan increases the outlay on industry in the scale of relative priorities. We also propose to allocate much more to transport and communications. Among the industries to be developed are such basic ones as iron and steel, aluminum, cement, mineral oils, fertilizers, and some important chemicals. In addition, we plan to expand industries like locomotives, shipbuilding, and machine tools. Each project has been worked out after a careful assessment of the technical aspects and the marketing prospects. In all these industries, there is to be a measure of state guidance and direction.

Recently, the Government of India re-enunciated its industrial policy in a statement which was widely appreciated and welcomed by the representatives of private enterprise. While this resolution on industrial policy demarcates the broad spheres of the public and private sectors, it lays emphasis on the need for cooperation between the two sectors for the promotion and development of industries. In agriculture, consumer goods industries, and some basic industries, the field is open to private enterprise, subject only to the pattern of development laid down in the Plan frame. Included in this category are cotton, jute, wool and silk textiles, paper, sugar, light engineering products, pharmaceuticals, drugs and chemicals, automobiles, and several other miscellaneous commodities produced in small or large-scale establishments.

Along with the development of basic industries, we want to build up small-scale and rural manufacturing to meet the needs of those people who live in villages—some 80% of our population. We realize that industry cannot thrive without a prosperous agriculture. Consequently, the total investment in agriculture and community projects was increased nearly 50%. Flood control, rural electrification, and the construction of dams for both irrigation and power will be in-

volved in these projects. Among social services, education has the
highest priority with investments in health following closely; labor
and labor welfare activities have also received attention.

WE WANT FOREIGN CAPITAL

I am frequently asked about our attitude toward foreign capital.
We welcome foreign capital within the broad framework of our
Plan. The investment of foreign capital is licensed to conform to an
order of priorities, in the same way as our indigenous private capital.
But once a foreign enterprise is set up in the country, there is no
discrimination against it. Indian and non-Indian concerns are treated
alike.

Foreign enterprise is free to remit its current earnings without any restriction and may repatriate all investments made in the
country after 1950 at any time the investors choose. India has had an
enviable record of meeting its foreign obligations, and its credit is
high in the world market.

We are eager to make use of the services of outside technicians and
to adapt their industrial knowledge to our problems. Several British,
German, French, Italian, and Japanese firms are now collaborating
with Indian manufacturers and the Indian Government in the establishment or expansion of various industries like steel, heavy electrical
equipment, and machine tools. Many American firms are participating technically and financially with Indian companies in the manufacture of sulpha drugs, dye stuffs, fine chemicals, textile machinery,
and plastics. Soviet, Czech, Rumanian, and Polish technicians are
aiding in steel, oil, and mining projects. Governmental relations with
foreign industries operating in the country have been businesslike
and cordial and there has been close and friendly cooperation between Indian and foreign experts and technicians. Both government
and private enterprise will require this kind of cooperation in an increasing measure.

Here is a large and growing area of economic cooperation in
mutual interest.

A BOLD EXPERIMENT

If the Second Five-Year Plan succeeds, as we trust and believe it will, it is expected to lead to the employment of about 10 million more people and an improvement of about 25% in the national income. It will produce an increase in the proportion of investment for economic growth from the present 6% or 7% of the net national income to about 10% or 11%.

Such a Plan could be regarded as a bold experiment if one considered only our resources. On the other hand, it looks like an unambitious one in the face of all our needs and demands. But, as President Eisenhower observed in another connection, we want to keep our feet firmly on the ground and our heads in the stars. We want to retain our vision without being visionary—by no means an easy task. While remaining conscious of our limitations, we want to realize our ambitions—and thus spur ourselves on to greater efforts. For the future of democracy in our country and the freedom and dignity of 370 million people is bound up with the success of these efforts.

QUESTIONS AND ANSWERS *

From the floor: Would you comment on the decision of General Motors to withdraw from India after 25 years of operating there?

Mr. Mehta: While it is true that General Motors and Ford have decided to close down, there are two or three other American companies which are staying on. One is Chrysler, which is collaborating with an Indian concern in Bombay in the manufacture and assembly of jeeps; another is Studebaker working with a Calcutta firm; and a third is Kaiser-Willys. Mercedes-Benz and Fiat and British concerns like Morris-Nuffield and Standard Leyland are also operat-

* In a subsequent meeting, Mr. Mehta answered questions pertaining to his formal presentation; this section of the chapter is drawn from the discussion which took place at this meeting. George P. Baker, James J. Hill Professor of Transportation, Harvard Business School, acted as moderator.

ing in India. Thus it is not a matter of unfriendly relations with non-Indian concerns. Briefly the facts are these:

> The policy of the Indian Government, even before our independence, was that there should be some collaboration between Indian and non-Indian manufacturers. Of course, each specific situation has to be considered on its merits, but this is the general policy. After our independence, the national government came to the conclusion that those plants which operate in India should gradually work up to a program of a major manufacturing nature, rather than remain mere assembly installations. Plans for these operations, which are to be completed in a certain number of years, are to be worked out with the consent of the government. Some of the American concerns were prepared to follow this policy, but General Motors felt that they would not be able to comply since the demand in India did not seem adequate to justify the establishment of manufacturing plants. There is no question of discrimination involved here, and General Motors itself has appreciated this point.

From the floor: Many industries are worried about expropriation of their facilities in India, without any compensation. Is their fear justified?

Mr. Mehta: The Constitution of India in its Article 31, which has been in force since 1950, declares that there can be no acquisition by the government without compensation. To illustrate our strict compliance with this provision, let me point out that the land reform program which we have undertaken has always provided fair compensation in government bonds for the landlords. So long as the Constitution of India is in force, the government cannot acquire anything without compensation.

From the floor: What method is used to determine the value of property to be acquired?

Mr. Mehta: Assessment of value always creates problems. The government appoints a tribunal to determine the figure. Sometimes the matter is turned over to the Ministry of Finance, which has all the data before it.

From the floor: Though you have given a very logical explanation of your government's socialistic views on the economic development of your country, isn't it true that your country would make faster progress if you adopted a more Western idea of profit and reward for effort?

Mr. Mehta: Our economy is still predominantly agricultural, and this area is wholly in private hands. It is true that we had to have certain controls in the postwar period because of various food shortages. The government had an obligation to provide a minimum amount of food and to see that it was distributed equitably. But as soon as the production of food increased, these controls were removed, and there are no controls on food in our country today. There has been no rationing for the last two years.

As far as industry is concerned, we welcome it in the private sector of our country. The volume of industry is still very small, but the bulk of it—cotton textiles, jute, sugar, heavy chemicals like soda ash, caustic soda, sulphuric acid, bicycles, sewing machines, automobiles, and hundreds of other products I could mention—are made by private enterprises. We have two steel plants, which are also in the private sector. Therefore, one cannot say that our economy is predominantly socialist.

It is true that we have nationalized certain services. Our railroad, for example, was nationalized long ago—in 1923–1933 when the British Government was in power. It was not done for any doctrinaire reasons. Two and a half years ago our airways were nationalized—and again it was not because of some rigid dogma but because we felt that the situation demanded it.

We have, therefore, what we call a mixed economy, in which certain things are done by the government and others are undertaken by private enterprise. We make our decision between the two according to the specific circumstances in each case. I can best illustrate my point with this striking example: After a severe epidemic in Bengal in 1943, when one million people died, we realized that we needed a plant for the manufacture of ammonium sulphate. Private enterprise was not interested in putting up such a plant at that time, so the government *had* to do it. We felt that the importance of providing the material for our people overrode any doctrinal considerations of public vs. private enterprise.

Our object, then, is to build a mixed economy in which both the government and the private sector participate. We want to maintain such incentives as are possible, set against the broad view of the nation's needs. We will always follow the democratic process in implementing our plans.

Let me relate this to the situation of American capital specifically. We have not had enough American capital in our country, and we want more. We do have some very good firms, like National Carbon Company (Union Carbide Corporation), Ludlow Jute Company, American Cyanamid Company, and Squibbs-Mathieson. There may have been occasional differences between manufacturers and government, which I believe occur even in the United States! But I do not think that these conflicts developed because of the way in which the business was managed or the conduct of the managers; fundamentally, our association has been cordial.

In considering this matter, one should appreciate the reasons for our national prejudice against foreign capital. Foreign capital and foreign domination have been combined in our country's history. The assignment of the East India Company, for instance, was to rule India, and foreign capital came into the country in that way. Consequently, it was considered an arm of foreign control.

Therefore, we feel strongly about not accepting any aid which we think might compromise our sovereignty or freedom. But unreasonable prejudice is ebbing, and so long as we hold to the principles embodied in our Constitution, we feel that there is no need to turn down help from countries which are friendly to us. The United States Government, for example, was most helpful in our First Five-Year Plan. No sensible Indian would say that the United States has failed to do what it could to enable us to implement our Plan.

In summation, then, we seek to fit foreign investment into our over-all plans, but we are not rigid in so doing. The particular requirements are matters for negotiation, adjustment, and understanding; and I personally believe that such arrangements cannot be determined by any set formula or treaty. The main element is mutual confidence. There are no short cuts, but, given mutual confidence and understanding, I am sure that programs which are satisfactory both to us and to American firms can be worked out.

WHY INVESTMENT IN LATIN AMERICA IS GOOD BUSINESS

Edmundo de Macedo Soares e Silva

THE RECENT HISTORY OF DIPLOMATIC RELATIONS between the United States and Latin America would fill pages, and one would hardly know what to wonder at most. Is it the spontaneous and invariable cordiality of our political agreements? Or is it the sincerity in the way we have approached problems affecting the unity of the Pan-American family and, at times, the very political stability of this hemisphere?

It is not surprising that the results have been generally so good on the official level, where men of such great merit have dominated the scene. These same constructive results, unfortunately, have not been obtained on the economic plane. Here we enter another field of Latin American relations, where the methods have been different and the consequences, accordingly, more disappointing.

Note: General Soares is President and Director, Brazil National Steel Company (Volta Redonda).

256

How can this unhappy contradiction be explained? I shall attempt to set forth an answer in these pages, but I will say at the outset that the principal reason is a lack of mutual understanding.

In Latin America not much is known about the geography and the history of the United States. And you in this country know even less about us. Personal contacts are rare, and prejudices based on assumptions that are not always correct are all too frequent. For instance, you may remember some of our immortal statesmen—Bolivar, Jose Bonifacio, and San Martin. But usually you remember only the unfavorable Latin American episodes. You forget the good things—such as the intervention of Ruy Barbosa in The Hague, and the immediate entrance of Brazil, following the United States, in the last two world conflicts.

It is customary for people in the United States to point to the occasional instability of Latin American democracies as a sign of social and political immaturity. But there are vital economic reasons as well —and it is in this area that the leaders of United States business can take action that will have favorable political implications as well as sound business results. Let us take a brief look at what Latin America has to offer.

NATURAL RESOURCES

Latin America covers more latitude than any other segment of the world. It is not all tropical country—outside of the Tropics are half of Mexico, the South of Brazil, almost half of Paraguay, all of Uruguay, and almost all of Chile and Argentina.

Even the tropical portion has extensive plateaus that counteract the latitude. Caracas, only ten degrees from the Equator, is 3,300 feet above sea level and has one of the most pleasant climates in the world. In Brazil, great mountain ranges put a vast area of our country at delightfully high altitudes. But so much for the climate. How about the people?

The population of Latin America is the most rapidly growing in the world—now 175 million; it will be up to 275 million in the next twenty years. Latin Americans at all levels of employment learn quickly, acquire a sense of responsibility, and produce satisfactorily. In addition, we have top men in all professions: medicine, law, engineering, and management.

In brief, Latin America possesses the area, the variety in climate, and the people necessary to attain great economic heights.

Next on our list of advantages are the resources of the soil. Because the Latin American nations have such a vast expanse in latitude and such high plateaus, they have a most varied land surface which ranges in climate from the frigid to the tropical. Since the tropical predominates, it is appropriate to examine this soil first.

The tropical earth is a great source of raw materials of vegetable origin, such as woods, medicinal plants, rubber, and fibers. Dudley Stamp, in his interesting book entitled *Our Undeveloped World*,* explains why the forests of lower latitudes have remained almost unexplored in an epoch of great wood shortages. He says that it is because the trees are of a different species—most of them hard woods of a type known as "tropical cabinet woods"—and so their use has been limited. Stamp's observations, however, express an old-fashioned idea that fortunately is now being modified. More and more uses are constantly being discovered for the tropical woods.

Latin America now has about 2.5 million square miles of such tropical forests, and 80% of this area is served by the great waterways of the Amazon Basin. Imagine the great potential that lies in this one asset alone—forests 83% the size of the whole United States!

The Latin American soils are of the highest productive value. The Andean plateaus, the well-irrigated valleys in many countries, the regions of volcanic origin, southern Mato Grosso, and the pampas of the Argentine, Uruguay, and Brazil are especially rich areas. Not content to let well enough alone, however, our agricultural experts are now studying the acidity of the soil, the destruction of organic materials by solar action, and the shallowness of the topsoil in for-

* Laurence Dudley Stamp, *Our Undeveloped World* (London, Faber & Faber, 1953).

ested regions. They are considering, too, the dangers of natural reforestation.

Tropical agriculture has progressed greatly, and food crops are both good and lucrative. Crops of international value—coffee, cotton, cacao, corn, rice, sugar cane, fibers, citrus plants, cocoanut, and bananas—have proved their economic worth and represent enormous riches. Thus the agricultural possibilities of Latin America range from the finest wheat and other grains of the temperate climates to the precious products cultivated only in the tropics.

Great soil potentials are not all that Latin America has to offer United States business. Let us consider its potential energy resources:

- Take hydroelectric power, which is estimated at more than 75 million horsepower. Only 6.5 million HP, or less than one-tenth, is now being utilized. (Incidentally, North America, excluding Mexico, uses less than one-fourth of its hydroelectric resources.) With the possibilities offered by modern civil engineering, this potential could be greater—and our water power is not generally limited by the usual winter season.

- Take petroleum with its tremendous resources. Production in 1950 was about 100 million tons, 40% greater than the United States output. Argentina, Colombia, Mexico, Peru, and Venezuela are already well-known as petroleum producing countries; now it is possible to add Bolivia and Brazil to the list. Brazil has developed its production in Bahia, and there are immense possibilities in the Amazon region.

- Consider coal. Clarence Field Jones stated that the reserves of coal in the Southern Hemisphere were small compared with those in the Northern Hemisphere, and that only Australia and South Africa had considerable quantities.* But do not be confused by the books!

The fact is that Colombia has extensive reserves. In the Andean region there is no place where coal *cannot* be found. Large subterranean deposits run across the country with especially rich

* Clarence Field Jones, *Economic Geography* (New York, The Macmillan Company, 1947).

veins in some areas, and reserves amounting to approximately 2 billion tons have been discovered 160 miles northeast of Bogota. Chile has mines to the south of Concepcion. In Mexico there is mineral coal in appreciable quantities, and Brazil, Peru, and Venezuela possess coal. The reserves of coking coal in Brazil are officially estimated at approximately 1.5 billion tons. Brazil uses its supply to make coke for the Volta Redonda steel plant, mixing it with coal imported from the United States.

So you see, Clarence Jones—and he was no different from almost all his contemporary geographers—was premature, and his statement is being disproved as the secrets of the Latin American subsoil are revealed.

• Take a look at Latin America's immense wealth in metal-bearing ores. Forget about our iron, copper, zinc, tin, and lead, which are well known and have already benefited the world economy. I am referring now to our manganese (in Brazil, Cuba, and Mexico especially), which is currently being substituted for Russian and Far East imports. In a short time these countries will be able to supply all United States needs. In addition, we have nickel, cobalt, titanium, aluminum, silver, bismuth, tungsten, rare earths, uranium, limestone, sulfur, fluorite, clays, and other refractory materials like magnesite and zircon. These ores are common in many of the countries and are either being fully exploited or initially developed.

What does all this mean? It means that the resources of the twenty Latin American Republics are of enormous significance. The kind of raw materials we have are already being utilized on an appreciable scale in the United States and in Europe. Hence there is no better investment anywhere in the world than in Latin America.

A GROWING MARKET

The resources that I have been discussing point to something more: the immediate importance of the Latin American market. I refer not only to the export market but to the consumer market as well. The latter is more important to the United States now than ever before because of the gradual loss of European and Oriental markets which it has suffered since the last war.

According to The Chase Manhattan Bank, production of goods and services in the twenty republics has now reached over $40 billion a year, double that of the mid-1930's. Imports have doubled, too, and the population—the number of potential customers—is increasing twice as fast as the world average. Chase also makes a prediction for the market of 1975: "Production in the neighborhood of $100 billion a year; population up more than 60% to about 275 million; imports from the United States totalling $7 billion—more than double the current rate." *

The struggle between the United States and the industrialized countries of Europe for the Latin American market is intense and will continue to be so. Up to now, Latin American imports have favored the United States. But this is being changed as Western Europe's position improves, both as a buyer and as a seller. Until now, the United States has maintained its role as the great seller, partly because of its tremendous capacity to import and to finance. I would warn, however, political change can radically alter that situation. For instance, the Chairman of your Senate Subcommittee on Appropriations for Agriculture has announced that he believes it is necessary to grow coffee or some similar plant in the United States. If this happens, each dollar withdrawn from the economies of the Latin American countries will be one dollar less with which we can buy from the United States.

The pattern of the Latin American capital goods import market has not yet been altered by industrialization. Take what is happening in steel production: we went from 300,000 tons a year before the last war to 2.2 million tons in 1954 (50% of this in Brazil), but our imports have not diminished in this time. We are still importing 3

* *Latin American Business Highlights,* a quarterly publication of The Chase National Bank, New York, September 1954.

million tons of steel every year, or approximately $400 million worth.

Industrialization does, however, alter the pattern of the consumer market. This was pointed out in the same Chase Manhattan Bank study, in these words:

> "As economic development changes the market, it changes the broad pattern of imports. The foreign exchange that Brazil saves on steel mill products and other items now produced locally, she spends on heavier imports of fuel and capital goods for her expanding industries. Fuel imports increased from 10% of the total before the war to 14% in 1952. At the same time capital goods climbed from 32% to 45%. *Raw materials and consumer goods declined in relative importance.* The same basic pattern shows up in the imports of Chile and Mexico when 1952 is compared with prewar years. The Argentine pattern is the same except that raw material imports registered a large gain instead of declining."

And yet, unfortunately for the long-term economic growth of Latin America, capital goods usually suffer the most when total imports must be cut. The theory is that these expenses can be postponed—but by so doing we postpone our economic progress. It is not easy to explain to our people that an expansion in steel facilities is more important than television sets.

FEATURES OF THE ECONOMY

These principal features of the geography and the market of Latin America lead us to a discussion of the chief characteristics of the economy of this vast region. The Latin American countries can be classified into three groups, according to the nature of their exports:

1. Countries of tropical agriculture—Brazil, Colombia, Cuba, Ecuador, and the Central American nations.
2. Countries of temperate zone agriculture—Argentina, Uruguay, and Paraguay.
3. Mineral-producing countries—Chile, Peru, Bolivia, Venezuela, and Mexico.

The external commerce of these twenty republics is dependent on the consumer's market in the more industrialized countries, which buys raw materials and agricultural products and sells manufactured goods and foodstuffs in return.

Exports of tropical foodstuffs increased substantially in the post-war era. Trade, especially with the United States, was steady until 1954. The terms of trade for coffee were favorable up to the recent decline in prices, partially caused by increased production, principally in Africa and Central America.

The temperate zone countries of Argentina and Uruguay, which had closer relations with the European countries, were handicapped after the last world war. The old Continent recovered slowly and fostered trade with those of its own colonies and territories that produced the same kind of goods as Latin America.

Now Europe is recovering and regaining the position it held in the past. Its sales of consumer and capital goods to Latin America are increasing, and it is already financing enterprises on reasonable terms. The Colombian steel plant at Paz del Rio and the Peruvian plant at Chimbote have French equipment and financing, and the expansion of the Brazilian alloy-steel plant (Acesita) is being equipped and financed by credits obtained in France and Germany.

Trade among the Latin American countries themselves is not yet very important because of the nature of their exports and the deficiency in their means of communication. However, the interchange has improved. Argentina's wheat, for example, pays for imports of coffee and manufactured goods from Brazil. Venezuela exports petroleum to Brazil. Nicaragua sends livestock to Peru. Chile supplies nitrates and copper and receives coffee, sugar, and cacao in return.

Taking the Latin American economy as a whole, its main characteristic can be stated this way: altogether, the Latin American countries do not have the products of exchange necessary to furnish them with the foreign credit indispensable to their development. With the exception of Venezuela, which has a large surplus from its exports of petroleum, none of the other countries can grow through exports alone. Thus there is a constant crisis of lack of exchange in the Latin American countries.

Let us look at Brazil, which is typical of the Latin American economy. Predominately a monoculture, depending on the international coffee market for the development of her internal economy, she has grave difficulties in maintaining the equilibrium in her balance of payments. While coffee production has increased, the consumer market has failed to grow. The slightest change in the terms of trade of this commodity seriously upsets the country's foreign exchange budget.

Because of United States overproduction, Brazilian cotton has been dumped on the market, with serious impact on the price. Our cacao has to compete with crops from Africa, where cheaper labor and other conditions can produce it at lower cost. The competition in vegetable oils from Africa and the countries of the Far East is also being felt strongly.

Practically speaking, Latin American mineral raw materials have only one market: the United States. And the swing in prices is frequent and violent, causing great disturbance among the exporters. These economic difficulties are reflected in the internal policies of the countries in crises, resulting in great losses in general prosperity and imbalance in international trade. That is why I say that all the potential difficulties in Latin America can be solved by sound foreign investments—both at the private and at the government level. Political disturbances in Latin America or anywhere else are generally a *result* of economic imbalance—not a *cause*.

POSSIBILITIES IN COLLABORATION

All these facts point to some clear conclusions as to the importance of collaboration between the United States and Latin America:

> The internal growth of Latin American countries requires an ever larger volume of investment.
> Exports of these countries are not increasing fast enough to allow them to finance this growth themselves.

Foreign investment is needed for two main reasons: to save internal financial resources for payment of previous external commitments, and to allow new growth.

But foreign investment effected only through financing, whether public or private in nature, is a burden for Latin America so long as the pattern of its export production cannot be changed.

The foreign investments of the greatest interest, then, are those that allow reduction of the pressure on the balance of payments, either by saving foreign exchange or by creating purchasing power in international means of payment. What I have in mind is investments destined to eliminate the so-called bottlenecks in production of power and improvement of the means of transportation.

Would such an investment policy be contrary to the interests of the United States? Let us see.

I venture to say that Arnold Toynbee is wrong in hinting that South America has little strategic importance at present. Its natural resources *are* necessary. Its human problems *do* deserve attention if the political stability of the Western Hemisphere is to be maintained.

The development of resources in the Latin American nations would create raw materials that the United States needs for its industry and its general well-being. The sales of these raw materials would give the Latin American countries greater means of exchange and permit them to increase their imports of United States products. The domestic production of consumer goods would raise the living standards of the people of Latin America, and in turn would stimulate increased imports of capital goods and services.

It is only through this policy of foreign investment that the Latin American countries can improve their capacity to import.

Consider Brazil again. Under normal conditions we *export* $1.5 billion worth yearly. This is a measure of our capacity to *import*. If the national economy does not develop—if we cannot improve our sources of power and transportation, explore natural resources, develop basic industries, and build consumer goods industries—our exportable production will not increase, and so our import capacity will remain at the same level. If exports do increase, however, import power will grow accordingly.

The United States has already adopted an investment policy in regard to Europe. The Marshall Plan did not have as its only objective the preservation of the culture of the Continent from which our forefathers came. It was also directed at economic reconstruction and at rebuilding the power to resist aggressions which are designed to destroy our concepts of life. The United States spent more than $50 billion for that purpose. Europe was reborn out of its ashes and became one of the most solid bulwarks for the defense of Christian civilization. At the same time, however, the United States created extremely strong competitors for its trade with Latin America.

And what about Latin America? During the same period, it received only $1.1 billion—2% of the total spent by the United States Government in its program of aid and assistance to foreign countries. Latin America needed, and still needs, this collaboration for the capitalization of its natural resources and for the revitalization of its economy, so hard-hit by the political and financial consequences of the last war.

Latin America's lack of sufficient foreign exchange to support a healthy international trade of goods and services has had two effects: (1) commerce has been handicapped and has fluctuated greatly, obstructing normal activities; and (2) we have experienced a surge of disorderly industrialization, which frequently takes advantage of an opportune market rather than creating definite values.

Drawing once more from a Chase Manhattan Bank's publication, *Business in Brief,*[*] we see that the investment rate is higher in Latin America than in other so-called underdeveloped areas of the world. However, as the article explains, ". . . the rate of population growth is higher, too. It averages 2.5% a year. So, even with a 3% per year rise in total production, living standards have been rising only about one-half of 1% annually since 1951."

The Europeans have shown perfect comprehension of the problem

---

[*] *Business in Brief,* The Chase Manhattan Bank, New York, April 1956.

and, in spite of their own difficulties, are organizing industrial enterprises with great future prospects in several Latin American countries. Often they collaborate with domestic capital. In Brazil, we have Mercedes-Benz, Bayer, Mannesmann, Kloeckner, Krupp, Schneider-Creusot, Volkswagen, and so on. One of the great consumers of American cars up to 1954, Brazil will now see the birth of an automobile industry of European origin in her territory.

United States businessmen often cite inflation and foreign exchange controls as factors against investments in foreign countries. It is necessary to observe that this state of affairs resulted largely from the postwar economic difficulties which I have already pointed out. But even in previous normal times we never had the desired investments in the necessary amounts. The United States currently invests less than 1% of its national income abroad; and of this total less than half is destined for the underdeveloped areas of the world.

A PROMISING POTENTIAL

Now I realize that great difficulties must be overcome to carry out the program which I have outlined. But the potentials are great, both in terms of improving the situation of an enormous area of our hemisphere and of increasing cultural and commercial relations with the United States.

The Latin American nations are convinced that the Americas should be one solid block; they are equally convinced that this is not possible without the strengthening of their own economies. Furthermore, only planned and continuous action in this direction will bring about lasting results. Emergency plans which are set up to overcome temporary crises can have only temporary effects. Economically responsible Latin Americans know that the establishment of an economy which will allow for their development will be equivalent to the creation, on a permanent basis, of a foundation which will cement permanently the political solidarity of the American Hemisphere—a solidarity necessary to defend our mutual personal convictions, our national institutions, and our way of life.

During the war, I frequently heard it said in this country that what was difficult to do would be done immediately and what was impossible would take a little longer. This philosophy should predominate now in relations between the United States and Latin America—but with one difference: in our relations there are only a few difficulties, and nothing is impossible.

SHOULD UNITED STATES CAPITAL GO ABROAD?

Sir Douglas Copland, M. Shafqat,
Walter Kotschnig, and UN Representatives

THE BURDEN OF LEADERSHIP*

MY ANSWER TO THE QUESTION posed in the title of this chapter—
"Should United States capital go abroad?"—is an emphatic "Yes!"
In expanding on that answer, I want to consider the matter from a
point of view which is somewhat broader than the issue of immediate self-interest.

Note: Sir Douglas Copland is High Commissioner of Australia to Canada;
Mr. Shafqat is First Secretary of the Pakistan Embassy at the United Nations;
Mr. Kotschnig is United States Deputy Representative to the Economic and
Social Council of the United Nations. John C. Baker, President of Ohio University and United States Delegate to the Economic and Social Council of
the United Nations, acted as moderator of the panel discussion on which this
chapter is based.

* By Sir Douglas Copland.

Needless to say, I think it is in the ultimate interest of United States businessmen to export capital. But I do not want to get into the question of investment at home versus investment overseas because each situation is different and must be determined on its own merits. Instead, I want to look at the wider picture of the world today and the responsibilities of all of us—particularly of the United States—to this world.

I recognize that this leaves me open to the challenge: "You come here as an Australian and talk about the responsibilities of the United States! Charity begins at home. Why don't you consider your own responsibilities?"

My reply is that we are doing this. I do not want to leave the impression that we have any great amount of capital to export; we have not. We are importers of capital. Nevertheless, we are trying to meet our international responsibilities through the Colombo Plan and the technical aid programs of the United Nations. All the countries of the free world are in this effort together and there is no way out; but the United States naturally has to bear much of the burden because of her great resources and capital supplies. Americans have to take a much more active part than the rest of us because of their position of leadership.

The economic world of today is like Gaul, which we learned in school was divided into three parts. There is the western sector, with America as the undisputed leader; the communist world, with its vigorous, developing economy; and the world of underdeveloped countries. We have to devise all our economic policies in relation to this framework.

The modern threefold world is new, entirely different from the one of a hundred years ago. It is even less like the one in which the countries of Western Europe were the great exporters of capital and the standard bearers of imperialism. In that world which is gone, everyone else was an appendage to Western European leadership.

What is the relationship between public and private enterprise in the new situation? The communist economy is, of course, committed to public ownership of everything of any importance, so the question of conflict between public and private ownership does not arise in their world. By the same token, the western economy emphasizes free enterprise. In the underdeveloped world, with its new nationalistic consciousness and aspirations and its urgent desire to lift the standards of living for all of its people with the utmost speed, it is inevitable that there will be large public investment. This is an inescapable fact. It is impossible to achieve rapid industrial expansion on a broad scale and raise living standards at the same time, unless it is done within the framework of a plan. And it cannot be done without a substantial degree of government investment.

The idea of "planning" is somewhat distasteful to us. The word implies total limitations on all types of economic activity and consequently appears to mean that our private enterprise system is weak and has failed. But to the underdeveloped country a plan is a beacon light, a guiding star in its present circumstances. Without a plan, no underdeveloped country will enter the promised land. Therefore, we have to rethink our attitude toward public versus private development to meet this new situation.

If the Free World is to compete successfully with the communist area, we must make far better and greater efforts in the underdeveloped countries. We must accept the fact that part of our assistance will take the form of public investment. We must realize that this public investment will be in the front line of development in those countries. It will establish the framework within which private enterprise will eventually take hold and prosper.

Of course, there will be varying degrees of public investment in the underdeveloped areas. In my own country, for example, a great deal of basic development is accomplished by governmental or semi-governmental authorities. Public investment is about 35% of the total. But that still leaves 65% for private activity, and we have plenty of examples of both local and foreign companies that have been growing very rapidly in the last ten years.

In the underdeveloped world, the planned frameworks are not yet altogether clear. But they are emerging and taking shape, and I am sure that they will be along the lines that I have sketched—a combination of governmental and private development. Capital exporting countries must therefore devise some permanent way in which the necessary capital can be supplied for government-sponsored ventures. At the same time, they must make sure that normal private investment by foreign and local businessmen can participate in the economy, in conformity with the laws and decisions of the countries concerned.

This is the situation with which we are faced, and it demands some fundamental adjustments on our part. It is equally important that the underdeveloped countries remain flexible as well, and resist the temptation to let the government assume all the responsibility. They are learning and experimenting; they may well find that a largely public economy is the sort of economy they want to have; or they may decide that less, rather than more, capital should be provided through the public sector. Be that as it may, these countries will have to do this experimenting and make these decisions for themselves, and we will have to find some meeting ground with them.

One thing is certain: we cannot get ourselves into a situation where we rigidly insist that private enterprise is the answer while they are staunchly maintaining that public enterprise is the right course to take. In the long run, my feeling is that neither of the two positions will prove to be the right one; I suspect that we will come to a compromise which we will discover together in the course of our experimentation.

It is difficult to predict the results of this testing process, but one thought along these lines might be worth raising. Suppose we were to blend the United States foreign aid program, the Colombo Plan, the efforts of the United Nations and all the other existing activities in the interests of economic betterment, into one great international agency, or group of agencies, with sections for technical aid by both private and public enterprise. Such a step might well lay the foundation for a permanently expanding world economy which would see the underdeveloped areas and the western world moving together and ultimately merging into one. Such a world would mean rising living standards and a better life for all.

OPPORTUNITIES IN PAKISTAN*

In Pakistan, we have tried to make clear that we are only too glad to accept foreign capital, and have acted to make certain that such investments are protected. But we feel that a general policy statement declaring foreign capital investments to be secure is perhaps not sufficient to satisfy prospective investors, particularly from the United States, so we have concluded a specific investment guarantee agreement with the State Department.

Insofar as our general policy is concerned, we have found it necessary to make major changes from time to time to adjust to the needs of investors. Our first approach was laid down in 1949; in a large number of industrial fields the share of control by foreign countries was held to around 50%. However, this policy did not stimulate the influx of much capital from abroad. Investments were slow in coming, even from Britain and other European nations with whom we had quite well-established commercial and industrial relations.

In 1954, the policy was revised drastically. We now offer foreign investors up to 60% of control over both capital and management in a large number of fields. As a matter of fact, it may be even more than 60% in industries which are essential for our country's progress. Nevertheless, we have still not had as active an interest as we expected in fields where we had hoped foreign investment would play a large role. This is particularly true in the basic industries such as power, chemicals, natural gases, steel, cement, and textiles.

This experience has led us to realize that Americans are not quite ready to enter a large number of fields abroad, though there are great opportunities for development and promise of substantial profits. They seem to feel that there are too many difficulties and risks involved in moving into areas like the Middle East, Southeast Asia, and the Far East. The adjustments which governments of underdeveloped countries would have to make in order to meet some of the implied demands of American businessmen might be more than they would

* By Mr. Shafqat.

care to undertake. However, I think we will eventually reach mutually satisfactory arrangements, especially since more and more United States companies abroad are now beginning to report to their colleagues that "it was not so far after all, and the hazards were not so many as we thought."

ADJUSTMENT AND COOPERATION *

There is no question in my mind that there are increasing opportunities for investment throughout the world. Quite a number of countries have changed their laws to facilitate the entry of capital from outside. But we hear more and more complaints at the United Nations that nothing is happening despite these changes. "We have improved our laws, but American capital is still not coming in," they tell us. And this fact, of course, reduces the pressure on these countries to make further changes.

This lack of response is most unfortunate, because the investment field is more promising now than it has ever been before. For a long time, the underdeveloped countries remained stagnant and offered very limited chances for investment. Now these countries are awake and want to develop just as far as they possibly can. To do this they are in need of private capital. At the same time, however, they are extremely sensitive about their independence and national sovereignty. The conditions which they place on foreign investments are stiffer, in some ways. Consequently, in order to take advantage of its enlarged opportunities, United States business has to be more flexible and adjust to the requirements which these countries establish.

If we are willing to cooperate in enterprises financed jointly by American and foreign interests, if we are willing to undertake training of the people in the country as a by-product of our investment, and if we go in with an eye to what these countries most need right now, the opportunities are unlimited. The latter point is most important. For example:

* By Mr. Kotschnig.

Traveling in the Far East recently, I came upon one country that wanted a basic chemical industry. An American firm was interested in moving in, but wanted to produce cosmetics for which there was a good market in the United States. If the company had been willing to work in the area of basic chemicals, producing the cosmetics as part of a larger effort, it would have had its license. As it was, the United States firm lost out on a good investment, and the Asian country had to look elsewhere for the chemical development it needed.

WHY INVEST ABROAD?

An Open Discussion *

From the floor: I constantly read reports which indicate that we are making new enemies all the time in the countries where we invest. The more we invest, the more we are suspected and the more hard feelings we create. The word I hear is "imperialism." We are accused of using our money to further the so-called "imperialistic aims of the American people."

Mr. Shafqat: Sometimes I suspect that public statements on political issues, in the U.N. and elsewhere, have misled many Americans into thinking that underdeveloped areas are hostile to foreign capital. Actually most leading statesmen from these countries agree on the desirability of such investments. But the international situation is such that they do not take a frank position in an open debate on inviting capital from a particular country or area.

We must remember that most of the underdeveloped countries are often in the dilemma of being expected to take sides between the great powers. They do not wish to take sides. They are untried and inexperienced, still trying to establish their own national identity, and engaged in the process of achieving domestic stability. They must be careful to forestall the accusation that they are playing into

---

* Businessmen present at the panel session on which this chapter is based raised certain questions which brought about the interplay of ideas reported more or less verbatim in this section.

the hands of either the communist bloc or the Western nations, because of the pressure from their people for "independence." They have to be extremely hesitant and thoughtful before accepting propositions that actually might be of great benefit to themselves as well as to the investor country.

Mr. Hadwen: * Canadian experience suggests that accelerated world economic development and more particularly recent Canadian economic progress would hardly have been possible without substantial foreign private capital investment by United States interests. This truism is illustrated by the course of Canadian economic history. By investment, of course, I do not mean governmental aid— I mean United States private capital participation in economic growth.

When you ask, "Is United States private foreign investment appreciated?", you raise an entirely different question. Let us be realistic; the businesses which invest abroad are primarily interested in profits from foreign sales. Their operations are not undertaken in the same way or for the same reasons as are international economic aid programs. Consequently, the concept of gratitude or appreciation is not really applicable.

It is fair to say, however, that large scale United States capital investment in Canada has been welcome and will continue to be welcome but that, while Canadians are pleased at the development of their country, they should not be expected nor are they asked to be appreciative or grateful for what are generally straight business transactions.

The Canadian attitude towards such investment is in part a reflection of the self-confidence of the Canadian Government. Canada believes that it can successfully and, I hope, to the mutual satisfaction of the legitimate United States and Canadian interests involved, integrate United States private capital investment into an economy whose development is, of course, the responsibility of the Government of Canada. Canadians have no fears on this score, nor, I think, need United States citizens.

* John Hadwen is adviser, Canadian Permanent Mission to the UN.

Sir Douglas: By and large, our experience has been that the reception we receive for a good business proposition in any mature country is a warm one. If you go out and do a job, minding your own business and staying out of politics, you will have no difficulty. But there are vast differences in attitude between, for example, the Netherlands and some of the less well-developed countries which have had no experience with foreign businesses operating within their borders.

In the latter situation, politics is mixed with business. You have to come in with something which is politically advantageous and will help make the existing government a little more stable in the process. Proposals along these lines will produce better relationships between private business and government.

As far as United States assistance is concerned, I have never noticed any tendency on the part of most countries to refuse American governmental aid, even though military and economic assistance have become intertwined. When Congress barks a little bit about the size of a foreign aid program, there are loud protests from the representatives of recipient nations. Naturally, some aspects are unpopular at times, but this is true in any endeavor. It is, after all, an uneasy head that wears the crown—and the Americans are wearing the crown now. You have to expect stories of unpopularity; no doubt they may even be partially true. But I do not think that it applies generally to American aid programs.

Mr. Epinat: * In France, the climate has become more friendly for foreign investment since World War II. There are no legal difficulties in the way—though there might be some psychological problems. I remember talking with a good old peasant friend of mine in 1948, when we were just beginning to feel the benefits of the Marshall Plan:

"What does Coca-Cola taste like?" he asked me. "Well," I replied, "it is like that medicine your mother used to give you when you were a child. Coca-Cola tastes very much like that." "I guess it is not

* Barthelemy Epinat is a Representative from France to the Economic and Social Council of the United Nations.

very good," he commented. "It isn't bad," I told him. "You get used to it." Nudging me, he said, "Don't you prefer Beaujolais?" I had to tell him, "Yes." Beaujolais, incidentally, is a light red wine.

The point of this story is that American investors have to be careful in their approach. If they try to tell everybody that the American system is perfect, and that everyone should drink Coca-Cola, they will set up psychological barriers. These barriers could ultimately have the effect of reducing investment opportunities, although the feelings, I am pleased to say, have not reached that point up to now.

Mr. Kopper: * Contrary to what may be the general impression, statistics show that the United States has made very substantial advances in its overseas investment program. Our experience, for example, is nothing short of phenomenal. We went out to the Middle East in 1933 when there was nothing but a large desert; now, twenty-odd years later, we operate the largest single American enterprise abroad. This growth has taken place in the midst of a grave political situation, where the attitude toward Americans generally has been hostile because of United States Government policy on the Palestine question.

Nevertheless, we have been able to abide by our rule of staying out of the affairs of the governments themselves. We have had minor difficulties with some of the Middle Eastern governments, of course. We will undoubtedly continue to have them, but despite these conflicts there can be no doubt that the total investment has been entirely worthwhile.

From the floor: We are hearing a great deal about the competition between Russian and United States or other western investments in some of the lesser developed countries. How do these developing nations feel about this? Do they favor one type of investment or one group over another? Are they playing one off against the other?

Mr. Pscolka: † I certainly am not the man to give here an answer

* Samuel C. Kopper is Assistant to the Chairman of the Board, Arabian Oil Company.

† Jaroslav Pscolka is a Representative from Czechoslovakia to the Economic and Social Council of the United Nations.

to the question of whether or not United States private capital should go abroad! But I do think that this question displays either misunderstanding or a lack of information.

Actually there are no Russian investments abroad. Take my country as another illustration: we do not export capital for direct investment but we do what we can for these countries in other ways. We can make available a special form of loan under a long-term agreement, for example, and supply capital goods. But we do not export capital for earning purposes, controlled by the foreign investor, nor do we settle down in any country abroad. We have a lot to do at home in building up our own economy, without getting into anything directly similar in other countries.

From the floor: Where can I get information about foreign investment opportunities and the various national laws in this field?

Mr. Kotschnig: There is ample material of this kind available through the United States Department of Commerce and through the United Nations. Also, most major banks will provide such material, and so will foreign consulates.

Part Four

FOREIGN OPERATIONS AND THE FUTURE OF CAPITALISM

BUSINESS LOOKS ABROAD AT ITS OPPORTUNITIES AND RESPONSIBILITIES

John C. Baker

IN 1946, SECRETARY OF STATE GEORGE C. MARSHALL spoke in Cambridge at Harvard Commencement and launched an idea which subsequently became the Marshall Plan. The plan, in essence, was to help Europe help itself. In Marshall's words: "Our policy is directed not against any country or doctrine, but against hunger, poverty, desperation, and chaos." This plan, as we all know, was an outstanding success and is still being talked about in many parts of the world. Without it, Western Europe today would not be a pillar of freedom, a staunch ally in the quest for a sound and durable free peace, and a flourishing economic center constantly achieving higher production levels.

Note: Mr. Baker, who acted as Chairman of the Conference, is President of Ohio University and United States Permanent Representative to the Economic and Social Council of the United Nations.

The time has come, however, when we must look beyond Europe. It is the fate of the entire world which concerns us now. I should like to stress the fact that this is not only a concern of government but a vital concern of business as well. The two outstanding world issues today are the preservation of peace and the need for a rising standard of living. American business and the United States Government must both be active participants in the fight to solve these problems.

In times of war American business has always played a significant and decisive role in international affairs. But in times of peace, unfortunately, both government and business seem to forget the place of business in foreign relations, and therefore business plays too minor a role in international economic affairs. At the present time, business is contributing to the maintenance of peace and higher standards of living only by limited participation and the payment of taxes. One of the most important questions being discussed in this book, therefore, is: What are the significant contributions that business today can make to national and international well-being? In other words, does business have both responsibility and opportunity abroad?

Behind the prosperity of our own country is a healthy and vigorous free enterprise system; it is only through the sustained operation of this system that our standards of living can continue to rise. What applies to the United States also applies to other countries. The Free World's welfare must be built on the foundation of strong, stable national economies—and this is where American business can and must do its part. I am not talking about the "dollar diplomacy" of past years. The world has changed greatly since that era: colonialism, as known then, is disappearing rapidly. Both business and government realize that our own security depends ultimately on the essential soundness of the international economy. The welfare of the world is also the welfare of American business.

Unfortunately, many Americans do not appear to understand these facts. Secretary of the Treasury George M. Humphrey has repeatedly proposed to Congress tax incentives and other aids to encourage United States capital and technical skills to go abroad. His proposals have had little success so far. Why is it that our country can mobilize more political support for taxes than for tax relief to encourage the capital investment and technical assistance which are so desperately needed overseas? Apparently many people believe that only corporation profits are at stake in Secretary Humphrey's proposals. This is a wholly untenable position today. Our system of free enterprise has made possible the present high standard of living in our country and in certain areas abroad. Free enterprise must be encouraged to serve mankind in other parts of the world. Such cooperation might supplement, or might even take the place of, gifts and loans.

To increase the standards of living in all parts of the world, two simple basic elements are required: capital and technical skills or know-how. American business has both the capital and the know-how, and it can, by exporting them, become part of the program to raise the standards of living and to preserve peace.

No nation, not even one as prosperous as our own, can long retain a position of leadership if it is not also a source of well-being to others. Large areas of the world are wavering between two opposing ways of life—one freedom and the other submission to the new tyranny of authoritarian government. We are now at one of these crucial periods in history with all the elements present which can lead to war, loss of liberty, and chaos, or to peace, freedom, stability, and a richer life for all. Dr. Alfred North Whitehead, for many years a professor of philosophy at Harvard, sensed this, I am sure, when he wrote: "The great political convulsions happen when the economic urge of the masses dovetails with some simplified ideal end."

Let us not be frightened by the facts but rather accept the great present-day challenge facing our country and especially business. This challenge is to aid the peoples of the world through sound economic measures in their struggles for peace, freedom, and a higher standard of living. These are the blessings of our civilization envied the world over. American business is in an ideal position to take leadership in this struggle. Here lie both the opportunity and the responsibility of business which have been discussed in the pages of this book.

BUSINESS RELATIONS ABROAD—CAN CAPITALISM SURVIVE?

Raymond W. Miller, The Right Reverend Monsignor L. G. Ligutti, Sidney E. Sherwood, and John B. Fox

CAPITALISM IS UNDER ATTACK in many places at this midpoint in the twentieth century. If it survives—and there is a real doubt whether it can—it will be because of the type of economic system which we have developed in North America and the skill with which we have described it to others.

Note: Mr. Miller, who makes the introductory remarks, is Visiting Lecturer on Business Administration, Harvard Business School, and acted as moderator of the panel discussion on which this chapter is based; Msgr. Ligutti is Observer of The Holy See to the Food and Agriculture Organization of the United Nations; Mr. Sherwood is Secretary, Export-Import Bank; and Mr. Fox is Director of Overseas Relations, Harvard Business School.

In 1951 I wrote an article for the *Harvard Business Review* on the affairs of Asia, in which I pointed out that men and women had been swept behind the Iron Curtain at the rate of 250,000 each day from 1945 to 1950. That trend has since been halted. But there is no reason to believe that the danger is over, because the United States has not been able to export its ideas in a way that people can understand. Our goods and our technical know-how are accepted; our beliefs and principles are too often rejected. As a matter of fact, "capitalism" is probably the most misunderstood and reviled word in the world today; our new type of "service capitalism" is too often confused with "exploitive capitalism."

It seems to me that there are three approaches we can take in acting to combat this hostility and clear up these misunderstandings. One is the philosophical and the public relations method; a second lies in the area of how we do business abroad, and how we conduct ourselves; and the third is in the field of education. The contributors to this chapter will examine each of these avenues and describe their own experiences as ambassadors of the capitalist system overseas.

NEEDED: A NEW ENLIGHTENMENT*

My comments in this chapter are based on observations and considered meditation about capitalism and the fundamentals of religion. By the term religion, I am not referring to any specific faith such as Christianity, Judaism, Buddhism, or Confucianism, but rather to the fundamental natural law which prescribes those moral standards which are universal.

These thoughts emerge from a great deal of travel and many talks with the leaders and the people in countless lands. I recently returned from a seven months' trip to the Far East, where I visited practically all the countries that are accessible to outsiders. Two years ago I journeyed through Africa, and two years before that I was in the Near East. In addition, I have spent a great deal of time in Latin America. As a matter of fact, I am very seldom at home!

* By Msgr. Ligutti.

Basic Purpose of Business

Socrates went about the streets repeating, "Know thyself," and he was made to drink hemlock. I hope I do not meet with the same fate, because I too should like to make a plea for self-knowledge. We must understand our basic goals before we can improve our methods for achieving them and win acceptance by other people.

Socrates asked questions—let me start by doing the same thing. What is the purpose of being in business? The answer is that each of us, as a human being, is a member of society, and doing business is the way many have chosen to help that society progress toward peace and a better living for all. Business, then, is a service, a means whereby we create material satisfactions for the individual and improve the general standards of society.

The real purpose of business is not accomplished through donations to charity and attempts at corporate do-goodism. Rather, it is achieved through a sense of justice and human dignity, a consciousness of social responsibility, and an unswerving loyalty to the principles of freedom and democracy. Underlying all this is a firm belief in God and the moral law.

These lofty moral-social purposes do not exclude a material reward —a well-earned profit for intelligence and diligence. But the separation of business from ethics is impossible. Theologically, man is not essentially and irrevocably bad, and businessmen do not act as if he were. "Do others before they do you" may be satisfying to a beast but it has not proved very satisfying to man.

A Bad Start

In spite of its ethical base, however, modern capitalism had a very bad start from a public relations viewpoint. The early captains of industry demonstrated little concern for the general welfare and well-being. If they recognized a higher purpose in their activity than the securing of an immediate profit, it was not obvious to the public. Helena Sara Zahler, in her book *Eastern Workingmen and National*

Land Policy, 1829–1862, comments on the shortsightedness of the first capitalists and their unwillingness to share the fruits of their prosperity:

"This period of the rapid growth of labor unions did not last long. But demoralized as it was by the panic of 1837 and the depression that followed, organized labor was sufficiently persistent to frighten conservative thinkers like Bishop Alonzo Potter and Francis Lieber. In a special Appendix to his widely used economics text, Potter denounced labor unions as "infidel," destructive of the rights of employer, apprentice, and unorganized worker, likely to create permanent class distinctions, and, worst of all, unmindful of the principle of supply and demand, one of the eternal laws of Nature and Nature's God. In spite of the Massachusetts decision in the case of *Commonwealth v. Hunt* that unions were not necessarily conspiracies in restraint of trade, a political philosopher like Francis Lieber still believed that unions led to "insufferable social tyranny, evil habits, and fearful crimes." Three years later, in 1845, the Philadelphia Board of Trade indicated its agreement with such reasoning by petitioning the Pennsylvania legislature to outlaw associations to raise wages." *

If the businessman's outright repudiation of the rights of workers was not enough to arouse public antipathy, the cause of capitalism suffered even more through the blatant egoism of some of the prominent industrialists of the age. In an article called "The Reserved Section," Wilbur D. Nesbit relates:

"At the time of the great anthracite coal strike of 1902, George F. Baer, head of the coal trust, was quoted as declaring: 'The rights and interests of the laboring man will be protected and cared for, not by labor and agitation, but by the Christian men to whom God in his infinite wisdom has given control of the property interests of this country.' " †

Nesbit's concept, in poetic form, of the way the early capitalists

---

* New York, Columbia University Press, 1941, p. 11.

† *The Cry for Justice,* An Anthology of the Literature of Social Protest, edited by Upton Sinclair, with an introduction by Jack London (New York, Upton Sinclair, 1925), p. 679.

viewed his opportunity for profit as a natural, inalienable, and unquestioned right, is worth quoting here:

> "In the prehistoric ages, when the world was a ball of mist—
> A seething swirl of something unknown in the planet list;
> When the earth was vague with vapor, and formless and dark and
> void—
> The sport of the wayward comet—the jibe of the asteroid—
> Then the singing stars of morning chanted soft 'Keep out of there!
> Keep off that spot which is sizzling hot—it is making
> coal for Baer!' " *

As the capitalist system has matured through the years, these early mistakes have largely been rectified. While the weaknesses of capitalism produced influential men like Marx, Engels, Lenin, and Stalin, and powerful forces like communism, socialism, and fascism, its strengths have built prosperity in large parts of the world. The fight for higher wages and better working conditions; the Encyclicals of the Popes, the *Rerum Novarum* of 1891, and the *Quadragesimo Anno* of 1931 issued in the interests of higher living standards; and the gradual adjustments brought about by larger consumer demands and increased markets—all this has had an effect and has produced the society we in the West know today. However, we must constantly remind ourselves that huge areas of the world have never experienced a capitalistic society and do not understand either the theory behind our system nor how it actually works. Some 60% of the earth's population—mostly tillers of the soil—remain untouched by the changes wrought in the West.

Changing the World's Opinion

There are, then, two jobs facing us:

- To make all capitalists—all businessmen—realize that enlightened self-interest is to their own advantage, that conducting their affairs with the higher social purpose of business in mind will

* *The Cry for Justice.*

produce the greatest benefits for themselves as well as for society at large.

- To show the world that modern capitalism *is* enlightened, that it has resulted in progress and improved living, and that it can achieve peace and prosperity for all.

We have made more headway on the first point than on the second. What is the world's opinion and judgment of capitalism and American democracy? Sad to relate, capitalism is often considered, even today, as one and the same with colonialism and human exploitation. If I found one place where this attitude persists, I found hundreds: in Indonesia, Japan, Korea, Formosa, Burma, Siam; it is even prevalent all over Europe.

In an article in *The New York Times* magazine entitled "For a New Foreign Aid Concept," Barbara Ward wrote:

> "One may ask ... how Soviet propaganda has continued to include the United States—the least imperialist great power in recorded history—in the imperialist smear. But the answer is clear. It relies partly upon 'guilt by association' brought about by America's link with its Western colony-holding allies.
>
> It also uses the lunatic syllogisms of Marxism—'all capitalists are imperialists. America is capitalist, therefore it is imperialist.' But it can also exploit a fact of colonial history not always understood in the West but painfully remembered in Asia.
>
> .... The Western powers, for instance, secured many of their semicolonial privileges in China by helping the Manchu Emperor to defeat the great Tai Ping revolt of the nineteenth century. Against this quite recent historical background, it has been easy for communist propaganda to interpret American support for Chiang Kaishek in the Chinese civil war as the re-entry point of 'Western imperial control' in China." *

An Indonesian leader explains his nation's anticapitalist feelings this way:

> "Nationalism in Indonesia is anticapitalist—largely because capitalism here is Western, and, specifically, Dutch. This is also one of

* March 11, 1956, p. 42.

the reasons why in Indonesia nationalism and communism can go hand in hand. Nationalism in Indonesia gains its chief support from an impoverished population, while capitalism is chiefly non-Indonesian, whether Western or Chinese. As a result of economic and social competition, racial differentiation has been accentuated and distorted into racial antagonism. Consequently it is easy for the communists to present their antiimperialistic and anticapitalistic agitation under the guise of patriotism and nationalism, and it is no easy task for the nationalists to detect the true nature of communism." *

We ask ourselves why we are so vulnerable. One answer can be found in an advertisement that appeared in *The New York Times* of June 12, 1956. The space was paid for by the *New Bedford Standard Times,* Basil Brewer, publisher. Here is the message:

"Strictly speaking ... foreign aid is national impoverishment. It is acceptable if it buys political advantages. Otherwise it is lunacy.

.... There would be less anti-Americanism in the world if America abandoned its philanthropic aspirations, its vocation of Santa Claus, its transcendental morality, and its missionary trappings, all its boy-scout gear, and if, at last, it followed openly and intelligently the policy of its own interest."

This sort of thinking is the best material for communist propaganda that we can supply. Tragically enough, the people in the United States who are paying for and supporting this kind of talk are honest, good, and sincere. They ought to be more intelligent, but they are not. They ought to know whom they are serving—what impact their words have around the world, and who is using them for what purpose. But unfortunately, they do not.

While I was in the Far East in the spring of 1956, the foreign pages of all the newspapers there were filled with the Autherine Lucy case. All the details were printed on the front pages, day after day, week after week, long after the furor had died down in the

* Sutan Sjahrir, "Problems the Country Faces," *The Atlantic Monthly,* June 1956, p. 119.

United States. There were also stories of the wetbacks in Texas and labor trouble in California—little items like these are exaggerated and built up by the communists for propaganda purposes.

Once I argued with a group of Chilean priests who were saying, "My, you people are slave-drivers—you pay your laborers so little." I pointed out that even if some were paid as little as fifty cents an hour—and very few are—they would still be collecting more money each hour than Chilean school teachers make in a day. But I fear the clerics remained unconvinced. Apparently they fail to appreciate the changes of the last fifty years. As Frederick Lewis Allen observed:

> "It has often been noted that when the orators of Moscow berate American capitalism and turn their invective on Wall Street, they are a couple of generations out of date; one might say, more specifically, that a typical communist propagandist of the 1950's sounds exactly as if he were reacting angrily to the news in the morning papers of March 3, 1901." *

Perhaps much of the difficulty America runs into can be boiled down to a problem in semantics. We describe our way of doing business as capitalism, and yet in much of the world this word connotes a system far different from the actual economic organization of the United States today. In the minds of too many people, capitalism stands for the self-seeking, unrestrained type of enterprise of the nineteenth century. William Ichabod Nichols, in his article, "Wanted: A New Name for Capitalism," argued that the phrase is outdated and no longer appropriate. He asked, "How shall we describe this system—imperfect, but always improving, and always capable of further improvement—where men move forward together, working together, building together, producing always more and more, and sharing together the rewards of their increased production?" † The author said that he had heard various suggestions, such as "the new capitalism," "democratic capitalism," "economic democracy," "in-

* *The Big Change, America Transforms Itself 1900–1950* (New York, Harper & Brothers, 1952), p. 80.
† *Reader's Digest*, May 1951, pp. 3–4.

dustrial democracy," "distributism," "mutualism," and "productivism," but he wondered if there might not be a better term. And he invited readers to write in their own suggestions. Nichols had 15,000 replies, and later remarked that never in his whole editorial experience had he touched so live a nerve.

It might be that by finding a new term to fit our business system we can facilitate our task of changing world opinion and turning hostility into acceptance. The fact is that United States capitalism is a veritable devil in the minds of many peoples. We may sell our products abroad, but our reputation is as low as one can imagine. We are mistrusted, we are accused of everything under the sun. We are crooks, we want to subjugate people, conquer them, make them pay through the nose. Modern decent capitalism, fair competitive service, lower prices, higher wages, better living standards, plus a fair and justifiable profit—none of these have been sold abroad as a part and parcel of our capitalist system.

A great sales job must be done in all the danger areas of the world. To save itself, capitalism must realize its social purpose—service to society—and act accordingly. It must prove that only through a system of honest competition can the greatest benefits be secured for all the people.

As individuals, we must be the best that we can be—perform, as executives, in a top-notch manner—to be, in short, good businessmen. What is a good businessman? A good businessman fits into a dynamic society, national, and international. He foresees the material needs of today but does not overlook the social needs of tomorrow. He exercises his intelligence, his foresight, his ingenuity. He seizes time by the forelock, he abides by the Golden Rule, and he is successful both at home and abroad.

GOVERNMENT LENDING AND UNITED STATES PRIVATE ENTERPRISE ABROAD *

I am tempting Providence in this chapter, because it is always dangerous to hold up a government institution as a model when writ-

* By Mr. Sherwood.

ing for a group of businessmen! Nevertheless, the government corporation with which I am connected has had some experiences in its financial dealings with foreign countries from which it has drawn certain policies which I believe are applicable, at least in part, to private business ventures in other countries.

As a matter of fact, the Export-Import Bank's operations are directly associated with the operations of United States businessmen engaging in foreign trade. As the principal foreign lending arm of the United States Government, the Bank facilitates and assists the country's overseas trade. Although we are one government agency that would like to see private capital assume the entire burden of financing United States overseas trade, we believe that we provide a real service by spreading our kind of capitalism in other countries in cooperation with private capital.

Financial Assistance through Loans

There are several ways in which the Bank fulfills this basic function. Perhaps the most important is the financial assistance which it provides to other countries that need United States equipment and services. These loans are sometimes made to the governments for necessary public works projects; sometimes they are made for private developments. In both cases, the Bank has found that the responsibility for the success of the project, including its management, is best placed with the borrower. In this way the borrowing country may take pride in the successful development of its own resources and can have no alibi for failure.

A good case in point is the Volta Redonda Steel Mill in Brazil. Back in 1942 the Brazilians came to the Export-Import Bank requesting a loan to build a steel mill which would enable them to develop their extensive iron resources. They admitted that they had no experience in making steel, but the facility was clearly needed. In making the loan, the Bank provided that the money would be available not only for steel-making equipment but also for the employment of steel engineers during the construction and early operational period. When the plant was in operation, the Brazilians hired a steel man from Pittsburgh as their general manager. He was distinctly *their* employee, not ours—and they took real pride in that fact. The president of the company was a Brazilian, and it was a Brazilian enterprise in the form of a mixed corporation. The result has been most satisfactory. More and more private Brazilian capital has come into the undertaking, and the company is producing over 40% of Brazil's steel needs. It has declared substantial dividends during recent years. Incidentally, Brazil is importing more steel products today than it did before the mill was built.

Although this was primarily a government undertaking at the outset, the same principles apply to private projects. Both borrower and lender must recognize that it is the country's own resources and industry which are being developed. The Arabian American Oil Company is an excellent example of this approach in the private sector of foreign investment. Their story is told elsewhere in this book, so I will not attempt to review their history, but I do want to mention some cardinal points in their policy which have been major factors in their success.

> First of all, the company recognized that the oil which it was pumping out of the Arabian desert was Arabian oil and that it enjoyed a concession from the Arabian government for the development of this resource. ARAMCO has succeeded in establishing the feeling in Arabia that it is in partnership with the Arabs. It has done this not only by having Arabs on its board of directors but by conducting an expensive and effective educational and training program for its Arab employees. When I was there a few years ago, some 25,000 Arabs were gainfully employed by the company, many of them receiving vocational training and education equivalent to a high school education in the United States. Promising young Arabs were being sent to the American University at Beirut for summer courses in economics, history, and languages.
>
> The company made it possible for some of its Arab truck drivers to purchase their trucks on an installment plan. I understand one enterprising businessman now has a fleet which he purchased over the years. He is operating these trucks under contract with ARAMCO. His story is a nice example of transplanting that essential element

of the American capitalistic system—the opportunity for the entrepreneur in business. It demonstrates a kind of capitalism in action that these people never knew existed.

ARAMCO is also maintaining an agricultural experiment station on the Al-Karj Oasis designed to show the Arabs what can be done with their land and water. In addition, the company supplies water and first aid on some of the caravan routes along the Tap line. All this activity has redounded to ARAMCO's benefit in the form of good will and greater security.

Government Participation with Private Capital

The risk of expropriation has been a real obstacle to the flow of United States private investment abroad ever since the end of World War II. In many instances the Export-Import Bank, by helping to finance private investment overseas, has been able to provide some political protection to the enterprise.

An example of this participation with private capital is the large line of credit that has been established for the development of a huge copper deposit in Peru. The history of that loan application is an interesting one. A large American copper company applied for the loan some time ago. At the time the Export-Import Bank felt that private capital could do the whole job. Furthermore, the copper supply situation was not sufficiently critical to require public money. Finally, we felt that there should be more private equity in the project.

Suddenly the long-run copper supply situation changed, and the company renewed its application for a loan. The project was going to cost over $200 million; they wanted $100 million for the purchase of United States machinery and equipment. The Bank advised the company that they would authorize the credit if the concern itself raised sufficient private capital to match the $100 million. It did so by joining with three other large American mining companies; the final investment came to well over $100 million in private equity.

Thus the government, acting through its Export-Import Bank,

served as a vehicle for private investment capital to open up a new source of copper for import into the United States. With the government providing some protection against the political risks by participating in the establishment of the enterprise, the private interests were placed in a position to undertake the risk.

The Bank also facilitates United States business relations abroad with so-called "exporter credits." The Bank picks up 60% of the notes of a foreign importer and requires that the exporter not only receive a down payment of 20% but also that he participate at his own risk up to 20% of the invoice value. This type of credit was primarily designed to place the United States exporter in a competitive position in those overseas markets where foreign competitors were able to extend longer terms by virtue of assistance from their governments, This situation was particularly critical during the recent transition from the sellers' to the buyers' market.

The Bank extends other forms of credit to assist United States businessmen in foreign trade and investment undertakings. I have mentioned these particular ones because they raise the fundamental question of how much government financial assistance is necessary as United States business expands overseas.

The expansion of such business relations is essential to the survival of the United States brand of capitalism.

Development in the East

Whether or not capitalism can survive depends largely on the direction which economic development takes in the so-called underdeveloped countries. I would stress particularly the countries of the Middle East and South Asia, because I am certain that Western businessmen are going to meet stiffer competition in these areas than anywhere else.

If United States business is to succeed in this part of the world, investors going into the area should keep one fundamental fact clearly in mind: they should recognize that there is a distinction between the United States brand of capitalism and the capitalism which the countries of the Middle East and South Asia have experienced.

United States capitalism has developed a flexibility which is part of the maturing process of any system. Specifically, it has shown the ability to adjust itself domestically to the social forces of the twentieth century. It has discovered that the good will of the community in which it operates is a tangible asset—that it is sound economics to invest money in maintaining this good will. If United States business can carry this line of thought abroad and can persuade people and governments in other countries that this is truly its basic philosophy, all doubts in my mind about the ultimate survival of our kind of capitalism will be erased.

But persuasion will not be easy because this is not the kind of capitalism which our friends in the East have known. They are acquainted only with a more primitive, early nineteenth-century brand. Whether colonial or native, private enterprise in these countries has generally been exploitive and unmindful of the social responsibility which a more mature United States capitalism has adopted as part of its basic philosophy during the last half-century.

These countries are just emerging from a long history of outside subjugation—economic, political, or both. They are on the threshold of independence. Because the capitalism they have known has been one of economic domination, frequently accompanied by political domination, all foreign capital has come to be suspect. In their minds, it is a potential threat to their newly won freedom. Extreme neutralism and nationalism are understandable products of their fear for that independence, and a Western business enterprise will not prosper in these lands unless it can overcome this psychological hurdle in the course of its negotiations and early operation.

A few years ago I served as financial consultant with the United Nations Economic Survey Mission for the Middle East. The purpose of this group was to see what could be done by way of economic development projects which might facilitate establishment of peace between the Arabs and the Israelis. At the start we had difficulty in getting the Arab governments to talk with us. Later I found out that they looked on this mission as a new and more powerful device for economic domination, coming in under a United Nations banner and backed by United States resources. They thought we were out to do what the former colonial powers could no longer do on their own. A local official told me that it was only after the Arabs became convinced of the sincerity of the men connected with the United Nations mission—when they came to realize that we had no sinister motives and were trying to help them on a partnership basis—that they felt they could place their confidence in us. I am sure private businessmen going into this part of the world will have the same sort of experience.

As I mentioned before, United States businessmen will encounter some very stiff competition in the Middle East and South Asia. European goods can be sold cheaper in these markets because of the shorter distances involved. But the intense competition we face from the powerful monolithic state to the north of these countries is much more important.

Although the structure of the Soviet Union is the antithesis of capitalism, it has recently found it expedient to adopt many of the traditional United States techniques of economic competition. It sends emissaries offering technical assistance, supports trade fairs, and uses all sorts of modern machinery. The result of all this is that communism may appear to be some kind of free enterprise assistance to the less sophisticated countries, and may even seem more appealing than the United States brand. It will take some doing on our part to meet this Russian competition; it will require the best efforts of government and business to deal wisely in the chancelleries and market places of the countries of the Middle East and South Asia.

Conclusion

The point I want to emphasize is that the major responsibility for seeing to it that a capitalistic structure based on free enterprise continues to thrive in this world lies with the United States businessmen and private investors abroad. In the long run, they will be the most decisive factor in creating and maintaining friendship or enmity between nations. I do not underestimate the effects of diplomacy and cultural interchange or the exchange of scientific knowledge or technical assistance, all of which, if properly conducted, can be potent factors in establishing a world where men may ultimately live in peace and prosperity. But there is no substitute for friendly economic intercourse between nations as a basis of mutual understanding and good international relations. Seldom in history has an international political agreement existed for long when there was no mutually profitable exchange of goods between the nations concerned.

As I said earlier, United States capitalism is successfully adapting itself to the forces of the twentieth century. I feel that the most encouraging evidence of this adaptation is our growing recognition that we are creating bigger and better markets for United States exports and better sources of products that the United States needs to import by helping to develop the economy of another country. If we continue to operate on this philosophy, the international economy will expand and develop. Thus can we lay the foundation for an ever-increasing interchange of goods produced by private enterprise.

THE ROLE OF EDUCATION*

Some seven or eight years ago, Dr. James B. Conant, then President of Harvard, was asked to visit Australia. At the same time, Erwin D. Griswold, Dean of the Harvard Law School, was invited to New Zealand. On the day of their departures for the South Pacific, Dr. Conant said to Dean Griswold, "God willing, I will meet you in Nandi"—the place where the air routes split, one going to Australia and the other to New Zealand. Several months later, their trip completed, the Conants were sitting in the waiting room in Nandi when who should walk in but Dean Griswold. Griswold spotted them across the room, dashed over, embraced Mrs. Conant, and shook hands with the President. He was so excited about this coincidence that he wanted to share it with someone, so he looked around the waiting room and saw three girls

* By Mr. Fox.

sitting there. Going over to them, he said, "Excuse me, I want to introduce myself. I am Erwin Griswold, Dean of the Law School of Harvard University." The girls made no response, but he went on undaunted. "And there is Dr. Conant and Mrs. Conant. He is President of Harvard University." There was a little pause and finally one of the girls said, "We are models from Dallas, Texas, and we are on the way back from Sydney; it really doesn't make any difference what your racket is, so long as you get a trip out of it!"

My racket is education, and I have had many trips because of it. On all these journeys, one question introduces itself into my thinking over and over again: do not the educational systems which exist in these areas have to be examined at the same time that we are trying to help these countries to develop further?

I well know how important Mr. Sherwood's field is. Credit and banking facilities are vital, and economic development is very significant. I agree with Monsignor Ligutti that the relationship between business and ethics must be demonstrated overseas. Many of the authors of this book have mentioned administrative practices which must be followed. But in the final analysis, if we do not move in with some clear-cut educational philosophy, we will only influence a small portion of the population.

By educational philosophy, I do not mean any specific techniques. I am referring to an approach which is based on and expresses the dignity and worth of individuals. For education in this nation represents our attempt, as best we can perceive and implement it, to help each individual realize his own role in the world, his own place in society, and at the same time to help him learn to respect others. The case history of the new business school in Turkey demonstrates what I mean in concrete terms.

Business Education in Turkey

In 1952 a group of men from the Ford Foundation went out to the Middle East. Two of them were asked by Turkish universities if they would assist in improving their educational facilities. The Ford Foundation then turned to the Harvard Business School for someone who could go to Turkey and explore the situation as it related to business education. Shortly thereafter, two of us undertook the mission.

Our job was to evaluate the attitude of the business community toward a school of administration similar to the Harvard Business School, and to find out what was already being done. For our part, we said that we were interested in an institution that would be distinctly Turkish in character, rather than an American importation. We had before us an example of the weaknesses in the importation approach, because we noticed that the patterns which already existed had been brought from France roughly seventy-five years ago. These plans, which worked well enough in Paris, were barely applicable to Turkey.

In addition, we tried to discover whether the personnel of the universities in Turkey were entirely satisfied with what was being done in the teaching of business administration. We soon found that they were somewhat discontented, dissatisfied, and anxious for change.

Our problem then became one of implementation. The first step was to make sure that the Turks themselves decided where this school should be located. I am convinced they would have been delighted to have us tell them where the school should go, but we resisted their pressure. We called a meeting of people from four different possible locations for the school, and laid the question in their laps. I do not think they had ever dealt with a foreigner on that basis before—but it worked. They decided that the school should be established at the University of Istanbul—so it was a Turkish decision, not an American one.

We then brought five teachers from the faculty at Istanbul University to be trained at Harvard in teaching and research methods— but *not* in content. We stressed the importance of student-centered education, because we felt it clearly exemplified our belief in the dignity of man and the worth of each individual's contribution.

The school is now under way; its first class entered in the fall of 1956. Though the Harvard Business School has continued to assist in its growth, it is entirely a Turkish institution, and there is no atmosphere of United States direction, interference, or "imperialism."

As I think about our experience in Turkey and recall the deep-seated problems which face these people and others like them in vast areas of the world, I am inclined to rephrase the question which I raised. I wonder if we can afford *not* to help establish educational institutions based on this philosophy as we go abroad with aid and investment?

QUESTIONS AND ANSWERS*

From the floor: Speaking as a citizen—and a businessman—of the Middle East, I can say that we are ready for American capitalism if you will bring it in the right spirit. We need money in our part of the world if we are to correct things that we know are wrong in our daily life, but the money must be accompanied by the values which have just been described.

Too often in the past United States business dealings have been tainted with nationalism, politics has been mixed with capital, and people have tried to use economic aid as a lever to force us to do things they wanted. I can give you a typical example:

> A leading American businessman—a corporation president—was sitting in on a meeting which was studying legislation that my country of Lebanon wanted to adopt in connection with the regulation of insurance companies. He disagreed with what we wanted to do, and finally said, "Gentlemen, if you decide to pass this legislation, I will have to go to my government and urge them to cut off all foreign aid for your country."

* Businessmen present at the panel session on which this chapter is based raised certain questions which brought about the discussion reported more or less verbatim on these pages.

From the floor: Why is there so much anti-Americanism in these foreign countries? Why do the people say, "Yankee, go home?"

Msgr. Ligutti: In the first place, anti-Americanism is not as widespread as some people here at home would have us believe. The few signs on the walls and the few newspaper criticisms do not express the general sentiments of the people.

Secondly, the negative sentiments are not so much anti-Americanism as anticapitalism. It is this latter attitude that we must counteract, and we should distinguish between the two.

Mr. Fox: One summer when I was working in Europe I thought I would put signs on my own luggage saying "Yankee, go home," because that is the way I felt quite often! I was certainly not the most popular man on the continent, and I think I know the reason why. As I moved around from place to place, I found all too often that I had been preceded by incompetent representatives of the United States. I don't pretend to be so overcompetent, but some foreigners with whom I talked clearly radiated the attitude of "Here is another damned fool American, come to tell us how to run things." Furthermore, red tape and inefficiency kept getting in the way. Many people I met did not know in advance when I was coming or what I was doing there. I think that the anti-Americanism which does exist can often be attributed to our failure to get the right kind of people for overseas positions and to plan our programs adequately in advance.

From the floor: On the basis of my experience as an American in Turkey, it seems to me that the answer to the question, "Can capitalism survive?" depends on the success with which the underdeveloped nations can solve their problems. The political and economic pressures that are building up because of the miserable economic conditions are tremendous. Unless they can be relieved, the survival of capitalism overseas is really in doubt.

From the floor: I travel about 200,000 miles every year and have visited many nations all over the world. In my opinion, the questions of segregation and capitalism have become needlessly confused and entangled. There is no logical relationship between the two.

If it had not been for the newshounds on radio and television, most people in the United States never would have even known about the Autherine Lucy incident. And yet this relatively minor occurrence is being discussed in the far corners of the world! I know we have a problem with this integration business in the South, but it is a problem that the South will have to solve for itself in the course of time. Progress is being made, and I can't see any need or reason for the situation to be considered or discussed outside the South. I certainly do not see how it affects this question of the survival of capitalism abroad.

Msgr. Ligutti: The Autherine Lucy case was played up and exaggerated purposely in the Far East. It was used by the communists as anti-American and anticapitalist propaganda—they link the two attitudes together. But the case was also discussed and criticized by many people who were not communists, nor even basically anti-American. Why? Because they consider our handling of the Negro question as one of the great weaknesses in our democracy, as indeed it is.

I recognize, of course, that there is a constructive side to race relations in the United States: that we are making progress toward the implementation of the ideal of human dignity in our dealings with one another. I realize, too, that the American scene is not dominated by racial conflict. But the fact is that most people in the world do not have such a sense of proportion about the segregation question. They are greatly concerned about it, and they magnify our failings. Therefore, we must be constantly aware of the impact which any and all of our weaknesses have around the world, and work diligently to clear up the inconsistencies which have developed between our democratic creed and the actual practices of our society.

From the floor: Why is the Soviet system doing so much better at public relations than we are?

From the floor: This is the price we pay for being a democracy. We distort and misrepresent our own reflection because of the variety of views we express. If we had a controlled press and radio, we could present a consistently impressive and noble face to the world, as the Soviets are able to do—temporarily, at least. But the truth will be known in the long run, and if the world is confused by what is going on here at times, the United States will have to balance this disadvantage against the freedom of speech and freedom of the press we value so highly.

Mr. Sherwood: There are several specific instances where the Russians have gotten the jump on us. For instance, the Export-Import Bank loaned several millions of dollars to Afghanistan for the development of a valley in the southern part of that country. When I was out there a few years ago, an official asked me if they couldn't use some of the money we had supplied to pave the streets. What they really needed in the long run was to improve their productive facilities—not to pave their streets—so we didn't feel able to comply with their request.

It will be ten years at least before the full value of this valley development project which we sponsored will be realized. But in the meantime, the Russians have gone in and paved the streets of Kabul, and the Soviet contribution was immediately evident. Maybe we were wrong not to go along with their wishes—certainly the communists beat us to the punch from the standpoint of public relations. In the long run, though, I think the people in Afghanistan will come to the conclusion that we are with them as partners because of the results that will be produced by the kind of programs we undertake. I hope this is not just wishful thinking!

From the floor: Speaking as a citizen of a foreign nation, I would like to challenge the way the question has been phrased for the authors in this chapter. Actually, it is not a matter of "Can capitalism survive?" The real question is "Can capitalism do more good for the people of the world than any other system?"

There is another point which ought to be made here, too. We all know what America has done for the rest of the world since the end of the war. We know that the United States has accomplished a great deal of good with its Marshall Plan aid, private investment, educational exchanges, and so forth. But it seems to work one way, with the Americans giving all the time. Many people resent being constantly on the receiving end. So I think the real task for America is to build up its bilateral trade with the rest of the world, and to let other countries help themselves in this way. Russia is very much on the move in this field today. Can America match them? Can the United States get across the partnership idea, and make it work?